D1627626

ULTIMATE EATLIST

THE WORLD'S TOP 500 FOOD EXPERIENCES... RANKED

Introduction

You'll need to jostle your way to the bar to order, poised for an opening to appear. *'Un pincho de anchoas con pimientos, por favor. Y una copa de chacolí. ¡Gracias!'* A small plate comes back with your first pintxo and a glass of Basque sparkling wine. *¡Salud!* Welcome to San Sebastián in Spain, one of the world's greatest cities to eat your way around. Sandwiched between the Bahía de le Concha and the city's river, the grid of narrow streets in San Sebastián's old town are packed with pintxos bars, each serving their own speciality of these Basque bites. In Bar Txepetxa on C/Pescadería, anchovies are the go-to snack. A few doors down at Nestor, it's a beefheart tomato salad dressed with just olive oil and salt, or a tortilla so sought after that you have to put your name down on a list for a slice. Further along C/Pescadería, Bar Zeruko's theatrical creations include a morsel of cod on a miniature smoking grill. It's as if the city has been designed to delight every sense – and your sense of adventure, as you meander from bar to bar, meeting different people, trying new and inventive Basque flavours.

Trips like this inspired Lonely Planet's Ultimate Eatlist, our collection of the world's most memorable eating experiences. Food and place are inextricably connected: local dishes evolved according to what grew nearby or what was in season. Occasionally a gastronomic genius will create a classic that is recreated in restaurants around the world: how many versions of salad Niçoise might ever have been made? But only on the French Riviera can you try it in its home and there, in the golden light and sea breeze, everything makes more sense – the tuna from the Mediterranean, the sun-ripened Provencal tomatoes. Thanks to migration and globalisation, it's easy to find kimchi in Los Angeles or manoushe in Melbourne but only in Korea or Lebanon can you dig down to their cultural roots. In these places, you don't just taste the dish but experience the whirl of people, languages, aromas and sounds that are unique to that destination. That's what makes each dish memorable.

So, how did we draw up our selection? First, we canvassed the Lonely Planet community – our writers, bloggers and staffers, a globetrotting group of people known to obsess over food and travel – for their most delicious discoveries. We also asked 20 chefs and food writers with an interest in world cuisines – from José Andrés to Andrew Zimmern – for their five favourite food experiences (see the coloured panels). With this long list to hand, we sought to rank the entries: where should you go for the world's must-have food experiences? Our team of expert food editors were aided by a panel – made up of chef and TV presenter Adam Liaw and food blogger Leyla Kazim – that evaluated the entries according to the taste of the dish, its cultural importance, and the special atmosphere of the location.

This book is the result of their deliberations. Looking at our top ten, it seems that shared, communal food experiences rated highly – pintxos in San Sebastián, dim sum in Hong Kong and sushi in Japan – and we wondered what caused this. Clearly, we enjoy eating food around other people with the extra local interaction and the sense of place these experiences offer. Perhaps the added variety also rewards the more intrepid gastronaut, who is not always completely sure what they're ordering...

Eating local has wider benefits too. Arguably, sustainability is higher when food is seasonal and grown in the vicinity, supporting local communities. An advantage of going to these places in person is that you can ask the server before ordering about the restaurant's sourcing policies – of seafood, which figures prominently in our top 20, for example – or where the ingredients come from. Vote with your dollar or yen or euro.

This book travels the world with an insatiable appetite. It takes in the culinary melting pots of London, New York and Melbourne, and also such don't-miss destinations as Lima, Singapore and the Yucatán. A few of the experiences we recommend are really off the beaten track: bush tucker in outback Australia or Faroese cuisine for example. But what they all have in common is that they will put you in thrilling touch with a place, its people and their way of life all thanks to some delicious food. In the Eat It! section of each entry we tell you exactly where to go to try each dish. Turn to our guidebooks and lonelyplanet.com for more detailed directions.

So, don't delay! Pack your passport (and loose-fitting clothing) and start ticking off your favourite food experiences from our Ultimate Eatlist.

Contents

1 Pintxos in San Sebastián **10**
2 Curry laksa in Kuala Lumpur **12**
3 Sushi in Tokyo **14**
4 Beef brisket in Texas **16**
5 Som tum in Bangkok **16**
6 Smørrebrød in Copenhagen **18**
7 Crayfish in Kaikoura **20**
8 Bibimbap in Seoul **21**
9 Pizza margherita in Naples **22**
10 Dim sum in Hong Kong **24**
11 Ceviche in Lima **26**
12 Pastéis de nata in Lisbon **26**
13 Oysters in Australia **29**
14 Cheese experiences in France **30**
15 Jerk chicken in Jamaica **32**
16 Lamb tagine in Marrakech **32**
17 Chilli crab in Singapore **34**
18 Moules frites in Brussels **36**
19 Peking duck in Beijing **37**
20 Pho on the Hau River, Vietnam **38**
21 Souvlaki in Greece **40**
22 Churros in Madrid **41**
23 Tapas in La Boqueria, Barcelona **42**
24 Gelato in Italy **44**
25 Hummus in Israel **46**
26 Fresh fish in the Seychelles **46**
27 Tarte tatin in central France **47**
28 Porcedu in Sardinia **47**
29 Beefburger in New York **48**
30 Köttbullar in Stockholm **49**
31 Fish and chips in Britain **50**
32 Tainan Night Market in Taiwan **52**
33 Steak tartare in Paris **52**
34 Ragù in Bologna **54**
35 Insalata Caprese in Italy **56**
36 Buffalo wings in Buffalo **57**
37 Bai sak chrouk in Cambodia **58**
38 Bakeries in Tehran **58**
39 Smoked salmon in Scotland **59**
40 Barbecued pork in Seoul **59**
41 Massaman curry in Thailand **60**
42 Fresh coconut in Fiji **61**
43 Baozi in Shanghai **62**
44 Midye dolma in Istanbul **62**
45 Beignets in New Orleans **63**
46 Masala dosa in southern India **64**
47 Irish stew in Dublin **65**
48 Kaiseki in Kyoto **66**
49 Domatokeftedes in Santorini **68**
50 Piri piri chicken in Mozambique **68**
51 Fattoush from Syria **69**
52 Doughnuts in Portland **69**
53 Pupusa in El Salvador **70**
54 Whitebait fritters in New Zealand **71**
55 Tiger prawns in Myanmar **71**
56 Samosas in India **72**
57 Sea urchin in Hokkaidō **73**
58 Spaghetti alle vongole in Italy **74**
59 Sunday roast in the UK **74**
60 Ikan bakar in Kuala Lumpur **75**
61 Chez Panisse in California **75**
62 Tapas in Seville **76**
63 Boeuf bourguignon in Burgundy **77**
64 Hainanese chicken in Singapore **78**
65 Bánh xèo in Ho Chi Minh City **78**
66 Korvapuusti in Finland **79**
67 Shakshouka in Tel Aviv **80**
68 Grilled octopus in Italy **83**
69 Elotes in Mexico **83**
70 Hot fudge sundae in the USA **83**
71 Khao piak san in Laos **84**
72 Gaeng keow wan in Bangkok **86**
73 Sourdough in San Francisco **88**
74 Doubles in Trinidad & Tobago **89**
75 Black-eyed pea fritters in Senegal **89**
76 Galette des rois in Paris
77 Dal in India **91**
78 Pumpkin custard in Phnom Penh **92**
79 Chilli-salted fruit in Vietnam **93**
80 Crab sandwiches in England **93**
81 Waffles in Belgium **94**
82 Toverhallerne in Copenhagen **95**
83 Mohinga in Myanmar **95**
84 Asado in Argentina **96**
85 Apple pie in the USA **98**
86 Jiaozi in Beijing **99**
87 Crêpes in Paris **99**
88 Miznon in Tel Aviv **100**
89 Po' boy in New Orleans **101**
90 White truffles in Piedmont **101**
91 Bush tucker in Australia **102**
92 Salmorejo in Spain **103**
93 Reindeer stew in Lapland **104**
94 Beef noodle soup in Taiwan **104**
95 Halloumi in Beirut **105**
96 Green chillies in New Mexico **105**
97 Clafoutis in Limousin, France **105**
98 Paella in Valencia **106**
99 Langoustines in the Comoros **106**

100–199

100 Cream tea in England **109**
101 Wienerbrød in Copenhagen **109**
102 Sachertorte in Vienna **110**
103 Balık ekmek in Istanbul **110**
104 Xiaolongbao in Shanghai **112**
105 Macarons in Paris **113**
106 Fondue in Geneva **114**
107 Summer pudding in England **114**
108 Feteer in Cairo **115**
109 Bhel puri in India **115**
110 Gado gado in Bali **115**
111 Nystekt Strömming in Stockholm **115**
112 Bratwurst in Germany **116**
113 Feijoada in São Paulo **116**
114 Muffuletta in New Orleans **117**
115 Glühwein and stollen in Germany **118**
116 Spaghetti carbonara in Rome **118**
117 Bánh mì in Ho Chi Minh City **119**
118 Knafeh in Beirut **120**
119 Vada pav in Mumbai **120**
120 Hotteok in South Korea **120**
121 Percebes in southern Portugal **121**
122 Boerewors in Johannesburg **122**
123 Assam laksa in Penang **122**
124 Llapingachos in Ecuador **122**
125 Mango sticky rice in Bangkok **123**
126 Kushari in Cairo **123**
127 Larb in Laos **124**
128 Cochinita pibil in the Yucatán **124**
129 Caviar in Moscow **125**
130 Lángos in Budapest **125**
131 Bouillabaisse in Marseille **126**
132 Scotch egg in London **128**
133 Fëgesë in Tirana **128**
134 Clam cakes in Rhode Island **129**
135 Humita in Argentina **129**
136 Ramen in Tokyo **130**
137 Choripán in Buenos Aires **131**
138 Keema matar in Chandigarh **131**
139 Fried chicken in Nashville **132**
140 Poke in Hawaii **133**
141 Raclette in the Swiss Alps **134**
142 Miso ramen in Sapporo **134**
143 Cong you bing in Shanghai **134**
144 Khichari in London **134**
145 Dal bhat in Nepal **136**
146 Egg waffles in Hong Kong **137**
147 Banitsa in Sofia **137**
148 Mapo tofu in Sichuan **138**
149 Cassoulet in Carcassonne **139**
150 Nordic cuisine in Copenhagen **140**
151 Pepperpot stew in Guyana **142**
152 Chicken muamba in Angola **142**
153 Cheesecake in New York **143**
154 Pierogi in Poland **143**
155 Makroudh in Algiers **144**
156 Icelandic lobster in Reykjavik **144**
157 Turkish delight in Istanbul **144**
158 Pa amb tomaquet in Catalonia **144**
159 Ćevapi in Sarajevo **144**
160 Rolex in Uganda **144**
161 Palusami in Fiji **145**
162 Haggis in Scotland **145**
163 Arbroath smokies in Scotland **146**
164 Sisig in the Philippines **146**
165 Fish amok in Cambodia **147**
166 Mansaf in Jordan **148**
167 Currywurst in Berlin **149**
168 Khinkali in Georgia **149**
169 Croque monsieur in Paris **150**
170 Polos curry in Sri Lanka **150**
171 Aperitivo in northern Italy **151**
172 Thukpa in Nepal **151**
173 Tom yum goong in Bangkok **152**
174 Umm ali in Cairo **152**
175 Tandoori chicken in Delhi **152**
176 Żurek in Kraków **152**
177 Dragon beard candy in Hong Kong **153**
178 Huevos divorciados in Mexico **153**
179 Syrniki blinis in Russia **153**
180 Picarones in Lima **154**
181 Eggs sardou in New Orleans **154**
182 Slow-cooked chicken in Senegal **156**
183 Tea eggs in Taiwan **156**
184 Chapulines in Oaxaca, Mexico **156**
185 Scallop pie in Tasmania **157**
186 Pork pie in the UK **157**
187 Escargot à la Bourguignonne in Dijon, France **158**
188 Halo-halo in Manila **159**
189 Harissa in Armenia **159**
190 Congee in Hong Kong **159**
191 Brigadeiro in São Paulo **160**
192 Jamón ibérico in Spain **160**
193 Paranthe Wali Gali in Delhi **160**
194 Cherry torte in the Black Forest **161**
195 Nyama choma in Kenya **161**
196 Pepparkakor in Sweden **162**
197 Taramasalata in Greece **162**
198 Lampuki pie in Malta **162**
199 Sopa de lima in Yucatán **162**

200 Greek salad in Athens **165**
201 Galette Bretonne in Brittany **165**
202 Romazava in Madagascar **165**
203 Bubble tea in Taipei **166**
204 Mopane worms in Zimbabwe **166**
205 Fatteh in Beirut **166**
206 Cannoli in Sicily **167**
207 Postre chaja in Montevideo **167**
208 Baghali ghatogh in Tehran **167**
209 Qabili palau in Afghanistan **168**
210 Cataplana de marisco in Portugal **168**
211 Maple syrup in Québec **169**
212 Fried green tomatoes in Georgia **170**
213 Convenience store chicken in Japan **170**
214 Paletilla de cordero in Mallorca **171**
215 Tarte au citron in France **172**
216 Metemgee in Guyana **172**
217 Kourou pie in Athens **172**
218 Clam chowder in New England **173**
219 Full English breakfast in London **173**
220 Chivito in Montevideo **174**
221 Langoustine in Scotland **174**
222 Khachapuri in Tbilisi **175**
223 Sandesh in Kolkata **175**
224 Cobb salad in Los Angeles **175**
225 Bryndzové halušky in Bratislava **175**
226 Baneja paisa in Colombia **176**
227 Katsudon in Japan **176**
228 Cha ca in Hanoi **177**
229 Maltby St Market in London **177**
230 Adobo in the Philippines **178**
231 Doro wat and injera in Ethiopia **179**
232 Airline food worldwide **180**
233 Leipäjuusto in Lapland **180**
234 Coffin bread in Taipei **180**
235 Soupe au pistou in Provence **181**
236 Cachupa in Cape Verde **181**
237 Harira in Morocco **181**
238 Salad niçoise in Provence **182**
239 Tartiflette in the French Alps **183**
240 Dulce de leche in Uruguay **183**
241 Anzac biscuits in Australia **184**
242 Töltött káposzta in Hungary **184**
243 Borscht in Russia **185**
244 Bakso in Indonesia **185**
245 Manti in Kyrgyzstan **185**
246 Moussaka in Athens **186**
247 Pigeon pastilla in Marrakech **186**
248 Gazpacho in Andalucía **187**
249 Lechón in the Yucatán **187**
250 Kapenta in Zimbabwe **187**
251 Orecchiette in southern Italy **188**
252 Shish tawook in Beirut **189**
253 Raan biriyani in Mumbai **190**
254 Café Schober in Zurich **190**
255 Suquet de peix in Catalonia **191**
256 Steamed crab in Maryland **191**
257 Ropa vieja in Havana **191**
258 Curried goat in Jamaica **192**
259 Pastrmajlija in Macedonia **192**
260 Manoushe in Beirut **193**
261 Nasi lemak in Singapore **193**
262 Torta di ceci in Tuscany **194**
263 Testi kebap in Cappadocia **194**
264 Pad ka pao in Thailand **194**
265 Crawfish boil in Louisiana **195**
266 Ta'amiya in Egypt **195**
267 Chicharrones in Cuba **195**
268 Beef rendang in Malaysia **196**
269 Wiener schnitzel in Vienna **197**
270 Tempura in Japan **198**
271 Quinoa stew in La Paz **198**
272 Tarta de Santiago in Spain **198**
273 Tacos al pastor in Mexico **198**
274 Lamian noodles in Lanzhou **200**
275 Bánh bao vac in Hoi An **201**
276 Arancini in Sicily **201**
277 Chai in India **202**
278 Acaí na tigela in Brazil **202**
279 Khao soi in Chiang Mai **203**
280 Giraffe Manor in Nairobi **204**
281 Takoyaki in Tokyo **205**
282 King crab with mac & cheese in Alaska **205**
283 Crab and dumplings in Tobago **206**
284 Mud crab fishing in Darwin **206**
285 Shingara in Bangladesh **206**
286 Poisson cru in Tahiti **207**
287 Laal maas in Rajasthan **207**
288 Risotto in Milan **207**
289 Lobster roll in Maine **208**
290 Kraftskivas in Scandinavia **208**
291 Ful medames in Egypt **209**
292 Yotam Ottolenghi in London **209**
293 Bò kho in Vietnam **210**
294 Sanuki udon in Kagawa **210**
295 Pom in Suriname **210**
296 Breakfast diners in the USA **211**
297 Goulash in Hungary **212**
298 Onigiri in Japan **213**
299 Wantan mee in Penang **213**

300–399

300 Hot dogs in Iceland **216**
301 Wagashi in Kyoto **216**
302 Yangshuo beer fish in China **216**
303 Salón de Chocolate in Quito **216**
304 Hangi in New Zealand **217**
305 Ngorongoro Crater Lodge in Tanzania **218**
306 Crispy duck in Hong Kong **218**
307 Seekh kebab in Islamabad **219**
308 Burritos in California **219**
309 Strawberries in the Netherlands **220**
310 Murgh makhani in Delhi **220**
311 Rillettes in France **221**
312 Nanaimo bars in Canada **221**
313 Ackee and saltfish in Jamaica **221**
314 Noryangijin fish market in Seoul **222**
315 Momo in Nepal **223**
316 Pap en vleis in South Africa **223**
317 Jollof rice in Nigeria **223**
318 Caña de azúcar in Lima **224**
319 Tiramisù in Treviso **224**
320 Semla in Sweden **224**
321 Ploughman's lunch in England **225**
322 Black risotto in Croatia **226**
323 Mas huni in the Maldives **227**
324 Rex Whistler restaurant in London **227**
325 Bún cha in Hanoi **227**
326 Yakitori in Tokyo **228**
327 Suppli in Rome **229**
328 Dobos torte in Budapest **229**
329 Mole in Oaxaca **229**
330 Crème brûlée in Paris **229**
331 Franceshina in Porto **230**
332 Weisswurst in Munich **230**
333 Ministry of Crab in Colombo **231**
334 Central Market in Adelaide **231**
335 Chili con carne in Texas **232**
336 Rasgulla in Bengal **232**
337 Ratatouille in Provence **232**
338 Cronuts in New York **233**
339 Machboos ala Dajaj in Kuwait **233**
340 Confiserie Sprüngli in Zurich **233**
341 Cazuela de mariscos in Chile **234**
342 Braais in Cape Town **235**
343 Avocado on toast in Melbourne **236**
344 Rou jia mo in Xi'an **236**
345 Fish taco in Baja California **236**
346 Hokitika Wildfoods Festival in New Zealand **238**
347 Casado in Costa Rica **238**
348 The Fat Duck in England **238**
349 Quiche lorraine in Paris **238**
350 Chalupa in Mexico **240**
351 Plate lunch in Honolulu **240**
352 Kaya toast in Kuala Lumpur **240**
353 Pljeskavica in Serbia **240**
354 Pudim in Brazil **241**
355 Egg hoppers in Sri Lanka **241**
356 Wonton noodles in Hong Kong **241**
357 Cuban sandwich in Florida **241**
358 Gulab jamun in northern India **242**
359 Bone marrow on toast in London **242**
360 Salteñas in Bolivia **242**
361 Haden mango in Miami **244**
362 Papabubble candy in Japan **244**
363 Bunny chow in Durban **244**
364 Barra in the Northern Territory **245**
365 Philly cheesecake in Pennsylvania **245**
366 Sardines mariées in Morocco **246**
367 Kokoda in Fiji **247**
368 Crab cake in Baltimore **247**
369 Corn soup in Trinidad **247**
370 Shojin ryori in Japan **248**
371 Seswaa in Botswana **248**
372 Nasi campur in Bali **248**
373 Bolinho de bacalhau in Brazil **249**
374 Ravintola Juuri in Helsinki **249**
375 Plov in Uzbekistan **249**
376 Bara brith in Wales **250**
377 Blaff in French Guiana **250**
378 Gâteau aux noix in the Dordogne **250**
379 Oysters rockefeller in the USA **251**
380 Biltong in South Africa **251**
381 Apricots in northern Pakistan **252**
382 Osteria Enoteca Ai Artisti in Italy **252**
383 Balti in Birmingham **252**
384 Hotpot in Chongqing **253**
385 Meat pie in Melbourne **254**
386 Vorschmack in Helsinki **255**
387 Chimney cake in Budapest **255**
388 Lahpet thoke in Myanmar **256**
389 Salt water taffy in the USA **256**
390 Éclade de moules in France **256**
391 Poutine in Montréal **257**
392 Okonomiyaki in Japan **258**
393 Vegetarian tacos in Los Angeles **259**
394 Cuy in Peru **259**
395 Ekiben in Japan **260**
396 Restaurant Les Cols in Catalonia **261**
397 Ice cream in New England **261**
398 Mitraillette in Belgium **261**
399 Roast meats in Hong Kong **262**

400 Hot dogs in Detroit **265**
401 Goya champuru in Okinawa **265**
402 Moreton Bay bugs in Brisbane **265**
403 Tamales from Mexico **266**
404 Roti cani in Malaysia **266**
405 Biang biang noodles in Xi'an **266**
406 Lox bagels in New York **267**
407 Wallaby tail soup in Melbourne **268**
408 Cashew fruit in Guinea-Bissau **268**
409 Spago in Los Angeles **268**
410 Koks Restaurant in the Faroes **269**
411 Kimchi in South Korea **270**
412 Restaurant Ulo in Greenland **271**
413 Marche Bastille in Paris **271**
414 Baojaam in Tallinn **271**
415 Chicchetti in Venice **272**
416 Tlacoyo in Mexico City **273**
417 Empanadas in Argentina **273**
418 Chlodnik in Poland **273**
419 Kobe beef in Kobe **274**
420 Goi cuon in Ho Chi Minh City **274**
421 Pizza slices in New York **275**
422 Akara in Lagos **276**
423 Schweinshaxe in Bavaria **277**
424 Gimbap in South Korea **278**
425 Black rice pudding in Ubud **278**
426 Flódni in Budapest **279**
427 Taco rice in Okinawa **279**
428 Pineapple cake in Taipei **279**
429 Pavlova in Australiasia **280**
430 Poulets de Bresse in France **281**
431 Yángròu pàomó in Xi'an **282**
432 Char kway teow in Penang **282**
433 Mozartkugel in Salzburg **282**
434 Tlayuda in Oaxaca **283**
435 Thali in India **283**
436 Mbeju and tereré in Asunción **283**
437 Eggs benedict in New York **284**
438 Manuka honey in New Zealand **285**
439 French baguettes in Paris **285**
440 Kalitsounia on Crete **285**
441 Chicken pepián in Guatemala **286**
442 Key lime pie in Florida **286**
443 Nasi goreng in Bali **287**
444 Pad thai in Bangkok **288**
445 Durian fruit in Malaysia **289**
446 Surf 'n turf in California **289**
447 Fried tarantula in Cambodia **290**
448 Mantu in Afghanistan **290**
449 Mince pies in UK **291**
450 Chicken tikka masala in Glasgow **291**
451 Elk in Norway **291**
452 Mochi in Japan **291**
453 Pork barbecue in North Carolina **292**
454 Chimaek in Seoul **293**
455 Dan dan noodles in Sichuan **294**
456 Salo in Ukraine **294**
457 Khuushuur in Mongolia **294**
458 Black pudding in Ireland **296**
459 Reuben sandwich in New York **296**
460 The Test Kitchen in Cape Town **297**
461 Black pepper crab in Singapore **297**
462 Cous cous in Marrakech **298**
463 NOA in Tallinn **299**
464 Hokkien mee in Kuala Lumpur **299**
465 Muskox in Greenland **300**
466 Pumpkin pie in New York **300**
467 Palmiers in France **300**
468 Bak kut teh in Malaysia **301**
469 Caplin and scrunchions in Newfoundland **302**
470 Trdelník in Prague **302**
471 Steak and kidney pie in London **303**
472 Baho in Nicaragua **304**
473 Borough Market in London **304**
474 Boulettes in Mauritius **305**
475 Lamingtons in Australia **305**
476 Mooncakes in Macau **305**
477 Obleas in Bogotá **306**
478 Bistecca alla fiorentina in Italy **306**
479 Banoffee pie in England **307**
480 Thieboudienne in Senegal **307**
481 Sai krok isan in Bangkok **307**
482 Sufganiyot in Tel Aviv **307**
483 Bouchons in Lyon **308**
484 Chicken and rice in Singapore **308**
485 Bò lá lot in Vietnam **309**
486 Chile relleno in Mexico **309**
487 Arepas in Venezuela **309**
488 Placky in Slovakia **310**
489 Lahoh from Yemen **310**
490 Alcapurrias in Puerto Rico **310**
491 Medianoche in Havana **311**
492 Shrimp and grits in Charleston **311**
493 Apple strudel in Vienna **311**
494 Espetinho in Brazil **311**
495 Simit in Istanbul **312**
496 Barmbrack in Ireland **312**
497 Soufflé in Angers, France **312**
498 Meloui in Morocco **312**
499 Knish in New York **313**
500 Stinky tofu in Taipei **314**

01–
99

© Lonely Planet / Mark Read

In San Sebastián bars such as Gandarias, left, traditional pinxtos (right) are piled high on the counter. Below: the sweeping beach and bay of San Sebastián.

© Shutterstock / Alexander Demyanenko

Classic bar-stool bites

Those salty-spicy beer buddies Buffalo wings hail from the New York town that bears their name.

page 57

A Scooby snack-sized sandwich, Uruguayan chivito was born of a happy accident.

page 174

Tokyo offers a host of bars on one strip where excess alcohol is soaked up with yakitori.

page 228

Bar-hop for pintxos on San Sebastián's streets

01

SPAIN // If there's a better way to explore a culture's cuisine than pintxos in San Sebastián, we'll eat our shorts. The tiny bites (known as tapas outside of Basque Spain) are best consumed with an accompanying drink, seeing as you'll be taking this particular culinary journey as a bar-hopping escapade through the streets of San Sebastián. Beginning their existence as small open sandwiches, pintxos can be experienced in many incarnations, from the traditional, piled-high toppings on bread, to molecular gastronomy renditions with flavours that defy what you see. Needless to say, almost every local ingredient is represented. It's hard to list favourites, but the simple examples are often the ones that blow your mind – battered white asparagus, a tuna and anchovy tart or maybe mushrooms braised with garlic. To get the full pintxos and San Sebastián experience, have a lazy day in the city and surrounds, take an afternoon nap, and then head out around 9pm. You'll never be more than a few minutes from your next bar, a whole new menu of tasty treats, and a whole new group of people eating and drinking – just follow their leads.

☛ TRY IT ! ***Ganbara comes recommended by Juan Mari Arzak – who could disagree? The battered white asparagus are essential.***

Choose your curry laksa stall beneath the towers of Kuala Lumpur

Below: curry laksa. Right, from top: the Kuala Lumpur skyline; barely a seat to spare at a city centre street restaurant.

MALAYSIA // Rich and creamy curry laksa is just about as tasty a bowl of food as you will find anywhere on the planet, but it's in Malaysia, and in particular in Kuala Lumpur, that you'll find some of the best ways of eating it. Here are fantastic little hawker centres tucked into the shadows of towering skyscrapers, and at Madras Lane, just off Petaling St, you'll come across competing curry laksa stalls vying for your attention.

Pick the one with the longest queue and when you have the bowl in your hands choose a plastic chair (make sure it's connected to the stall where you bought your laksa or you'll be in trouble) and begin the swoon-worthy, sweat-inducing process of eating. Come again the next day to try the neighbouring stall's version. A heady mix of spices and flavours (such as fresh turmeric, galangal, chilli, candlenut and shrimp paste) go into the curry mix, which, when combined with coconut milk, creates the signature fiery orange appearance of the noodle soup. Two types of noodles (thin rice and thick egg), along with shredded chicken, shrimp, cockles, tofu puffs, bean sprouts, a sprinkling of fresh chilli and mint and a squeeze of lime, make up the rest of the lip-smacking ingredients. It's an only-in-Malaysia experience.

EAT IT ! *From the hawker stalls along Madras Lane, off Petaling St, Kuala Lumpur.*

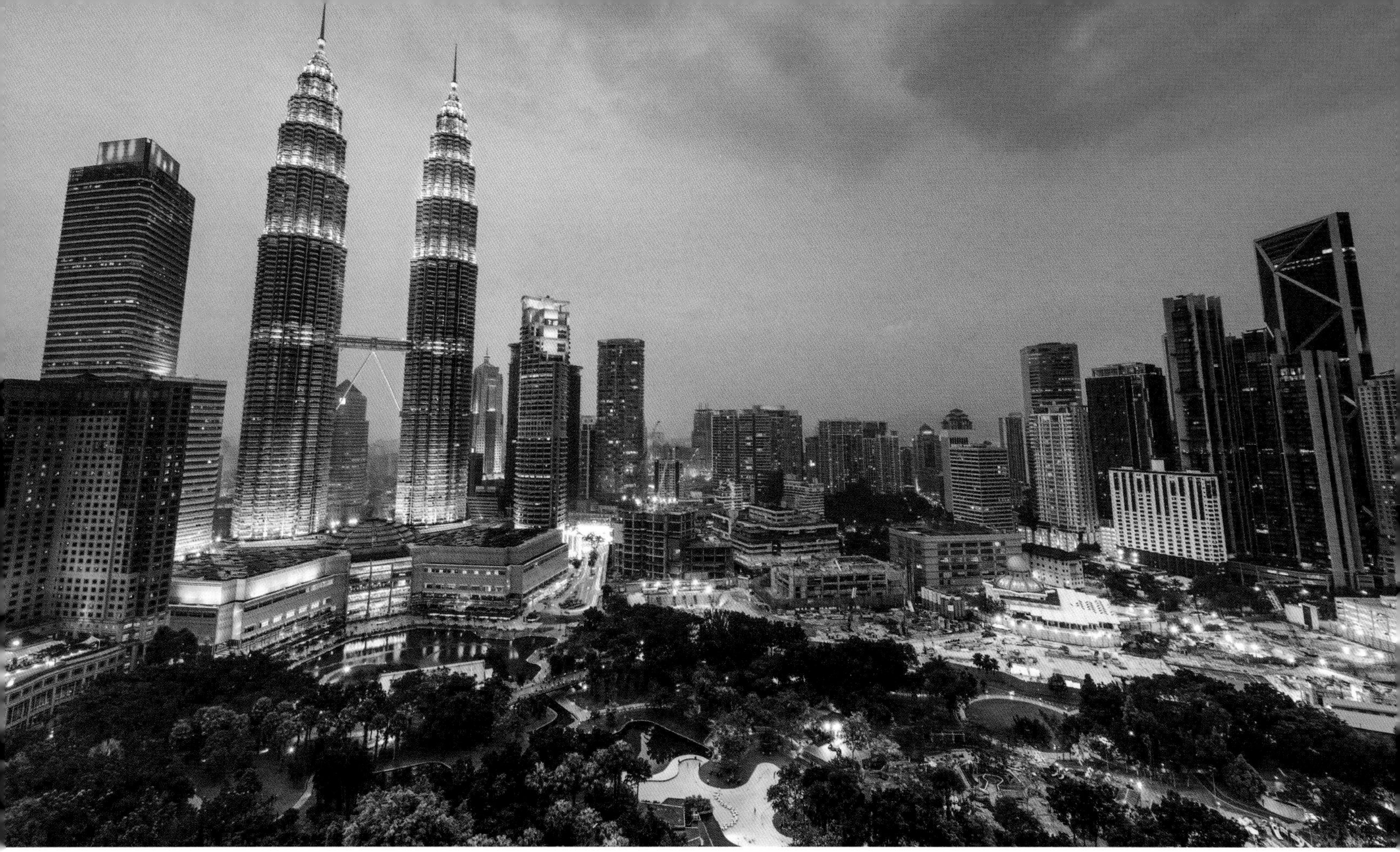

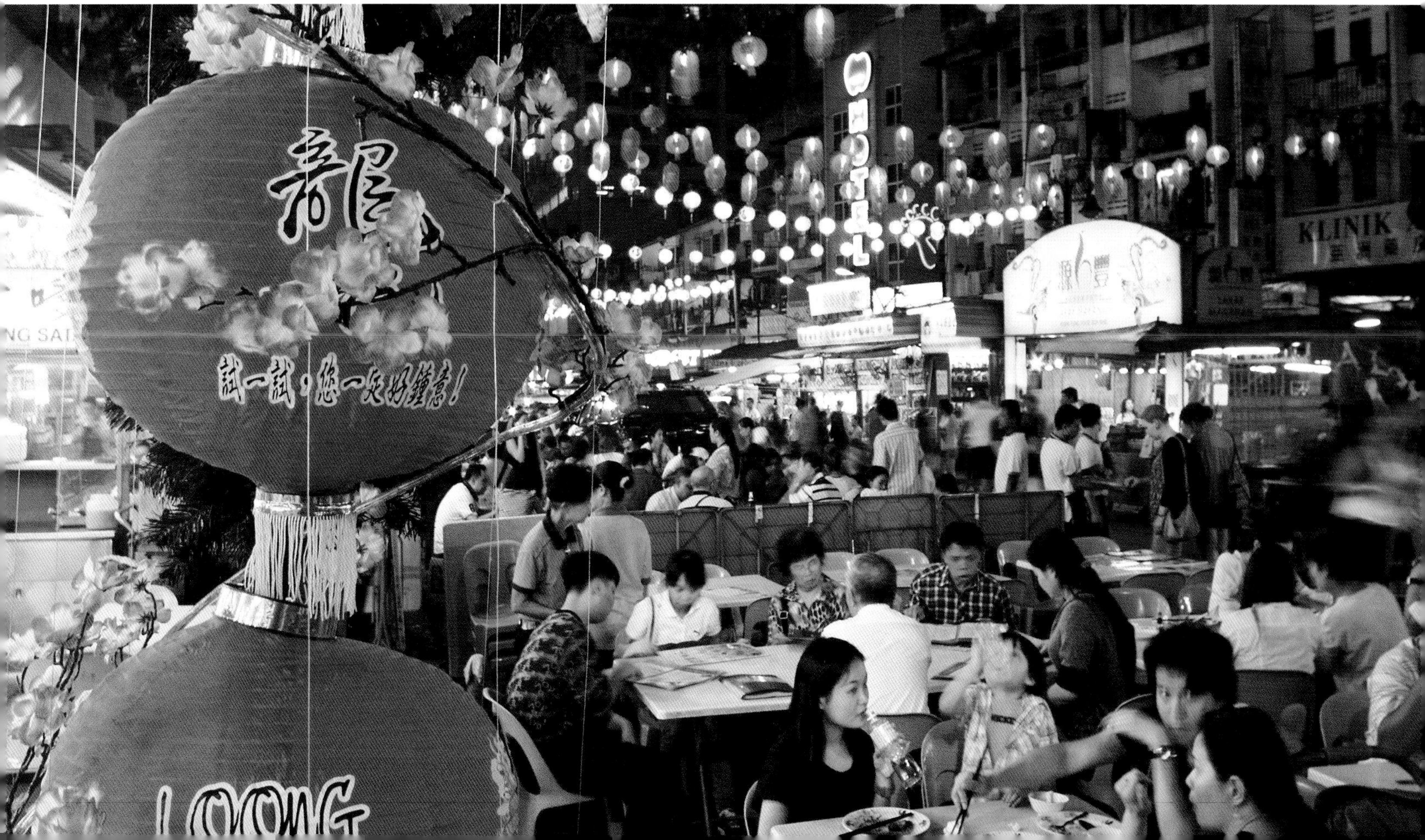
龍
試一試，您一定好鐘意!
HOTEL
KLINIK

Roll up for a sushi masterclass in a traditional Tokyo setting

03

Where the chefs are a spectacle

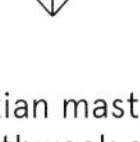

Egyptian masters slap, thwack and pull at pizza-like feteer dough in Cairo.

page 115

The lamian noodlemakers of Lanzhou are natural-born performers.

page 200

Papabubble is as much about its kaleidoscopic kitchens as its candy treats.

page 244

JAPAN // We want to say that if you're going to eat sushi in Tokyo, go to Sukiyabashi Jiro or Sushi Saito, but the inordinately long waiting lists to get in to either restaurant take the shine off the experience. That said, if your fairy godmother (aka hotel concierge) waves a magic wand, do not miss your chance; the sushi mastery on show at both places is undeniable. In the absence of a fairy godmother, however, there are some superb sushi restaurants in Tokyo that dish up life-changing experiences without the wait. Cases in point include Manten Sushi Marunouchi and Jūzō Sushi.

Most top-end sushi chefs will serve their sushi *omakase* style, which just means you leave it to them and they will select, prepare and serve your sushi as they see fit. Don't kick back and relax just yet, though – there are some etiquette rules to abide by. Firstly, when your fresh piece of sushi is placed in front of you, pick it up with your hands, not chopsticks, and don't dip it in soy sauce or ask for any extra wasabi. The chef has seasoned the offering, so it is something of an insult to modify the flavour. Between courses it's fine to use chopsticks to pick up pickled ginger and the *oshibori* (hand towel) to clean your fingers.

Take your time and interact with the chef; it's such an intimate setting and a perfect opportunity to learn more about this ancient culinary artform. Remember to pay attention to the rice as well as the fish. Sushi masters spend years perfecting their rice and consider it as important as all the other ingredients. Soak it all in – the tradition, the skill, the respect, the service, all amounting to the quintessential Japanese dining experience.

EAT IT ! ***Manten Sushi Marunouchi, 2 Chome-6-1 Marunouchi, Chiyoda; Jūzō Sushi, 2 Chome-4 Asagaya Kita, Suginami, Tokyo.***

Below: a sushi chef prepares a plate in his Tokyo restaurant. Left: the hard-to-resist fruits of such skilled labour.

Take your time and interact with the chef; it's a perfect opportunity to learn more about this ancient culinary art

Is Texan beef brisket worth the four-hour queue? Hell yeah!

04

USA // The folk in Texas know their barbecued meats. So when they line up for four or more hours to get some, it has to be special. That's the situation at Franklin Barbecue, in Austin, six days a week. Franklin's menu includes pulled pork, ribs, sausage and more, but the main attraction is its smoked beef brisket. It keeps it simple, rubbing the meat with a mix of salt and black pepper, and cooking it 'low and slow' in oak-wood smoke until it's fall-apart tender and encased in a thin, salty crust. It's a juicy, smoky Texas classic, judged best in class by the Texans themselves. Plenty of outsiders are fans too, including Anthony Bourdain ('the finest brisket I've ever had'), Barack Obama (skipped the line, but paid for everyone behind him) and Kanye West (tried to skip the line, got bumped). You could drive to Lockhart, the state-legislated 'Barbecue Capital of Texas', and be back in the time it takes to get into Franklin's. But the queue is good fun, you can have a beer and meet some friendly Texans while you wait, and damn, that brisket is good.

EAT IT ! ***Queues have been known to form at Franklin's at 5am, for an 11am opening. So get there early! 900 E 11th Austin, Texas.***

Supreme salads

You'll only really know how good Greek salad can be when you've tasted the Athens original.

page 165

A dish born of experimentation, LA's Cobb salad is named after its culinary creator.

page 175

There are many variations on salad Niçoise but only one place to eat it: the French Riviera.

page 182

Som tum: the Bangkok street salad that packs a mighty punch

THAILAND // Rarely does a salad generate so much hype, but then *som tum*, or green papaya salad as many of us know it, is no ordinary salad. *Som tum* is a bang! of flavour – it's sour, salty, sweet and intensely fiery. It's also texturally extraordinary, combining the crunch of peanuts with cool slivers of pale green papaya and carrot, and small, sweet, juicy shrimps and tomatoes. It's sold from street vendors all over Thailand, but is particularly beloved in the capital, Bangkok, where it feels like there's a seller on every corner.

Grabbing a plate of *som tum* on the street, amid all the traffic chaos and the stifling heat, is a rite of passage for visitors to the city, but if you would prefer to revere your salad in relative peace and quiet, the restaurant Som Tam Nua, at the Siam Center on Siam Square, has a worthy version – tamed slightly for Western palates but still delicious. Somtum Der in Silom is also excellent, and you can adjust your spice level to taste – be warned, however, as the spiciest salad will blow your socks off.

EAT IT ! ***From street vendors in Bangkok, or at Som Tam Nua, Siam Center, Siam Square; or Somtum Der, 5/5 Saladaeng Rd, Silom, Khet Bang Rak; both Bangkok.***

Clockwise from top: the interior of Franklin's; owner Aaron Franklin; a market trader in Bangkok; Thailand's hot *som tum* salad.

© Wyatt McSpadden / Courtesy of Franklin's

© Lonely Planet / Matt Munro

Grab a slice of smørrebrød, Copenhagen's bread of heaven

06

The great bread bake off

↓

There's even a museum dedicated to Boudin sourdough at its flagship San Francisco bakery.

page 88

↓

Bara brith is a fruity bread favourite at teatime in Wales, even if some claim it to be a cake.

 page 250

↓

Ireland's take on the above, barmbrack has its own place in the country's folklore.

 page 312

DENMARK // Want to know what the best thing is since sliced bread? Danish *smørrebrød*, that's what. Take a slice of rye bread, put some butter on it and then heap it with whatever tasty ingredients you like. Actually, it's not that simple. There are some rules to *smørrebrød* that help to elevate it to something beyond just a piece of bread with toppings. Firstly, thin toppings go on first, followed by the bulkier kind; secondly, when eating more than one kind of *smørrebrød* at once (and this is nearly always the case, good luck stopping at one) you start with the slice that features herring, move on to fish, then meat and finish with cheese. This carefully choreographed sequence is designed to gently walk your palate through the flavour combinations, so that one never overpowers the other.

If you've never had *smørrebrød* before there are some classic combinations you'll see all over Denmark: pickled herring, onion and dill; mayonnaise, boiled egg, shrimp, dill and lemon; roast beef, pickles, onions and horseradish; blue cheese, apples and bacon, for example. But these are just a tiny sample of the almost limitless number of toppings.

At Copenhagen's *smørrebrød* institution, Restaurant Schonnemann, which has been serving up the open-faced sandwich since 1877, the presentation is so delicate and refined it resembles sushi in style. Try the following for an ultimate *smørrebrød* experience, otherwise known as the world's best sandwich degustation: herring marinated in dill cream with capers, onions and a fried egg; smoked salmon and smoked halibut with a crab and mayonnaise salad, tomato and basil; a breaded cutlet of pork with apples, thyme and onions; and finally, camembert with blackcurrant jam. And to drink? Why, there's only more than 140 different schnapps, aquavit and genevers to choose from. That should do nicely.

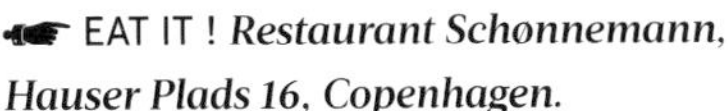

EAT IT ! ***Restaurant Schønnemann, Hauser Plads 16, Copenhagen.***

Your smørrebrød is served (left); there are strict rules governing its presentation (below) despite the huge variety of toppings.

At Copenhagen's Restaurant Schonnemann, the preparation of smørrebrød is so delicate and refined it resembles sushi in style

© PhotoImage / Alamy Stock Photo

07

Visit the New Zealand coast where the crayfish is so good they named a town after it

NEW ZEALAND // On the east coast of New Zealand's South Island, about two hours' drive north of Christchurch, is the picturesquely situated town of Kaikoura. Famous for the abundance of marine life present off shore, with sperm whales, dolphins and seals often spotted close to land, the town's name derives from the Maori words 'Kai', meaning food, and 'Koura', meaning crayfish.

Trading on its namesake are numerous fresh seafood vans up and down the nearby coastline. Of these, one of the oldest, and best, is Nin's Bin. A 20-minute drive from the centre of town, this basic blue and white converted caravan has a few wooden picnic tables scattered outside where locals and well-informed travellers hunker over fresh crayfish and mussels with a view over the Pacific Ocean. Nin's Bin prepares its crayfish with butter, garlic and a sprinkling of parsley, letting the fresh and sweet flesh shine. Add a squeeze of lemon, throw in a cold beer and hope for a sighting of sperm whales, and you'll have a perfect afternoon.

EAT IT ! *Nin's Bin, Kaikoura, South Island.*

08

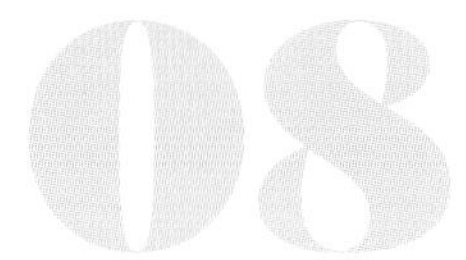

Bibimbap: the South Korean bowl food that's every body's best friend

SOUTH KOREA // Korea's meal in a bowl is pretty much flawless food. Beef and sautéed vegetables such as shiitake mushrooms, spinach and courgettes are piled on to warm, white rice and flavoured with spicy chilli paste and an *umami* fermented soybean paste, topped with either a raw or fried egg. There are two main types of *bibimbap* – *jeonju*-style, which comes in a cold bowl, and *dolsot*, which comes in a piping-hot earthenware bowl – making it the perfect dish for any season. Whichever one you choose comes to you like a display meal, with all the ingredients fanned out over the rice, so take a moment to admire the pretty culinary spectacle and know that the ingredients are chosen for specific reasons. The red of the chilli pepper represents your heart, the green vegetables are for your liver, the yellow of the egg yolk is for your stomach, black or very dark items (mushrooms or soy sauce) are there for your kidneys, and the white rice is for your lungs. Now dive right in, mix the whole lot up and give your insides a boost.

EAT IT ! ***Seoul's city streets are awash with restaurants serving bibimbap, find your own favourite.***

© Gary Blake / Alamy Stock Photo

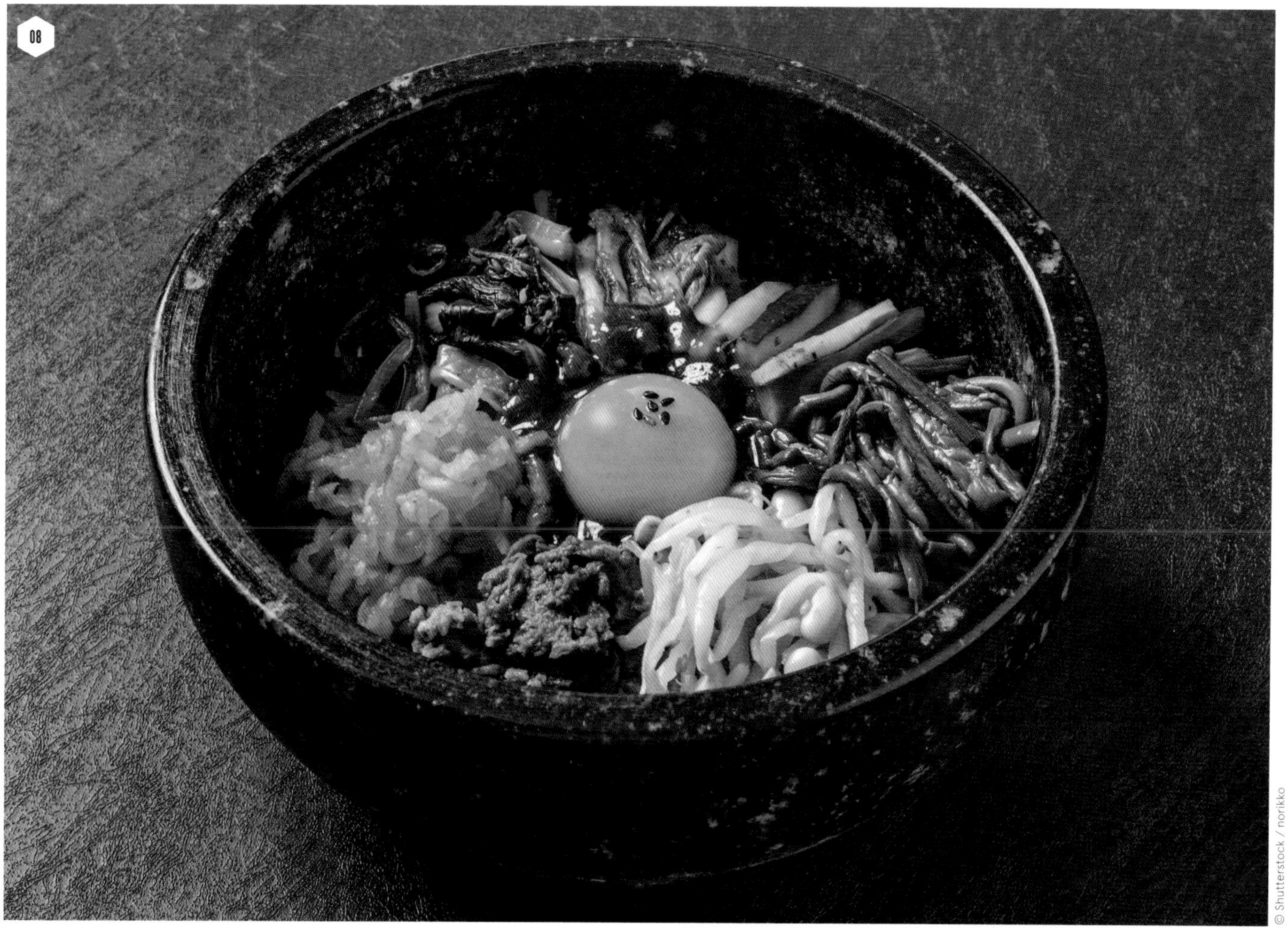

© Shutterstock / norikko

© Lonely Planet / Susan Wright

Clockwise from left: another one for the oven at Naples' Pizzeria Bellini; the tomato, mozzarella and basil margherita; its home city of Naples.

Italian classics

As any Bolognese knows, the true rich, meaty sauce, ragù, is served with tagliatelle.

 page 54

Spaghetti carbonara can trace its lineage to Rome, where it's eaten citywide.

 page 118

Italy's fashion capital owes risotto alla Milanese to the nearby rice fields of the Po Valley.

page 207

© Lonely Planet / Susan Wright

© Getty Images / Michele Falzone

Sing the praises of pizza where the margherita took form

09

ITALY // The world is forever indebted to Italy for inventing the pizza. While there are infinite numbers of ways it can be prepared, there's one version of our worldwide food obsession that will always stand prouder than the rest: the original margherita pizza from Naples. To eat margherita here is reminiscent of a religious experience – you'll find zealous disciples of specific restaurants. It's believed the worldwide phenomenon was first created when a local baker prepared dinner for the visiting King Umberto and Queen Margherita in the 19th century. Legend has it he made three pizzas, and the queen was taken with the flavours of the tomato, mozzarella and basil version, in the colours of the Italian flag. From then on it has been named in her honour. So where to eat it? One of the longest-standing establishments and a true master of the margherita is Di Matteo. The huge cerulean-tiled pizza oven fires out light and stretchy toasted pizzas that fly out of the door to pizza-lovers on their own personal pilgrimage and locals who appreciate the exalted position they find themselves in. If the queue is too long at Di Matteo, stroll the streets and find your own place of worship.

☛ EAT IT ! *At Di Matteo on Via dei Tribunali 94, Naples.*

Hone in on Hong Kong for quintessential dim sum

CHINA // Dim sum (translated as 'light snack') is served all over the world, but nowhere does it like Hong Kong. In fact, Hong Kong's dim sum is a destination in itself. Dim sum (also known as *yum cha*, which translates as 'with tea') has evolved from the traveller ritual of stopping for tea and snacks while on the road into the world's best brunch.

In Hong Kong you can sample your dim sum as simply or as extravagantly as your predilections go. At multiple locations across town, DimDimSum does its titbits traditionally – you'll find that the *siu mai* (steamed pork dumplings), *har gow* (steamed shrimp dumplings) and *char siu bao* (BBQ pork steamed buns) are all excellent. The atmosphere is buzzing with students, travellers and lovers of dim sum on a budget. At the other end of the spectrum are the Michelin-starred establishments like Duddell's and Fook Lam Moon. At the painfully elegant Duddell's the classics are given an elaborate twist; think pork and shrimp dumpling with scallop and caviar, or a deep-fried pork and shrimp wonton with foie gras. By contrast, Fook Lam Moon's mood is classic Cantonese but still serves Hong Kong society's elite with offerings that come with small unexpected flourishes, such as the *siu mai* with crab roe or the steamed squid with curry sauce.

Whether jostling for elbow room at budget restaurants or sitting in classy surroundings as silent carts glide towards your table, Hong Kong dim sum is the definitive version to try before the proverbial bucket gets kicked.

EAT IT ! ***DimDimSum, 26-28 Man Wui St, Jordan; Duddell's, Level 3 Shanghai Tang Mansion, 1 Duddell St, Central; Fook Lam Moon, 35-45 Johnston Rd, Wanchai.***

Hong Kong's Temple Street Night Market (right), where you'll be able to feast on delicious dim sum (below).

廟街
Temple Street
ASIAN CURRY KITCHEN
DVD
AV

11

See why ceviche made Peru famous for its food

PERU // In 2017, Peru had two restaurants in the world's top 10, which won't come as a surprise to anyone who has been to the country and tasted the food, in particular its standout dish, ceviche. For the uninitiated, ceviche is raw fish (or other seafood) marinated in citrus, most commonly lime or lemon, or a mix of the two, which serves to not just flavour the fish but break apart the amino acids, rendering it 'cooked'. As well as the citrus, ceviche is seasoned with chilli, onions, salt and coriander. In the humming metropolis that is Peru's capital, Lima, you won't have to walk far before coming across a *cevicheria*, but because Lima sprawls for kilometres along the Pacific coastline we've got a couple of suggestions to save your legs. Tiny Al Toke Pez has a loyal following for its uncomplicated approach to the classics and for its fervent adherence to freshness... oh, and it's cheap. If you're prepared to fork out more money for your fish then La Mar is hard to go past; the surroundings are classy and the classic ceviche here is delicious, but have some fun too and try something out-of-the-box, such as the *carretilla*, made up of octopus, jumbo squid, sea snails, limpets and clams.

EAT IT ! ***At Al Toke Pez, Av Angamos Este 886, Surquillo; and La Mar Cebicheria, Av Mariscal La Mar 770, Miraflores; both Lima.***

Big city pastries

↓

Take your pick of Iranian sweet treats during morning baking at a Tehran patisserie.

 page 58

↓

Vienna's imperious Sachertorte is best enjoyed at the hotel that still guards the recipe.

 page 110

↓

If you think macarons are everywhere you haven't been to Paris, where they are as plentiful as they are perfect.

 page 113

12

Swing by a Lisbon pastelaria for the ultimate egg tart

PORTUGAL // 'Bom dia.'
'Bom dia, tem pastéis de nata fresquinhos?'
'Claro, vão ser quantos?'
'Um por favor. Pensado melhor... levo dois. Obrigado!'
It's a conversation that happens every day on the streets of Portugal: visitors and locals alike are lured into pretty neighbourhood pastry shops (*pastelaria*) by the thought of a fresh *pastel de nata* and walk out with not one but two or more. Pair them with a cup of coffee for a perfect pick-me-up on your sightseeing tour.

Many countries have their own take on the egg tart, but in Portugal the simple formula has reached sweet perfection: the puff pastry shell flaky and crisp at the edge, the egg custard soft and sweet but not cloying, and the whole thing small enough to devour in a few bites. The *pastel de nata*, or *Pastéis de Belém* to give it its original name, was purportedly created centuries ago by monks but you won't have to trek to a monastery to find one these days – in pastry-obsessed Portugal it can feel as if there's a *pastelaria* on every street corner.

EAT IT ! ***Lisbon's Pastéis de Belém makes pastéis de nata to the same recipe it acquired from the neighbouring Jerónimos Monastery way back in 1837.***

A yellow tram on the streets of Lisbon (top), where pastéis de nata (right) can be found everywhere. Far right: the interior of Rafael Osterling's El Mercado (see p40).

12

© Courtesy of El Mercado / Pierre Monetta

© Nigel Parry

Eric Ripert

Eric Ripert is a French chef and TV personality, noted for his innovative seafood dishes. Ripert founded New York's Le Bernardin, one of the most celebrated restaurants in the world, and has authored four cookbooks, including his latest, My Best.

01

POMEGRANATE JUICE, BODH GAYA, INDIA The fresh pomegranate juice you find at street stalls in the small villages outside Bodh Gaya, India, is the best you will ever try.

02

GANJANG-GEJANG, SOUTH KOREA I always seek out this traditional dish of raw crab marinated in soy sauce when I'm in Korea – it's a must!

03

ANYTHING AT ALAIN DUCASSE'S LOUIS XV, MONACO The dishes at this three-Michelin-starred restaurant in L'hotel de Paris on the French Riviera are out of this world. It's over-the-top luxury and an incredible dining experience.

04

MASHED POTATOES, JAMIN, PARIS I first tried Joel Robuchon's famous mashed potatoes many years ago. Jamin has since closed but you can still find it at any one of his many ateliers around the world.

05

ANYTHING AT RYUGIN, ROPPONHI, TOKYO I was so impressed by everything in this restaurant, from the intimacy of the space to the refinement of the dishes.

Slurp down Tasmanian oysters straight from the ocean

13

AUSTRALIA // Whether you chew first or swallow 'em straight down, as an oyster lover you owe yourself a pilgrimage to the bivalve mollusc mecca that is Tasmania. For fans of fresh shellfish, the whole east coast is a dream destination, from beautiful Bruny Island in the south to the spectacular Freycinet Peninsula in the north. While the largest concentration of oyster farms is around the southern capital of Hobart, the trip north heralds breathtaking scenery perfect for a seafood romance. With the Freycinet National Park occupying most of the verdant peninsula, you'll find yourself immersed in granite rock formations jutting above soft sandy beaches and tranquil bays opening onto the Tasman Sea. Operating within the wetlands and estuaries of this pristine country are the Pacific oyster farms that have made the region a beacon for seafood aficionados. At Freycinet Marine Farm you can buy a dozen oysters straight from the sea to enjoy at a nearby beach or at the farm's own picnic tables. Or take a tour to see how the industry works firsthand, from incubation to grading.

Cultivated in Japan for centuries, jumbo-sized Pacific oysters were introduced to Australia in the middle of the last century and became an instant hit for their thick, meaty flesh and speedy maturation. Feeding on aquatic algae and nutrients, oysters have a healthy concentration of vitamins and minerals, including one of the highest natural concentrations of zinc, which is great for the immune and digestive systems. In the early 2000s, Italian scientists found that oysters contain certain amino acids that may promote libido, lending credibility to the legend that they are an aphrodisiac. So whether you prefer them raw, drowning in Tabasco, or with just a dash of lemon juice, eat your Tasmanian oysters with pride.

EAT IT ! ***Freycinet Marine Farm at 1784 Coles Bay Rd offers tours, farm sales and a mouthwatering seafood menu.***

Left, Wineglass Bay in Freycinet National Park is close to many of the local oyster farms, where you can also learn to shuck oysters safely.

Singular shellfish

It's what's on the inside that counts. Never more so than when eating sea urchin in Hokkaidō, Japan.

page 73

Blistering barnacles! You'll find boiled percebes on menus in southern Portugal.

page 121

The Ministry of Crab in Colombo is truly a centre of crustacean excellence.

page 231

Enjoy the freshest possible seafood at an oyster farm on the beautiful Freycinet Peninsula in Tasmania

From left: camembert from a rural French fromagerie; food stalls in the Dordogne; a Paris cheesemonger slices into his wares.

Where eating is an education

↓

What more is there to know about the spicy currywurst sausage? Visit its Berlin museum to find out.

☛ page 149

↓

Allow Aboriginals to walk you through the bushland fare of Australia's Northern Territory.

☛ page 102

↓

New Zealand's Bay of Islands honey shop tutors in the many benefits of manuka honey.

☛ page 285

© Lonely Planet / Matt Munro

Choose from three of the finest French cheese experiences... or enjoy them all

14

FRANCE // There are endless ways to enjoy French cheese, but these are our three favourites. To begin with, the king of cheese, Roquefort. Visiting the caves of Roquefort-sur-Soulzon feels like an anachronistic exercise; all the cheeses are lined up in the 2km-long Combalou Caves as they have been for centuries. It's the history and specificity that gives Roquefort its characteristic tang and creaminess, and getting to taste-test it at the place of inception is magical.

Secondly, the cheese trolley at Le Grand Véfour in Paris. When you're able to tear your eyes away from the opulent old-world décor with its frescoed ceilings, red velvet banquettes and gilt mirrors, you'll spy the cheese: a plethora of sheep, goat's and cow's, from the piquant to the nutty. The attentive and knowledgeable staff can talk you through all your options.

And thirdly, French cheese on your own terms. Cycle to a *fromagerie* in a rural village where you purchase your cheese, buy a bottle of champagne, find a shady, secluded spot in the countryside and let yourself be transported to the other side.

EAT IT ! ***Combalou Caves, Roquefort, Roquefort-Sur-Soulzon, Aveyron; Le Grand Véfour, 17 rue de Beaujolais, 75001 Paris.***

© Shane Luitjens / Alamy Stock Photo

15

© Shutterstock / Curioso

16

15

Jerk chicken: the Caribbean heat in Jamaica's capital

JAMAICA // Jamaica's favourite fiery rub has made the leap to countless destinations worldwide, so wonderfully addictive are its tongue-tingling spices, but eating it over chicken on home soil is still the best way to taste this Caribbean speciality. The dish developed when Spanish-owned African slaves escaped into the mountains and joined with the local Taino population. Traditional recipes evolved through the use of indigenous ingredients and before you know it... jerk chicken! A long list of seasonings goes into a jerk rub, most importantly pimento and scotch bonnet peppers. The heart-quickening blend is liberally applied to the chicken and thoroughly rubbed into the skin, and the result is left to marinate for a few hours (minimum two), before pieces of the bird are grilled and smoked over a fire which has been fed with fresh green branches from a pimento tree – the true secret of this fusion dish.

EAT IT ! *In wooden huts, surrounded by lush greenery, at the Pepperwood Jerk Center, 2 Chelsea Ave, Kingston.*

16

Complete a feast for the senses in Marrakech with lamb tagine

MOROCCO // Marrakech is filled with beauty at every turn, and nowhere more so than in the cobbled alleyways and souks of the ochre-hued medina. The energy of the streets is intoxicating. There's the scent of cinnamon in the air, a frenzy of pedestrians, and a constant racket from market-stall holders, traffic and touts. Lose yourself long enough to work up an appetite for Morocco's most famous meal, the tagine. In the traditionally decked-out restaurant at La Maison Arabe, diners sit beneath a hand-painted ceiling, ornate chandeliers and carved wooden windows, all to the gentle sound of a tinkling fountain in the flower-filled courtyard and live Arab-Andalucian music. So relax and enjoy your mint tea while you wait for the tagine to arrive. And boy, is the succulent meat and spice dish worth the wait. In fact, if you can't contemplate leaving the dish behind, sign up for the restaurant's four-hour cooking class and take the memory with you.

EAT IT ! *At Le Restaurant at Hotel La Maison Arabe, Derb Assehbi, Marrakech.*

© 500px / Sabino Parente

3389

Salute the glorious rise of Singapore's new culinary classic, chilli crab

17

From below left: throughout Singapore, from Lau Pa Sat hawker centre to Chinatown, chilli crab has become a signature dish.

SINGAPORE // From humble beginnings – it was first sold from a pushcart in the 1950s – Singapore's flagship, finger-licking and fiery crab meal is now an essential stop on anyone's culinary tour of the Lion City. The crab was originally cooked with bottled chilli and tomato sauces, but these days restaurants develop their own sauces from scratch, and they range from sweet and slightly spicy to knock-your-socks-off hot. There are seafood restaurants all over the city serving signature chilli crab, but it's fun to get your hands dirty at the long-standing No Signboard chain. Like the dish itself, No Signboard started simply, as an establishment so basic that it had no name. Now there are numerous outlets around town. Its crab comes with the option of adjusting the spice level to taste, but we think that chilli crab should pack a zing, so don't be shy. When the plate arrives at your table, roll up your sleeves – it's a creamy, messy, hands-on free-for-all. And when all the soft, juicy meat has been carefully extracted from the shells (it's acceptable to suck out anything you can't reach), grab a couple of *mantou* (steamed buns) to soak up all the remaining sauce.

EAT IT ! *At No Signboard Seafood, 414 Geylang Rd, Singapore.*

LUCKY
CHINATOWN
L4D
DOTA
幸運牛車水
AVIVA
24

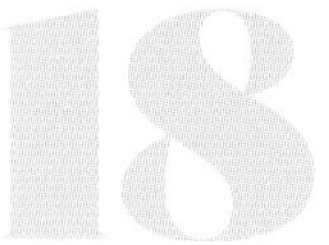

Chalk up an authentic meal experience with a plate of mussels from Brussels

BELGIUM // There's an esoteric joy in experiencing an internationally celebrated meal in its home country; and in Belgium, nothing will make you feel more like you're in the moment than *moules frites*. The traditional way to prepare *moules frites* is to pair these jewels of the sea with diced shallots and garlic mixed with white wine and cream. The accompanying fries are always that – fries, not chips – and the whole meal just wouldn't sing without a side of famous Belgian beer. You won't have any trouble finding *moules frites* in Belgium's capital, Brussels, but it's hard to go past the legendary Le Zinneke, where there are nearly 70 different variations on offer. The range is staggering, from simple alternatives to the classics like mussels with beer, chicory and cream, to more adventurous combinations such as sake and hot chilli. Le Zinneke mussels are sourced fresh daily from Zeeland and its food is prepared under the umbrella of the slow food movement, with great respect paid to organic ingredients and the sourcing of local products.

☛ EAT IT ! ***Roll up your sleeves and start building your very own midden! Le Zinneke, Place de la Patrie 26, 1030 Schaerbeek, Brussels.***

Take your table for a culinary spectacle in the hometown of Peking duck

CHINA // Caramel-coloured birds hanging in Chinese restaurant windows all over the world are a now-iconic sight, but it wasn't until the mid-19th century that cooks started to hang the duck to let the fat drain and create the intensely crispy skin that makes the dish so famous. In Beijing (or Peking), where the dish was born, a duck-eating experience can range from cheap and cheerful to high-end gastronomy. The best lies somewhere in between... like at Siji Minfu. Here the balance is struck between comfortable modern dining and old-school technique. Go for the whole bird and pay the extra for the premium duck (it's fatter and juicier). When roasted, the duck is brought to your table and the carving performance begins. First, they remove the head, followed by the crisp skin, then the meat is laid out on a plate. The carcass is removed, wheat pancakes are brought to the table, and it's time for you begin the assembling process: dip the duck in a salty hoisin sauce, then add pickles, and slivers of spring onion and cucumber. Wrap it up and place the parcel in your mouth. Swoon.

EAT IT ! *Siji Minfu, 32 Dengshikou W St, DongDan, Dongcheng Qu.*

All aboard a floating river market for pho on the go in Vietnam

20

VIETNAM // At Can Tho, the largest city in Vietnam's Mekong Delta, human industry bumps up against the waterlogged fecundity of the delta jungle. Life here is centred upon the Hau River, a major distributary of the Mekong, the city spilling on to its banks, with houses on stilts edging over the muddy waters and on to the river itself, most notably at its famous floating markets, the largest of which is Cái Răng. The action at Cái Răng starts early, with buyers and sellers exchanging fruit, vegetables and money from boat to boat. Among the nautical scrum, smaller vessels peddle sweet Vietnamese coffee and hot food. It's easy enough to get a ride on a boat from downtown Can Tho to visit the market, but it does mean setting out as early as 5am, so these river-borne food carts come as a godsend. And not just for a caffeine kick – some offer full-blown meals, including Vietnam's favourite breakfast dish, pho.

In fact, there might not be a better place to eat pho. After all, roughly half of the food produced in Vietnam comes from the delta, so the ingredients here are all super-fresh (and south Vietnamese pho is famously more generous with garnishes and condiments than its northern counterpart). A large part of the fun is watching someone drawing steaming beef broth from a large pot and combining it in a bowl with noodles, bean sprouts, spring onions, Thai basil and other garnishes, all retrieved from different containers, while balancing on a small boat. The acrobatic challenge does nothing to diminish the intoxicating aromas and flavours of meaty soup, basil, hoisin, chilli sauce and fresh lime that make this one of the world's great breakfasts. Finish off with fresh pineapple from a snack boat and you're in heaven.

EAT IT ! *Dodge the big tourist boats and book your trip to Cái Răng on a small sampan, so you can get much closer to the action (and snack boats).*

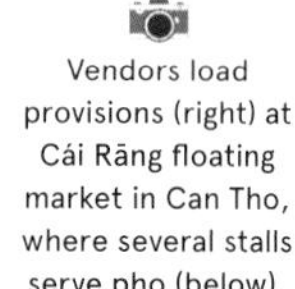

Vendors load provisions (right) at Cái Răng floating market in Can Tho, where several stalls serve pho (below).

21

Souvlaki: the grilled meat aroma of Athens after dark

GREECE // It's late-night in Athens and the aroma of herby grilling meats is seductively beckoning you towards open doorways and the hubbub of local conversation. The Greek take on the nocturnal flatbread sandwich format is fresher and healthier than most. A *souvlaki* is composed of grilled meat (chicken, pork, lamb or even beef), a crunchy salad of tomato, red onion and cucumber and some refreshing *tzatziki*, all wrapped in a large soft flatbread. The meat is the crucial ingredient (and the key difference from the *gyros*, which uses meat sliced from a rotisserie). Skewers of small chunks are grilled and flavoured with herbs, salt and lemon juice. Vegetarians are not forgotten: a grilled halloumi *souvlaki* is an equally wondrous end to a legendary night out in Athens.

EAT IT ! *In swanky Kolonaki head for Kalamaki Kolonaki at Ploutarhou 32. Or in Gazi, Elvis offers a shot of booze with your souv.*

21

Martin Morales

Martin Morales is the chef-founder of London's Ceviche Soho, Andina in Shoreditch, Casita Andina in Soho and Ceviche Old St. He has written two cookbooks Ceviche - Peruvian Kitchen and Andina: The Heart of Peruvian Food.

01

'RAG STEAK', BOGOTÁ, COLOMBIA This is a steak filled with salt and oregano, wrapped in a cloth, and then thrown into hot coals. Minutes later a succulent steak is revealed. I learned to cook it at Andres Carne de Res.

02

BARBECUED LAMB, FETHIYE, TURKEY At a local restaurant in Kayakoy, lambs are reared metres from your table – choose the parts you want and cook it on your own barbecue. Served with salad and fresh bread.

03

BLACK SQUID INK RICE, PONTEVEDRA, SPAIN O Boccoi on the waterfront in Combarro the black squid ink rice is beyond spectacular. It has the freshest and deepest squid ink flavour – don't miss it!

04

CALDEIRADA DE PEIXE, ALENTEJO, PORTUGAL Find a casual wood cabin style restaurant on a desolate Portuguese beach, such as Restaurante A Ilha, and sit outdoors to enjoy this classic fish soup.

05

CEVICHE PISQUENO, LIMA, PERU EL MERCADO DE RAFAEL OSTERLING My favourite restaurant in Peru represents Lima with its exquisite ceviches; the tuna and avocado ceviche is a recent highlight.

© Lonely Planet / Matt Munro
© Lonely Planet / Mark Read

22

Care to share chocolate and churros in Madrid?

SPAIN // Madrid in winter is the epitome of romance. But when you've had enough tramping through the frosted beauty of Buen Retiro Park, or shopping the side streets around the Plaza Mayor, it's time to get your frozen nose out of the biting breeze and to dip your *churros*. Served with a sinfully decadent bowl of rich chocolate dipping sauce, *churros* are essentially long, thin fingers of deep fried, sugar-crusted doughnut. Traditionally, the dough is piped into a large bowl then fried until it becomes crispy on the outside. *Churros* are the perfect antidote to Madrid's winter weather, but be warned. When the moment comes and there is only one *churros* left on the plate, it will be a test for even the strongest friendship.

EAT IT ! *Madrid's Chocolatería San Ginés at Pasadizo de San Gines has served churros since 1894, and offers a choco hit 24/7.*

St JOSEP
LA BOQUERIA

Graze your way around the best of Barcelona in bustling La Boqueria

23

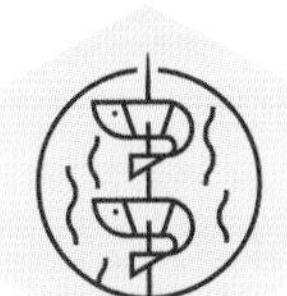

Marvellous markets

↓

The smells, sounds and general sensory assault of Tainan night market are unforgettable.

page 52

Complement a trawl through Copenhagen's Toverhallerne with a craft beer from its on-site brewery.

page 95

The fruits of the deep come in every shape and species at Seoul's Noryangjin fish market.

page 222

SPAIN // Standing shoulder to shoulder with locals in a Barcelona bar, sipping on sangria and picking at small plates of tapas, is one of life's greatest pleasures. The other mind-blowing Barcelona tapas experience is exploring the living, breathing Spanish food pyramid that is La Mercat de Sant Josep de la Boqueria, also simply known as La Boqueria.

The tapas stalls don't generally start serving until lunchtime so that gives you hours to wander around the fresh food stalls building up an appetite. There are kaleidoscopic displays of fresh fruit, imposing *jamón* stalls with huge legs of hams in various states of ageing, cheese, eggs, pastries and bread, and a gob-smacking amount of seafood. The popularity of this working market makes it a bustling affair, but part of the fun is in watching locals buy their groceries and travellers using their limited Spanish to buy slices of *jamón Ibérico*.

When your feet start to protest, head for the bars. Ramblero is the place to go for seafood tapas, fresh oysters, scallops, mussels and more – the *esqueixada* of cod (salad of salted cod with tomatoes, onions, olive oil, vinegar and salt) is heavenly. Next stop, the best-known of the market tapas restaurants, El Quim de la Boqueria (expect to have to wait for a free stool; the place is unbelievably popular). The defining dish here is the eggs fried in lots of olive oil with baby squid, but you should also load up on the wild mushrooms in port wine. Finally, head to Bar Pinotxo to sample the chickpeas and blood sausage.

Yes, it can be extremely busy inside the market. But the gates open at 8am (Monday to Saturday) so arrive as soon as you can to experience it (and the food) at its best.

EAT IT ! ***Ramblero; El Quim de la***

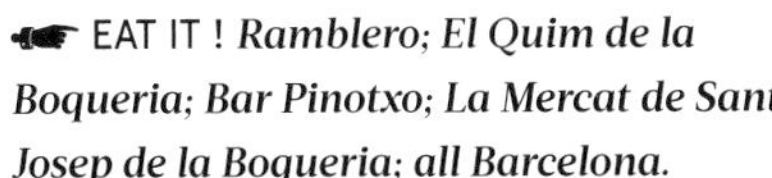

Boqueria; Bar Pinotxo; La Mercat de Sant Josep de la Boqueria; all Barcelona.

The famous gate to Barcelona's La Boqueria market (left), in which El Quim (below) is one of the hugely popular pitstops for snacks.

See kaleidoscoic displays of fresh fruit, jamón stalls with huge legs of ham, and a gob-smacking amount of seafood

At an Italian gelateria, ice-cream is a thing of artisanal beauty

24

ITALY // Sure, walking along cobblestoned streets grasping an ice-cream, with brilliant blue skies overhead and gorgeous young people buzzing past you on Vespas, can make everything in life seem brighter and more vibrant. But that's not the only reason why gelato in Italy is the best tasting ice-cream in the world.

Gelato's lower fat content puts much more emphasis on flavour ingredients and, unlike so much ice-cream, the good stuff here isn't treated like an indefinitely frozen asset, it's made anew every morning – which brings fresh, local, seasonal produce to the fore in spectacular fashion. So you get pistachio made from nuts grown in the foothills of Mt Etna, and strawberry flavour made using the Verdura Valley's ripe wild strawberries starts to appear in April and May. Citrus, Amarena cherries, chestnut and hazelnut are all regional, seasonal, must-sample flavours too.

Not every *gelateria* is staffed by artisanal gelato makers, but there are a couple of dead giveaways that indicate you're in the right spot. Flavours such as pistachio and banana should look pale, not fluorescent. And the gelato makers should look bleary-eyed – they've been up since the crack of dawn, after all.

EAT IT ! *Every ice-cream lover has to try fresh gelato served in a brioche bun at Noto's legendary Caffè Sicilia at least once in their life. Corso Vittorio Emanuele 125, Noto.*

Below: your pistachio and hazelnut gelato is served. Right: sun and lemon gelato by the sea near the Bay of Naples.

LISTINO PREZZI
PICCOLA (SMALL) € 1,50
GRANDE (LARGE) € 2,50
Il Gelato

25

Hummus: in which the humble chickpea becomes a social event

ISRAEL // We're in dodgy territory assigning hummus to a particular country. So, before we go any further, big shout out to Lebanon, Syria, Palestine, Egypt, Turkey and Cyprus. For this list, though, we're going with Israel's. At its most basic, hummus is a creamy dip made from chickpeas, tahini, lemon juice and garlic, but for disciples it is so much more. In Israel it's also a social event to be savoured, so gather your mates and get stuck in. Toppings for Israeli hummus are inventive; try fried mushroom and aubergine, fava bean paste with tahini and a boiled egg, and *hummus basar,* which is hummus with fried, minced beef. Each is served with fresh pita bread and quarters of white onion, the only acceptable ways of getting the hummus into your mouth.

EAT IT ! ***If you become paralysed by indecision head to reliable Abu Hassan (also known as Ali Caravan), 1 Dolphin St, Yafo, Tel Aviv.***

© Bon Appetit / Alamy Stock Photo

25

26

© Lonely Planet / Mark Read

26

Snack on fresh grilled fish in paradise

SEYCHELLES // Palm-fringed beaches, granite boulders, crystal waters and shimmering coral are the constant allure of the 115 islands that make up the Seychelles. So it's little wonder that the fish around the nation's paradisiacal perimeter are spectacular. Numerous beach restaurants and vendors across the archipelago offer you the heart and soul of Creole cuisine. Pick from the freshest snapper, rabbitfish, jackfish and sailfish caught by local fishers aboard one of the bobbing boats you see on the aqua waters. Dashed with a subtle blend of chilli, ginger, garlic and lemon, your catch is grilled to perfection. Refresh your palate with water straight from the coconut available from a neighbouring stall. Then pinch yourself, you're in heaven.

EAT IT ! ***At sunset, mix with locals at Beau Vallon Beach and absorb the smoky aroma of grilled Creole creations at the stalls lining Mahe's lively Beau Vallon Beach.***

27

How a happy accident in a French hotel gave the world tarte tatin

FRANCE // In the popular version of the story behind this upside-down apple tart, Stéphanie Tatin, co-owner of Hotel Tatin in Lamotte-Beuvron, rescues a burning panful of apple pie filling by laying puff pastry on top and sticking it in the oven. The blend of rich, caramelised apple and crisp pastry base is so well-received that it becomes the hotel's signature dish. *Et voila*! Track forward 120 years and *tarte tatin* is a national institution. Hotel Tatin's restaurant was modern at the time of the tart's invention and, like its recipe, doesn't seem to have changed much. Its quaint dining room, with timber furniture, dusky pink carpet and draped windows, has just the right *grand-mère* quotient for enjoying a fat slice of oven-warm upside-down apple tart.

☛ EAT IT ! ***Hotel Tatin has accommodation too. It's a great base for exploring the heavily forested Grand Sologne region and the Loire Valley. 5 Avenue de Vierzon, Lamotte-Beuvron.***

28

Celebrate with Sardinians and a slow-cooked porcedu

ITALY // Most people associate the Italian island of Sardinia with fish, but the mountainous interior offers some of its most mouthwatering dishes, and *porcedu* is right up there: a whole suckling piglet, cooked for hours over a fire stoked with myrtle leaves, thyme, oregano, mint, basil, bay leaves, marjoram and apple wood chips. It's a labour of love that showcases not just the best of local produce but the Sardinians' independent nature and appreciation of their beautiful landscape. The work that goes into the preparation means that it's a dish most commonly served at celebrations, so do your best to get invited to a local's wedding or birthday party to sample meat that's juicy and tender from hours of slow turning over a gentle heat, with crispy and salty skin, all served up on a huge platter covered in myrtle leaves.

☛ EAT IT ! ***Befriend a local to score an invite, or try a B&B like Agriturismo la Sorgente Localita Annunziata, Castiadas, Sardinia.***

29

Welcome to New York, where the bun and the beef combine sublime

USA // This fast-food staple has hotly disputed origins, with Germany claiming first dibs. The city of Hamburg was, indeed, the first to make a meat steak from minced beef, garlic, onion, salt and pepper. But they didn't put it inside a bun. The Americans are sticking their flag in that one and have turned the invention into a national passion. The bun itself has been upgraded so you'll find brioche and ciabatta in addition to the crowd-pleasing sesame seed bun. Weighing in on the best burger debate is a dangerous game but we stand by New York as the place to sate cravings. Burgers in the Big Apple are big business, and new places with creative additions to the meat patty pop up all the time. At Bill's Bar & Burger you'll find the signature cheeseburger is as tasty as a burger can be: six ounces (170g) of beef, cheese, pickles and lettuce. If you like your burger extravagant then try an Emmy Burger, from Emily in Brooklyn: dry-aged beef, cheddar, charred onions, cornichons and a Korean-style sauce, bookended by a pretzel bun.

EAT IT ! *Bill's Bar & Burger, Bill's Rockefeller Center, 16 W 51st St (also Downtown at 85 West St); and Emily, 919 Fulton St, Brooklyn.*

30

There's nowhere like the motherland for a plate of genuine Swedish meatballs

SWEDEN // Sweden's fantastic meatballs, or *köttbullar*, are popular from Malmö to the Arctic Circle, though Stockholm is nominally the *köttbullar* capital, by virtue of the number of options it offers for experiencing the dish. Wander the circuitous laneways of the medieval old town, Gamla Stan, with its quirkily symmetrical golden and ochre-coloured buildings, or the elegant cobbled streets in the heart of the city, and you'll find a restaurant serving *köttbullar* the traditional way. The meatballs are made with a mix of pork and beef mince – sometimes reindeer, especially up north – plus breadcrumbs and allspice, and lodged in a shallow bowl of smoothly whipped potato with meaty, creamy gravy poured over. Sides of sliced pickled cucumber and tart lingonberry sauce cut through the richness of the cream. For a dish designed as fuel for workers facing down the Scandinavian elements, it offers a sophisticated balance of flavours. Until you've been to Sweden, you've never really tried *köttbullar*.

☛ EAT IT ! ***Köttbullar* doesn't appear on the printed menu at Tranan at Karlbergsvägen 14 in Stockholm, but the place is famous for them.**

© Shutterstock / Millionstock

© Getty Images / Johner Images

© Lonely Planet / Matt Munro

PD304
BONNIE LASS

The freshest fish and chips in a sublime Scottish scene

Left, a fishing boat waits for the tide to rise in Stonehaven harbour. Below, fresh fish and chips can be served in newspaper or on a plate.

Made in England

The right method of serving cream tea - scones, jam and clotted cream - is a matter of national debate.

page 109

Now a standard in Indian restaurants across Britain, balti curry was conceived in Birmingham.

page 252

Wash down your steak and kidney pie with a pint of local ale in a London pub.

page 303

UK // The romance of the sea is keenly felt at Stonehaven, in northeast Scotland. Its pebble-strewn beach traces a kilometre-long bay; sailing boats bob in the harbour; rockpools teem with crabs and sea stars; gulls ride on the breeze; and in the distance, the leaden horizon of the North Sea. Completing the scene, halfway along the beach is The Bay Fish & Chips, whose fish is wild-caught from Marine Stewardship Council-certified stocks, with the name of the boat that supplied the day's catch displayed on a board. The potatoes for its chips are sourced from a potato merchant in nearby Potterton. Considering the setting, the sustainability and the beautifully cooked fish, is it the best fish and chip shop in the world? The constant queue suggests so.

Of course, saying the best example of Britain's national dish is in Scotland may ruffle a few feathers. For one thing, most accounts have the dish originating in England in the 1860s, either in London, at the shop of Jewish immigrant Joseph Malin, or in Lancashire, as invented by entrepreneur John Lees. Whatever the truth, there are great fish-and-chip shops the length of Britain. The next question is cod or haddock? Cod is thought to be the more sustainable option today, but look for MSC-approved sources.

EAT IT ! *Default order: battered cod, large chips, Irn-Bru. Beach Promenade, Stonehaven, Scotland.*

Add a shake of the vinegar bottle to thick, white fillets of fish in a crisp, deep-fried shell of batter and hot, fluffy chips

Stay up till dawn amid the delights of a Tainan Night Market

32

TAIWAN // In a place synonymous with street food, Tainan is the undisputed food capital. Affectionately known as the 'city of snacks', it's the birthplace of coffin bread and *danzai* noodles, and you can expect to find celebrated street vendors on almost every corner. But it's the fabled night markets that will leave you gobsmacked. Nothing prepares you for the sensory overload as you enter these fascinating farragoes of crowds, heavenly smells, bright lights and banners advertising rows of stalls serving culinary treasures from Taiwan and beyond.

Here you'll find Singapore *laksas*, Thai sweets and Indian rotis alongside stalls for Taiwanese stinky tofu, spicy duck blood, oyster omelette, green onion pancakes, milkfish soup, fruit skewers and every type of bread. The markets are sprawling, loud, insanely popular and represent a genuine melting pot of cultures, tastes and traditions. The two biggest, Hua Yuan and Dadong, have plenty of shopping stalls and games stalls (think old-school water balloon shooting) to keep you occupied between snacks – and at Dadong you can munch along with the bizarrely entertaining spectacle of its unique outdoor night auction.

EAT IT ! *Go family-friendly at game-centric Dadong Night Market. No 276, Section 1, Linsen Rd, East District, Tainan City.*

Parisian perfection

A fabulous Breton import, crêpes are sold from street stalls all over the capital.

page 99

We've tracked the ultimate croque monsieur to an elegant Left Bank bistro.

page 150

Where else to get your fix of crème brûlée than in magical Montmartre?

page 229

Book a table in a classic Parisian bistro and order the steak tartare

FRANCE // Like croissants and baguettes, cigarettes and red wine, steak tartare in a Parisian bistro is as French as it comes. And before you protest about clichés and caricatures remember there is such a thing as a culinary classic, and France has a whole market basket full of them. So be prepared to surrender yourself to some truisms in the City of Love. At Le Bar Romain in the 9th arrondissement there is a whole section of the menu dedicated to different tartares, from tuna and salmon to beef with herbs, onions and salmon roe or beef tenderloin with balsamic vinegar, parmesan, onions and capers. They all sound enticing but the reason you're here is for the original, the beef tartare with chopped onions, capers and herbs – simply adorned with parsley potatoes or a fresh green salad. The texture of the meat is soft with subtle seasoning, and there's added bite from the onions and tartness from the capers. Beyond the balanced flavours you'll be eating your tartare under carved wooden ceilings and Renaissance paintings lit by sparkling chandeliers, with, of course, a glass of champagne at hand.

EAT IT ! ***In the sparkling, classic Parisian brasserie that is Bar Romain, 6 rue de Caumartin, Paris.***

A vibrant Tainan night market (top), where all manner of treats simmer and sizzle (right). Far right: steak tartare is served.

32

© StockFood / The Picture Pantry

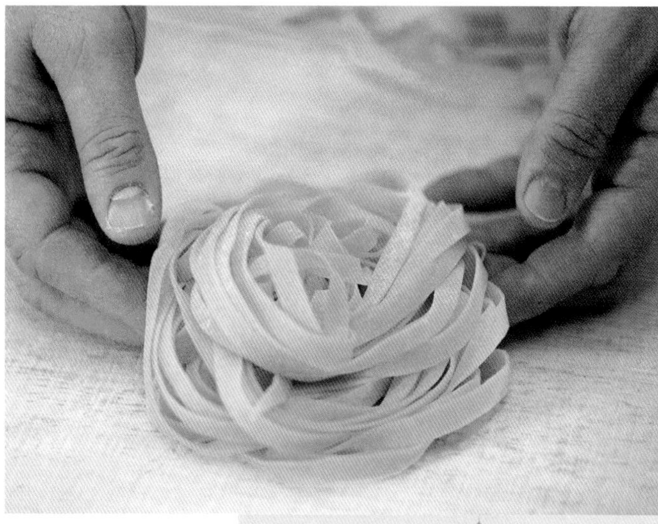

From left: tagliatelle is prepared at Bologna's Ristorante Diana; the historic cityscape; ragù as traditionally served.

Disputed dinners

The Indian states of West Bengal and Odisha are at odds over which invented sweet rasgulla.

page 232

Who created the cake in honour of Anna Pavlova causes arguments in the Antipodes.

page 280

Eastern or western? Not so much an origin dispute, more a disagreement on prepping North Carolina BBQ.

page 292

© Lonely Planet / Susan Wright

Know your Bolognese from your, well, Bolognese

34

ITALY // No, this is not spaghetti Bolognese. We're warning you, don't ask for spaghetti with your ragù in Bologna or you will be met with withering looks, eye rolls and disappointed head-shaking. This is because the meat and tomato sauce we've come to know the world over as Bolognese is not known as such in Bologna, it's just ragù and it's served with tagliatelle, never spaghetti. The reasoning behind this is that the rich, meaty sauce sticks much better to a wider style of pasta. So here's what goes into a traditional *tagliatelle al ragù* in its home town. At least two types of meat (usually pancetta and diced beef) and often some minced veal and pork; onions, carrots and celery; red wine and beef stock; and tomato paste. It's served over lightly salted tagliatelle with some grated Parmesan cheese.

It's not that you'll never enjoy a spaghetti Bolognese again. It's just that once you've tried the real deal in the place it was invented, you might find that you're one of those people who spontaneously shoots withering looks when someone suggests spaghetti with their ragù Bolognese.

☛ EAT IT ! ***At the traditional Ristorante da Nello al Montegrappa in the historic city centre. Via Montegrappa 2, Bologna.***

35

© Getty Images / svariophoto

35

35

Keep it simple with an insalata Caprese on the sun-kissed isle of Capri

ITALY // Sunshine, a terrace table, a pink-hued sunset and the perfect *insalata Caprese*: more often than not, the simple things in life are the best. The Isle of Capri, which is within a stone's throw of Sorrento off Italy's west coast, is where this simple salad originated. It's all about the match-making: a soft buffalo mozzarella off-setting the fruity tang of large ripe tomatoes, freshly picked basil leaves and a slug of punchy Italian virgin olive oil – the colours of the Italian flag. A Caprese salad doesn't really need anything else.

The simplicity puts all the responsibility on to the ingredients, just as it should be in Italian cooking. What matters is that the ingredients are local, seasonal and the very best that they can be. A tasteless greenhouse-grown tomato, rubbery mozzarella or bland, mass-produced olive oil will all be found out. Get it right and enjoy *la dolce vita* for an evening on Capri.

EAT IT ! *Terrazza Brunella at Via Tragara, 24 has a terrace with views of the sea and Capri and does a decent insalata caprese too.*

36

Pull up a bar stool in Buffalo to understand why the chicken wing became a spicy snack staple

USA // To put it bluntly, Buffalo wings are a bar snack. Eat them anywhere other than a bar and they will taste like, well, like what they are: the worst part of the chicken, slathered in butter and cayenne pepper. But eat them in their natural habitat – in a saloon with a televised hockey game blaring in the background and a few empty bottles of lager in front of you – they are transformed into the single greatest dish on the planet. Buffalo is the upstate New York city where they're said to have been invented in the 1960s. Wings fanatics, however, hail Anchor Bar owner and believed creator Teressa Bellissimo as a saint for having birthed the salty-spicy beer pairing. The Bellissimo family has insisted the dish was accidental and yet this combo is now even more linked than a burger and fries. Buffalo wings have transcended their main ingredient to become a simple vehicle for delivering taste bud-destroying spiciness, as wing-eating contests and bar menus often use them to showcase their unholy sauce concoctions.

☛ EAT IT ! ***While versions of 'wings' are served in bars worldwide, Anchor Bar, in Buffalo, New York, is Buffalo Wing mecca.***

37

Greet the Cambodian morning with a bowl of bai sach chrouk

CAMBODIA // Savoury, filling bowls of soup, noodles and rice, often slurped down by the side of the road on the way to work, is how millions of Southeast Asians start their day. In Cambodia, you'll have jump-starting breakfast options such as *nom banh chok*, rice noodles with fish and a green curry sauce, or *kuy teav*, a rice noodle soup made with pork or beef bones, but it's the aroma of the simple *bai sach chrouk* that will make your mouth water. Pork, marinated in coconut, is slowly roasted over open flames on small makeshift BBQs before being placed on rice with a sprinkling of spring onions. It's served with pickled cucumber, carrot, ginger and daikon and a bowl of clear chicken broth. Sweet, sour, salty, smoky and totally delicious.

EAT IT ! ***At any of the busy breakfast street stalls in Phnom Penh, between 7am and 9am (after that they're usually sold out).***

37

© Austin Bush

38

© Getty Images / Andrew Peacock

38

Find all Iranian life gathered in a Tehrani bakery

IRAN // It's a common morning sight in Tehran; customers leaving their favourite bakeries with a precariously teetering tower of pastry boxes, packed with freshly baked bread and all sorts of flaky delights and sweet treats. In a country obsessed with food and with a culture that prides itself on hospitality, Iranian bakeries are a metaphor for life. Locals visit their favourite shops every day to stock up on *lavash*, *sangak* and *barbari* – varying forms of flatbread eaten with everything. And these days they're equally likely to be seen leaving one of the new breed of internationally inspired patisseries with a decadent collection of delicate cakes, biscuits, tarts, macarons and other sweet pastries, all taken straight home to share out among family and friends over tea sipped through sugar cubes.

EAT IT ! ***There are many patisseries and bakeries to choose from, but you could start with Orient Café, Darvazeh Dolat No 16, Tehran.***

39

Find absolute peace in a Scottish salmon smokehouse

UK // Picture an old brick kiln on an island off the Scottish coast, smoke curling slowly from a hole in the roof, and inside, rows of pink salmon fillets hanging over smouldering piles of whisky-soaked wood. Imagine the smell of the smoke entwined with the sweet fishiness of the salmon, and the sound of the waves. No wonder cold-smoked salmon from the Outer Hebrides, with its buttery flesh touched by the aroma of that smoke, is a popular choice for 'best in the world' – it comes from a place so peaceful, so patient, that if you visit, you might never complete that half-composed tweet about #slowfood. You could go on a yoga retreat and eat wholefoods... or you could go to Scotland and eat smoked salmon with the odd glass of single-malt. Your call.

EAT IT ! *Hebridean Smokehouse smokes salmon over peat, beechwood and whisky-barrel oak. Clachan, North Uist, Scotland.*

40

Grill, wrap, eat, repeat: barbecued pork in Seoul

SOUTH KOREA // Seoul offers an intoxicating mix of the past (ancient shrines, imposing city walls, wooden houses), the present (you'll hear this week's K-pop chart-topper everywhere you go) and the future (South Koreans use cutting-edge tech as if it's oxygen). But among all that time-travelling, there's something timeless about sitting in a restaurant here, a grill at the centre of your table, wisps of meaty smoke in the air and piles of immaculately prepared ingredients at your disposal. There are many ways with Korean barbecue meat, but none beat *samgyeopsal* – fatty slices of pork belly grilled with garlic, onions, chilli and kimchi, wrapped in lettuce and perilla leaf. For the barbecue novice it's easy to prepare and delivers a flavour hit that'll have you marvelling, and then pulling together the ingredients for another one.

EAT IT ! *Jeju Abang is known for pork BBQ, as are several of its neighbours on the BBQ Alley near Jongno 3-ga station (take 4th exit).*

© Lonely Planet / Austin Bush

© Lonely Planet / Austin Bush

41

Dive into a deep and rich Massaman curry in Bangkok

THAILAND // In common with many Southeast Asian cities, eating out in Bangkok is one of the best culinary adventures imaginable. On every street, alley and canalside you'll find countless vendors' carts selling both the familiar - the likes of *moo ping* meat skewers, pad thai, and *tom yum goong* - to the utterly unique - like black sesame rice dumplings in hot ginger, taro root ice-cream or Massaman curry. This latter is unlike most Thai food, replacing sweet and light flavouring with dense, heavy spices more common to Central and southern Asian dishes. Cardamom, cinnamon, cloves, star anise, cumin, bay leaves, nutmeg and mace flavour the unctuous curry sauce, but that could be any old curry, right? What gives the dish its unique flavour is the clever comingling of these spices with more local ones; galangal, white pepper, shrimp paste, tamarind and coconut cream are all added to the mix, as well as roasted peanuts, to create yet another reason to explore Bangkok's truly original food scene.

EAT IT ! ***Hang out at W Market global food courtyard near the Phra Khanong BTS station with live music, street artists and a beer.***

© 500px / Oliver Saved

42

Fresh Fijian coconut in paradise

↓

FIJI // Sometimes a life-affirming food experience can just be about eating a fresh coconut on a beach with views over turquoise water. In Fiji, winsome wood-and-straw resort huts known locally as *bures* face the Blue Lagoon in the Yasawa Islands, where a vibrant world of marine life sits below the sea's surface. How to perfect this moment? Perhaps that little gift from Mother Nature, a fresh coconut, plus straw, nothing else: cold, sweet and refreshing.

☛ EAT IT ! ***From a sun lounger while marvelling at the fortunate position you find yourself in.***

43

Stuff your days in Shanghai with stall-bought baozi

CHINA // Sweet or savoury, these little fist-sized doughy buns are just right for breakfasts on the go. Grab one from the ubiquitous street-side stands or in one of the hundreds of restaurants that serve them citywide. The traditional *baozi* most commonly come stuffed with BBQ'd pork, either plain or heavily spiced, but there are many popular vegetarian varieties with tasty things such as mushroom, pak choi, leek and tofu; and there are sweet options too, stuffed with red bean paste or custard. In recent years the *baozi* business has been through a hipster transformation, with new stores and stalls opening up and serving innovative fillings like Korean fried chicken, Japanese *okonomiyaki*, and BBQ pork with apple and sweet and sour lotus root.

EAT IT ! *There are thousands of baozi stalls, shops and restaurants throughout the city, but for the modern take, try Baoism, at 150 Hubin Lu, Hubindao Mall, B2, Room E30, Shanghai.*

43

© dpa picture alliance / Alamy Stock Photo

43

© Marti sans / Alamy Stock Photo

44

End the night in Istanbul with classy clubbers' pick-me-up, midye dolma

TURKEY // Here's how to eat a *midye dolma*. First go out to a club or bar in one of the happening districts like Beyoğlu, Karaköy and Şişli or Beşiktaş. Then, when you're worn out from dancing, head out into the night and follow the locals, who will lead you to the stuffed mussels with wedges of lemon sold from street carts all over Istanbul. Inside the shiny black shell sits the juicy mussel, on top of rice seasoned with cinnamon, pepper and cumin, and sometimes pine nuts and currants. Locals eat these mussels all day, but they're especially popular as a late-night post-clubbing or bar snack. Join in by squeezing lemon over your mussel and rice, eating it in one mouthful straight from the shell.

EAT IT ! *After enjoying Istanbul's famous nightlife at any street stall where you see locals lining up.*

José Andrés

José Andrés pioneered the small plate movement in the USA, through his many restaurants, including Minibar in New York and e by José Andrés in Las Vegas.

© Our Local Commons

CRAB, MARYLAND, USA
The Bethesda Crab House does them perfectly – lots of Old Bay and nothing else. This tastes like home to me.

SANCOCHO, PUERTO RICO
As a volunteer with #ChefsforPuertoRico, I served a lot of this simple, hearty stew with beef and vegetables, commonly found in homes throughout the country.

CAVIAR, RIOFRÍO, SPAIN
This tiny village in Granada has the best organic caviar in the world. I take a slice of jamón ibérico, a spoonful of caviar, and fold it up — we call it a 'José Taco'.

TANGERINES, OJAI, CALIFORNIA
The Tangerine Man grows delicious kishu mandarins — so juicy and sweet. And you can order online, so you don't have to go to Ojai to get it.

UNI, HOKKAIDO, JAPAN
I came here with my friend Nobu Matsuhisa and he took me fishing for sea urchin. The roe from there has so much umami it's like you are kissing the sea.

Bite into a beignet for a taste of that Big Easy beat

USA // It's magical how a simple, deep-fried square of choux pastry can be so much greater than the sum of its parts. The hot crunch of the outer crust, the chewy doughnut centre and the mountain of silky powdered sugar it's buried under combine to make the New Orleans *beignet* a dessert to die for. Part of the same French-Canadian migrant story that delivered Cajun culture to Louisiana, these hot, sweet treats are especially popular in the city's French Quarter, where the streets buzz with the energy of local bands and, presumably, some kind of *beignet*-fuelled collective sugar-rush.

EAT IT ! ***Join the throng at the 150-year-old Café du Monde for classic New Orleans beignet and a coffee-and-chicory café au lait.***

© Jim West / Alamy Stock Photo

Masala dosa: your culinary saviour in southern India's urban sprawls

INDIA // Amid the swirling, noisy rush of a south Indian city street, with the crowds and cars, auto rickshaws and close tropical air pressing in on you, the delicate crunch, subtle tanginess and aromatic spiciness of a fresh *masala dosa* can feel like a cool breeze. No matter where you are, from frenetic Mumbai in the west to, um, frenetic Chennai in the east, you'll see people stepping out of the human current to snack on delicious rice-crêpe-wrapped parcels of potato curry. At any time of day too – they are eaten for breakfast, lunch and dinner, or any time in-between. The *dosa* is made from a fermented batter of ground rice and lentils, cooked thinly on a griddle until crispy on one side but soft and light on the other, the resulting crêpe folded around a filling of potato, onion, curry leaves, turmeric and mixed spices (the masala), and usually served with coconut chutney. Ask a dozen Indians where to get the best *masala dosa* and you'll get a dozen answers, but spend any time in the south and it won't take long to draw your own conclusion.

☛ EAT IT ! ***To balance flavours and stay clean, spread coconut chutney on the dosa, tear off a small piece and drizzle with sambar.***

47

© Getty Images / Nazir Azhari Bin Mohd Anis / EyeEm

© Shutterstock / T.Slack

47

© thegingernomad / Stockimo / Alamy Stock Photo

47

Brighten dark Dublin days with a bowl of Irish stew and a pint of the black stuff

IRELAND // On a winter's day, with the rain lashing down, the temperature in single digits and the sky permanently set to dusk, life contracts to Ireland's pubs and intensifies with talking and laughing, inky-black pints of Guinness, and a willingness for singing and dancing. It's the craic – facing down grim weather and dark days with simple joy. The natural culinary accompaniment is Irish stew, a dish that similarly makes magic with whatever's to hand – in its purest form, mutton or baby goat cooked with potatoes and onions in water; increasingly, lamb is subbed in, and ingredients like parsley, carrots, leeks and pearl barley, to soak up the watery broth, are added. It's the definition of warming, hearty and filling. You can season the stew with salt, but the flavour is best enhanced by eating it in one of those pubs, with one of those pints of Guinness, and friends. Many cultures locate the romance of food in hours of preparation and myriad ingredients; for the Irish, the romance is in the eating and whatever happens around it.

EAT IT ! *Dublin's The Brazen Head, 20 Bridge St Lower, is Ireland's oldest pub and serves a classic Irish stew. Any questions?*

Show ritual appreciation for the delicate balance of kaiseki

48

JAPAN // Fine-dining degustations and beautifully crafted, Michelin-starred plates of food are everyday affairs in Japan, but *kaiseki* is an order of magnitude above these. At the upper end of the eating scale, it can easily run to tens of thousands of yen, but is worth it. Not just a meal and about more than presentation and taste; *kaiseki* is the realisation of the Japanese *omotenashi* – which translates as 'wholehearted hospitality'. The chef's purpose in serving *kaiseki* is to convey ultimate respect to the guest. It's an exquisite embodiment of Japanese culinary skill, veneration and appreciation, and is something that should be experienced at least once in a lifetime.

The city of Kyoto is the home of *kaiseki*, where these extraordinary meals are usually served in a *ryokan* (a traditional inn with tatami-matted rooms). Each chef prepares the *kaiseki* in a slightly different way, largely because the meal is an artistic expression of esteem and a celebration of seasonal produce, so no two *kaiseki* meals are ever the same. Saying this, there are still some rules that your chef will follow (this is Japan, after all). The courses you can expect to be served are an appetiser with sake; a dish that is simmered; sashimi; a course known as *hassun*, which is designed to be an expression of the season; a grilled course; and a rice dish. The progression of edible magnificence culminates in a dessert and a matcha tea ceremony. Set aside a whole day to luxuriate in the event, and to show the chef your appreciation for such a superb and discerning offering.

EAT IT ! *At Kyoto Kitcho Arashiyama, 58 Sagatenryūji Susukinobabachō, Ukyō-ku; or Gion Karyo, 605-0074 Kyoto Prefecture.*

Kyoto, home of such aesthetic delights as Ginkaku-ji temple (right), is also where you'll partake in the edible art of kaiseki (below).

49

Watch the sun go down in Santorini with a plate of domatokeftedes

GREECE // How can a humble tomato fritter taste so good? Perhaps it's the beauty of Santorini or the tiny, vibrant, cherry tomatoes that grow on the volcanic island – whichever, this is the best place in the world to sample *domatokeftedes*. Harvested year-round, the tomatoes have a distinctive flavour due to the mineral- and nutrient-rich soil they grow in, and are at their juiciest from June to August... which should work out nicely with your Greek island holiday plans. Tavernas across the island serve the fritters as part of an ouzo meze, and the locals know best, as these lightly fried balls of tomato, feta, red onion, parsley, mint and oregano are a perfect accompaniment to a spectacular evening sunset and swig of an aniseed aperitif.

EAT IT ! ***Most traditional island tavernas feature domatokeftedes on their menu, pick one with a great view and tuck in.***

50

Feast on spicy piri piri chicken on a beach in Mozambique

MOZAMBIQUE // The enticing smell of spicy chicken on a smoky grill, intermingled with paprika, lemon and garlic marinade seasonings and spices, is near-impossible to resist. And why would you? Possibly because you'd have to drag yourself away from one of the beautiful beaches that Mozambique can lay claim to, along with this signature dish with a spicy kick. If you're lucky, you won't need to leave the beach; fiery piri piri chicken can be found at beachshack stalls as well as roadside barbecues, cafes, restaurants and street stalls in major towns. Best of all, you can help the local economy too: the tender butterflied bird pairs perfectly with a cold Impala beer, the first commercial beer to be made with cassava instead of barley, which has boosted the country's agricultural economy and provided jobs.

EAT IT ! ***At roadside BBQs, or if you fancy a restaurant then Piri Piri, Av 24 de Julho, Maputo, Mozambique, is a sound bet.***

51

Fattoush with friends: a tribute to Syria and the salad gone global

SYRIA // We're giving this salad to Syria but it's found all over the Levantine region. The ingredients of toasted flatbread, sweet tomatoes, fresh vegetables and herbs, lemon juice and sumac make it perfect for the searingly hot temperatures in the Middle East. It's best eaten in a street-side Damascus café, which is sadly not possible now, nor likely to be in the immediate future, but we're talking about the oldest continuously inhabited metropolis in the world, so it will be back. Syrians eat *fattoush* by placing some of the ingredients into a lettuce or vine leaf and wrapping it up into a little parcel. In lieu of tasting the salad in Syrian surrounds, prepare a huge plate for friends, serve some hibiscus flower tea, *zouhourat*, and toast to Syria's future.

☛ EAT IT ! ***This is an everyday food available throughout Syria, the wider Middle East and indeed most big cities around the world.***

51

52

Let a bacon maple doughnut put a spell on you

USA // Portland: environmentally sustainable land of fine coffee, great beer and wine – and the Bacon Maple Bar from Voodoo Doughnut. Queues continue to form outside the cult downtown doughnut shop for its whacked-out technicolour creations (presented in a pretty pink box). There's the vegetarian Grape Ape, a raised yeast doughnut with vanilla frosting, grape dust and lavender sprinkles. Or the Viscous Hibiscus and the pot-inspired Maple Blazer Blunt, dusted with cinnamon sugar and with ember-like red sprinkles. But the king of the 'nuts might be the Bacon Maple Bar, a raised yeast doughnut with maple frosting decorated with two crispy rashers of bacon. Sweet, savoury and doughy – what's not to like? If you feel guilty, burn off some calories on a Biketown shared bike.

☛ EAT IT ! ***Voodoo Doughnut has three Portland stores: 22 SW 3rd Avenue and 1501 NE Davis St. Or via food cart and bicycle delivery.***

52

53

Pick your favourite El Salvadorian pupuseria and devour its signature snack

EL SALVADOR // You've tried *quesadillas* and *arepas*, now it's time to settle into a *pupuseria* with the locals and spoil at least three of your senses with the addictive El Salvadorian *pupusa*. These thick, round corn tortillas are stuffed and pressed on to a hot comal grill until toasty. Of the numerous different fillings, the most common are cheese, refried beans, chicken, *chicharrón* (fried pork skin), and *revueltas* (a combination of beans, pork and cheese), but the tortillas are also filled with seafood varieties, mixed vegetables and even sweet versions with berries. Savoury *pupusas* always come served with a side of coleslaw known as *curtido* and a tomato salsa which cuts through the richness of the dough. This delicious dish is sold on street corners and in restaurants, but best of all is to eat it in the dedicated cafes known as *pupuserias*; you won't have any trouble finding one anywhere in the country – the fun comes in finding your favourite.

EAT IT ! ***Anywhere in El Salvador, though the pupusa has spread to the US and Canada, where you'll find them in most big cities.***

54

Lakeside in New Zealand, net some whitebait fritters

NEW ZEALAND // Every August, keen whitebaiters set up their scoop nets in rivers, streams and lakes across New Zealand for the short season when it's permissible to catch these little freshwater fish. At Lake Onoke in the North Island's Wairarapa region, the fisherfolk set nets around the lake shores hoping for a hefty haul. The season is regulated in order to ensure the protection of the different species which seems to add a certain fervent excitement to the preparation of one of New Zealand's most loved snacks – the whitebait fritter. They are prepared by adding whole juvenile fishes to beaten egg, flour and salt before being pan-fried in butter. Pair some with a Martinborough Sauvignon Blanc at Lake Ferry Hotel on the lakefront.

EAT IT ! *At the Lake Ferry Hotel, 2 Lake Ferry Rd, South Wairarapa Coast.*

55

Recline in your beach chair and await your tiger prawns

MYANMAR // The white sand of Myanmar's Ngwe Saung beach stretches for miles, broken only by palm trees on the shoreline and beach chairs and umbrellas dotting the sand. It's a laid-back tropical idyll where visitors swim, snorkel and sunbake. To the north are smart resorts, to the south budget hotels and a backpacker vibe, and between them the village of Ngwe Saung, where you can grab a bite to eat... but what do you do if the gentle whoosh of the waves on the sand is too hard to leave? Don't worry, the locals have got you covered. It won't be long before a food vendor approaches your spot and you can buy the lightly charred BBQ tiger prawns that sit in a plate on their head. Sure, it's a bit bizarre, but you won't be arguing with the taste.

EAT IT ! *Ngwe Saung Beach, Ayeyarwady region, Myanmar.*

Refuel on a samosa – one of India's most successful exports – while seeing Kolkata's sights

INDIA // With the sights, sounds and, yes, smells, of India swirling about you, these chewy, mildly spiced parcels are ideal on-the-go street food. Hold one safely in one hand, while checking directions in your guidebook with the other. Every region in India has its own version of the samosa, from the Punjab, where the filling is dominated by potatoes and peas; to Gujarat, where finely chopped potatoes are mixed with cabbage; via Karnataka, where onion and minced mutton are popular; and Delhi, where fillings go off the rails with the likes of moong dal in the mix. But we're plumping for the Bengali samosa in Kolkata – known here as a *shingara*. Its mix of potatoes, peas, cauliflower, chillies, a dash of cumin and peanuts or even, in the posher sweet shops, cashew nuts, is a total winner. As a sightseeing pick-me-up in the former capital of British India, nothing can beat the pairing of a cup of chai with one of these flaky pastries.

☛ EAT IT ! *Try Tewari Sweets in Bara Bazaar for some of the best samosas in Kolkata, or head for the 19th-century Mrityunjoy Ghosh & Sons sweetshop on Sarat Bose Road.*

56

Slice and scoop a sea urchin during the Shakotan Peninsula's ocean harvest

JAPAN // There aren't many foods that look less appealing to eat from the outside than the spiky little sea urchin, otherwise known as *uni*. The contrast between the urchin's thorny exterior and the delicacy inside makes the experience of eating one a bit of fun. On the northern Japanese island of Hokkaidō, you'll find some of the freshest, most delicate and delectable sea urchin there is. Hokkaido specialises in two types: *bafun uni*, which is rich, creamy and intensely orange in colour; and *murasaki uni*, which is sweet, subtle and a yellowish hue. *Uni* obsessives will tell you to visit Hokkaidō's Shakotan Peninsula for harvesting season from mid-June to mid-August. Small seafood restaurants throughout the peninsula will all have *uni* on the menu during this time, and because the urchin is at its freshest it's best to try it raw and unadorned. Once the prickly exterior has been sliced apart, reach in and scoop out the alien-looking edible roe sacks and pop them in your mouth; there is no taste like it.

EAT IT ! ***In seafood restaurants on the Shakotan Peninsula, Hokkaidō. Mid-June to mid-August is when to make your pilgrimage.***

58

Bask on an oceanside terrace in Positano with a plate of spaghetti alle vongole

ITALY / On the Amalfi Coast, where the sun shines into crystalline waters and on to plunging cliffs with picturesque swimming coves, where pastel-hued villages cling to mountainsides backed by lemon groves and terraced vineyards, sits sun-bleached Positano: a classic coastal town with steep, winding streets, fashionable boutiques and a thriving food scene. The cuisine here is based on simple techniques and fresh local ingredients. *Spaghetti alle vongole* (spaghetti and clams) is the perfect embodiment of this style of eating and we can't think of a better way to live *la dolce vita* than to sit on a Positano restaurant terrace with a bowl of this pasta and a glass of crisp white wine. It's a perfect balance of the sea and the land, a representation of place and a spectacular meal to go with your summer afternoon by the water.

☛ EAT IT ! ***In Positano, or anywhere in coastal Campania.***

© 500px / Francesco Riccardo Lacomino

59

Make a British weekend of it with a Sunday pub roast

UK // Fewer and fewer people in Britain start Sunday with a trip to church, but the roast lunch is still a lock. For visitors, it's a must-do experience. It doesn't matter whether you're in a centuries-old, windowless pub in London or at a large country inn with tables sprawling over a lawn, you'll be among friends and families laughing, drinking beer and tucking into plates of hot sliced roast beef or pork, Yorkshire pudding, roasted potatoes and assorted veggies, all slathered in gravy. Warming, filling and indulgent, it's comfort food par excellence. But more than that, it's a reassuring experience, a weekly ritual where the nation stops time, staves off the start of the working week and lives in the moment. Grab a plate and take your fill.

☛ EAT IT ! ***After you've tried the local pub(s), go haute cuisine at Yorkshire's Michelin-starred Star Inn. Main St, Harome, near Helmsley.***

© Shutterstock / mikecphoto

60

Ikan bakar: Kuala Lumpur's seafood sizzle

MALAYSIA // Follow the lunchtime crowds in thrall to fragrant clouds of smoke blooming from the colourful *ikan bakar* (grilled fish) stalls nestled on the edge of Kuala Lumpur's Urban Orchard Park. This is the unassuming epicentre of the city's most seriously sizzling seafood. Each stall has at least one enormous cast-iron skillet on to which you can order your selection of fresh seafood, such as catfish, stingray, mackerel and squid. The stalls' points of difference are their side dishes and the marinades they use for the fish. Before being cooked, seafood is wrapped in banana leaves to retain flavour and hold it together. It's an experience just to watch the skillet cooks flipping and turning the green packages as they ensure each one is cooked just so.

EAT IT ! *With such an abundance of stalls offering their own take on ikan bakar there is no such thing as too many fish; try them all.*

61

© PhoodFotog / Alamy Stock Photo

60

© Shutterstock / thefoodphotographer

61

Tick one off your foodie bucket list at Chez Panisse

USA // It's a measure of the influence of Chez Panisse that the approach to 'California cuisine' it has championed since 1971 – local, sustainably farmed ingredients, prepared using a fusion of cooking styles – is now synonymous with Western cooking. It remains committed to those ideals today, and serves world-class food, driven by the seasons. There's a French influence, but really this place is 100% Bay Area. From the locally sourced produce to the bonhomie born out of its remit to emulate a boho Berkeley dinner party, it's northern California on a plate. Chez Panisse occupies the same old Arts and Crafts house it always has, renovated but with the dark-wood warmth of the original, and co-founder Alice Waters still plays a hands-on role.

EAT IT ! *Order à la carte upstairs or, better, eat downstairs, where there's a new set menu every day. 1517 Shattuck Ave, Berkeley.*

62

Sample the wonderful tapas bars (and sherry) of Seville

SPAIN // Every Spanish city has a superb selection of tapas bars but Seville offers something special: it's set in the sherry-producing heartland of Andalucía. Start your day discovering the city's centuries of history at the Real Alcázar and the world's largest Gothic cathedral. Then work up an appetite wandering the medieval streets until you find yourself at a small tapas bar. Now, it's time for another education.

Years of experience and refinement have gone into the delectable titbits that the Spanish serve with a small glass of something. And when that drink is an austere, aged manzanilla, a bone-dry fino, or deep amontillado, the food and wine pairing becomes next-level sublime.

The experience is also about the wildly social Spanish ways. Eating and drinking great food and wine is a national passion and conversation is an essential element. Whether you stumble onto a picturesque square with a hole-in-the-wall bar or hunt down an establishment with a stellar reputation, don't hesitate to ask locals for sherry or tapas recommendations: '*¿Qué me recomiendas?*' (what's good?).

The following plates should be on your must-try list. First, la Bomba (aka 'the Bomb'), a sphere of soft, mashed potato, crumbed and fried and served with an aioli mayonnaise and a spicy tomato sauce. Next, authentic acorn-fed Andalucian *jamón ibérico*. Then a simple *gilda* – a lollipop of anchovies, chilli peppers and green olives; fried or grilled *chipirones* – tiny sweet whole squid, served with lemon; grilled razor clams or prawns; and lastly, a plate of *albóndigas*, succulent meatballs.

This selection of Spain's best tapas is just some suggestions for your next bar crawl, the joy of which will be in finding your own favourites.

EAT IT ! ***A classic Seville hang-out is El Rinconcillo (right)at C/ Gerona 40. Or try the traditional Las Teresas (left) at C/Santa Teresa 2.***

Feast on the purest boeuf bourguignon in its Burgundy birthplace

FRANCE // To eat true *boeuf bourguignon*, you just have to go to Burgundy – with its rolling green hills, winding rivers and canals, vaulting Romanesque churches and stately châteaux. Oh, and delicious red wine and beef. *Boeuf bourguignon* is simple local food, first cooked by peasants in the Middle Ages with whatever ingredients they had to hand, and so built around the specific flavours and textures of the local produce. The wine has to be Burgundy, the local pinot noir, full-bodied, ideally with fresh red berry flavours, a distinct earthiness and a hint of spice. You'll see the beef everywhere, munching on those rolling green hills – the broad-shouldered, white Charolais cattle – so revered for its tender, lightly marbled meat that it's celebrated in various local *fêtes du Charolais*. You'll find *boeuf bourguignon* on the menu wherever you go in Burgundy. The dish is popular as a home meal but if you can't score an invitation to someone's house, numerous restaurants in the region's capital, Beaune, do their own version of the 'true' dish.

EAT IT ! ***We'll plump for 21 Boulevard, 21 blvd Saint-Jacques, Beaune. Its dining room is in a 15th-century stone wine cellar.***

63

64

Hainanese chicken: the dish that encapsulates Singapore

SINGAPORE / The almost monochromatic presentation of Hainanese chicken rice hides the complexity of its taste, which is like a metaphor for Singapore's own personality; what comes across as so clean and simple on the outside masks a profusion of complex components below the surface. The meal originated in the southern Chinese island of Hainan, where small, bony chickens were cooked until Cantonese cuisine introduced firmer, larger white chickens that were easier to cut and eat. To prepare, the whole bird is poached, and the liquid then flavours the rice, along with ginger, pandan leaf and garlic. The sliced meat is drizzled in sesame oil and soy sauce, and the final flourish comes in the form of a trio of sauces: hot chilli, ginger and a dark soy.

☛ EAT IT ! ***At Tian Tian Chicken Rice in the Maxwell Food Centre, 1 Kadayanallur St, Singapore.***

64

65

65

Head south to savour Vietnam's crispy pancakes

VIETNAM // Vietnam's gloriously crispy, yellow-hued *bánh xèo* pancake is a culinary must-try when visiting the south, where the savoury pancake is thinner and crispier than in the north. Southerners use more coconut milk and turmeric to achieve this. The other ingredients include whole prawns, pork, bean sprouts and mung beans, which are added to the pancake in the pan before it is removed from the heat and folded in half. Break off a piece of the pancake, place in a lettuce leaf, add herbs, and roll. Don't forget to dip it in the small dish of fiery *nuoc cham* sauce, before popping it in your mouth. The dish is so popular in Ho Chi Minh City that you'll find it just about everywhere, although Bánh Xèo Muoi Xiem and Bánh xèo 46 are two of the best.

☛ EAT IT ! ***Bánh Xèo Muoi Xiem, 204 Nguyen Trãi, Phuong Pham Ngũ Lão; Bánh xèo 46, 46A Đinh Công Tráng, Tân Đinh; both HCMC.***

Amanda Hesser

Amanda Hesser is the former food editor for the New York Times magazine, the author of several cookbooks, and co-founder of the wildly popular online cooking site Food52.

© James Ransom / Food 52

HORSERADISH-INFUSED VODKA, PORTLAND, OREGON At Kachka, a Russian restaurant, you get many tiny dishes and lots of vodka. It was amazing – peppery but vivid.

EGG HOPPERS, SRI LANKA You can find these lacy coconut crêpes with an egg fried in the centre throughout Sri Lanka.

BISCUITS AND STRAWBERRY JAM, NEW ORLEANS, LOUISIANA
In the French Quarter there's a small inn called Soniat House. Every morning they deliver biscuits hot from the oven, with homemade strawberry jam with whole fruit suspended in the jelly.

WHITE PIZZA, OLD FORGE, PENNSYLVANIA
I grew up eating this pizza. It has a layer of dough, American cheese, another layer of dough, olive oil, salt and dried rosemary.

LOBSTER ROLL, AMAGANSETT, NEW YORK
There are lots of different versions, but this one from the Crab Shack – on the north side of Long Island's Route 27, between Amagansett and Montauk – is my favourite.

A word in your ear: visit Finland on korvapuusti day

FINLAND // To proclaim *korvapuusti* as a national obsession is to downplay the significance of the humble cinnamon roll in Finnish society. Not only do these buns have their own national day (4 October) but truth be told, before the Finns got serious about their coffee, cafes were ranked in proportion to the size of their buns. The origin of these cinnamon and cardamom delights is a mystery, although many argue that cinnamon rolls were first created in Sweden (in fairness, every Scandindavian nation has staked a claim) - but we've selected the Finnish version because they're loved so much here. *Korvapuusti* translates as 'a slap on the ear', possibly because they look like one. But don't let that put you off.

EAT IT ! *Duck into the 19th-century Café Regatta, Merikannontie 8, for a friendly Finnish vibe in Helsinki's cutest cafe.*

© Getty Images / Rae_The_Sparrow

Find a shakshouka to suit at breakfast in Tel Aviv

67

ISRAEL // By now you've probably spied *shakshouka* on a Western cafe menu, you may have even baked your own at home; it's one of the multitude of irresistible Middle Eastern recipes that have made the leap to the international food scene. So, what makes a *shakshouka* in Israel so special? It's the years of love, dedication, experimentation and refinement that have gone into making the dish what it is today. In trying *shakshouka* at its source you're sampling not just the baked eggs with spiced tomato sauce, chilli peppers and onions, but a complex culinary journey.

Most recipes call for chilli and cumin, but then the spice list gets bespoke. Some keep it simple with just a hint of salt, pepper and perhaps some cinnamon, and others go all out with smoked paprika, caraway seeds and even harissa. This is the real beauty of *shakshouka* – other than the need for it to be served in a cast-iron pan with a side of bread for mopping up the sauce, it can be customised within an inch of its original existence.

In Israel's vibrant food-loving funhouse of a city, Tel Aviv, there are tasty versions of *shakshoukas* everywhere – with aubergine or tofu instead of eggs, as well as the traditional kind with inventive inclusions such as chicken shawarma and hummus, or goat's cheese and salami. One of the best places in the city to try *shakshouka* is at the bustling foodies' heaven, Carmel Market. The Shukshuka restaurant here has no less than nine variations of the brekkie fave, from meatballs to Moroccan tuna, and it takes care of vegetarians and vegans too. In a city that demands stamina, there's just no better way to kick-start your day.

EAT IT ! ***In the sunshine at Shukshuka, Carmel Market, Tel Aviv.***

In Tel Aviv, the shakshouka dish (right) is the perfect complement to the city's vibrant cafe culture (below).

68

Grilled octopus by the Med is the Amalfi Coast ideal

ITALY // Famous for impossibly picturesque towns atop verdant cliffs, the shoreline of the Amalfi Coast is also an octopus's garden – you won't find a more memorable place to sample this seafood. The quality of the produce is world class, its freshness guaranteed and its cooking perfect – the cephalopods are plucked from the Mediterranean and grilled to perfection with just a hint of seasoning and zest to bring out the zing. Whether dining on the *terrazzo* or snacking on the beachfront, the taste is as delightful as the view.

EAT IT ! ***Visit Da Vincenzo amid the pastel-hewn perfection of Positano for outstanding octopus with artichoke. Viale Pasitea, 172/178, Positano.***

69

Sink your teeth into a Mexican elote

MEXICO // Even in a country as blessed with glorious street food as Mexico, *elotes* are a rare treat. Whole cobs of corn are skewered at one end, boiled or lightly charred over hot coals and doused with a combination of butter, lime juice, chilli powder, grated Cotija cheese, mayonnaise and Mexican *crema*. So, Mexico on a stick, basically. *Elotes* are sold from food carts and food bikes all over the country, most commonly after dark, when their citrus-and-chilli zing make them the ultimate post-tequila snack.

EAT IT ! ***If a condiment-smeared face puts you off elotes, try esquites – the corn is shaved into a bowl and eaten with a spoon.***

70

Oh, happy days: America's hot fudge sundae

USA // In the scrapbook of defining images of 20th-century USA, there's a photo of teenagers on a date at an ice-cream parlour. Between them, a bowl is loaded with vanilla ice-cream, smothered in hot chocolate fudge sauce, spiked with a couple of wafers and topped with a cherry. In the window, a neon sign flashes. In the corner, a jukebox plays 'Donna' by Ritchie Valens on repeat. Such is the nostalgia for this all-American scene that old-school ice-cream parlours still exist across the US. Now all you need is a date.

EAT IT ! ***Join the likes of Al Capone, the Beatles and the Rolling Stones and try the homemade sundaes at Chicago's legendary Margie's Candies, 1960 N Western Ave.***

68

69

Customise your khao piak sen early morning in Laos

71

Khao piak sen (below), rustled up in the street-stall kitchens of Laos (right), is a popular breakfast soup.

LAOS // There is no better place to kick off your day in Laos's ancient Luang Prabang than roadside with a steaming bowl of *khao piak sen*. Join kids on their way to school and men and women on their way to work slurping their noodle soup to a soundtrack of tuk tuks, motorbikes and morning markets. Your bowl of thick soup will arrive at your table in a flash, and in it you'll find a thick bed of fresh-made noodles made from rice flour and tapioca starch, fried garlic, slivers of ginger and spring onion, coriander, and most likely a boiled egg and some pork meatballs. Specify 'no offal' before you sit down if you're not partial to cubes of pig's blood, liver, kidney or heart.

And this is where the fun begins because, as with well-known noodle and rice soups in neighbouring Vietnam, you customise the flavour of your breakfast to your liking with the extensive choice of condiments and sauces on your table. Choose from fresh lime, chilli, fish sauce, pepper, soy sauce, sugar and many more. The salty, spicy, sweet and satisfying combination is so addictively delicious that the best breakfast stalls sell out before 9.30am, so forget about the lie-in.

EAT IT ! *At any street-side stall with a spare plastic chair, Luang Prabang.*

© Lonely Planet / Catherine Sutherland

Left: did we mention that gaeng keow wan was hot? Below: a street market in Bangkok, where you'd be advised to try the green chicken curry (right)

A world of curry

↓

A jackfruit-based polos curry by the beach in Sri Lanka is practically paradisaical

page 150

↓

Malaysia has become the epicentre of beef rendang, created in Southeast Asia

page 196

↓

The butter chicken favourite, murgh makhani, was the brainchild of a Punjabi chef in Delhi

page 220

© Lonely Planet / Austin Bush

© Lonely Planet / Catherine Sutherland

Above all else in the Land of Smiles, eat up your green

72

THAILAND // Trying to choose one dish above all others from a cuisine as fantastic as Thailand's is like trying to pick a favourite child, but if it came down to only eating one Thai dish for the rest of our lives, then we'd have to go with *gaeng keow wan*, or green chicken curry. The spiciest of the coconut-based curries, its green colour comes from the small green chillies which are pounded into a paste along with a spice and herbs list as long as your arm. In the heaving foodie heaven that is Bangkok you can find *gaeng keow wan* just about everywhere, and once you start exploring you'll see that each restaurant does things a little bit differently, from slight variations in the consistency of the sauce to the use of different vegetables. Some restaurants will serve you a bowl of rice on the side and others rice noodles. At the old-school, hole-in-the-wall Sanguan Sri in Lumphini you get an authentic green curry experience – it's hot, the place is packed with locals, waiters whiz back and forth at pace and when the curry arrives at your table with a bowl of fluffy jasmine rice, everything falls into place and you realise you're having the Thai food experience of your dreams.

EAT IT ! ***At Sanguan Sri, 59/1 Witthayu Rd, Lumphini, Pathum Wan, Bangkok.***

73

Sourdough in San Francisco: learn the legends of the loaf

USA // The Boudin sourdough empire began in the hopeful hands of Californian goldpanner Isidore Boudin in 1849, and is now so well-established that its daily bread is served at numerous locations across San Francisco. The best place to try the stretchy, springy, crusty loaf is the striking warehouse HQ at The Wharf. Here you can watch the bakers at work, tour the Bakery Museum, shop at the market and eat as much sourdough as you can get your hands on. The menu features baguette beef burgers, classic sandwiches such as tuna salad, chicken and cranberry, sourdough pizzas, and divine soups, stews and chillies like clam chowder or shrimp and andouille sausage – all served in hollowed-out sourdough loaves.

EAT IT ! *At the bakery flagship, Boudin at the Wharf, 160 Jefferson St, San Francisco, California.*

© Tribune Content Agency LLC / Alamy Stock Photo

© Daniel Di Paolo

© Shutterstock / pansticks

74

Double up on fried flatbread during carnival in the Caribbean

TRINIDAD & TOBAGO // Port of Spain goes into overdrive during Carnival season, when restaurants, bars and clubs do a roaring trade all night long, and steel-pan band rehearsals in empty car parks offer the chance to hear the intricate compositions created by pannists for hundreds-strong bands. To survive such a rollicking good time, you'll need some sustenance. Enter the Trinbagonian double – a spicy chickpea curry known as a *channa*, sandwiched between two pieces of hot, fried flatbread. The curry is pimped with a hot pepper sauce, some mango *kuchela* relish and tart tamarind. It's as messy as it sounds but will keep you going till the morning, when you'll be ready for another one – or two. They don't call them doubles for nothing.

EAT IT ! *At any time of the year from the Breakfast Shed, Wrightson Rd, Port of Spain, Trinidad.*

© Shutterstock / Sergio TB

75

Dance to the tune of black-eyed pea fritters in Senegal

SENEGAL // Black-eyed pea fritters – aka *accara* – are widely available across West Africa, but one of the most evocative places to eat them is around Senegal's Embarcadère just north of Place D'Independence, before boarding the ferry to the Isle de Gorée. Deceptively light, its mix of skinned black-eyed peas, onions and baking soda, deep-fried by vendors manning Dutch pots on street corners across Dakar and the rest of Senegal, seems simple. But the resulting crunchy, light and fluffy fritter, akin to a beignet, is utterly addictive, especially when dipped into or eaten with *sosu kaani*, a feisty sauce made with tomatoes, onion and habanero or scotch bonnet chillies, and seasoned with bay leaf, garlic, salt and pepper.

EAT IT ! *If not near the ferry to Gorée then along avenue Pompidou. It also works as a substantial snack served in a baguette.*

© StockFood / Chatelain, Sonia

© Getty Images / Kim Rogerson

76

As any Parisian will tell you, galette des rois is a cake fit for kings

FRANCE // The fact that they only appear in patisserie and boulangerie windows for a short time in January creates an air of exclusivity to this sweet treat that Parisians find impossible to resist. What began in the 14th century as part of a feast celebrating the Epiphany, or Three Kings' Day, on 6 January has turned into a month of Christmas and New Year cheer. At the centre of this is the flaky, layered pastry with a rich, creamy frangipane filling known as Galette des Rois, or 'King's Cake'. Part of the cake's long-standing appeal is the tradition of hiding a *feve* (originally a broad bean) within its sweet almond-meal centre. Finding the *feve* signified good luck. Today the *feve* is more likely to be a tiny figurine, the finding of which entitles the beneficiary to wear the paper crown and be king for the day. You can often spot the Galette des Rois by the adornment of the decorative gold paper crowns, but you'll be just as easily led by the steady stream of patrons exiting the bakery with excited smiles on their faces.

EAT IT ! ***Join the locals for a glimpse of the king – and grab a baguette while you're there. Régis Colin, 53 rue Montmartre, Paris.***

Indian dal: the ubiquitous dish that feeds a nation of millions

INDIA // Just how does such a simple thing as a lentil turn into a national dish and essential addition to any gastronomic occasion? Dal is undoubtedly India's culinary leveller and collective comfort food, a meal that is eaten at humble street stalls, high-end restaurants and everything in-between. Whether you eat it among the chaos of Delhi's streets or in the air-conditioned cool of a restaurant, this is a food for the people, by the people. The best dals are cooked for hours for maximum creaminess and most include Indian spices such as cumin, turmeric, garam masala, chilli, mustard seeds, ginger and garlic. In *tarka dal* the spices are fried in ghee and added to the creamy mixture, giving it a smoky flavour; *dal makhani* from the Punjab region of north India is made with black lentils and red kidney beans with butter and cream for extra richness; and in the south the *sambhar dal* is generously heaped with seasonal vegetables. You get our drift, there are seemingly endless varieties and combinations of types of split peas and different spices in this Indian staple, all of them worth seeking out.

EAT IT ! ***Anywhere and everywhere throughout India.***

77

© Tim Gainey / Alamy Stock Photo

77

© Lonely Planet / Matt Munro

Curtis Stone

Celebrity chef and TV personality Curtis Stone is currently the host of My Kitchen Rules. He is also the chef-owner of Los Angeles restaurants Gwen and Maude.

HOMEMADE PASTA; ITALY
While exploring Europe with my best mate when we were 21, we ended up at his family's home in Francavilla, Italy. I learned to make fresh pasta from three generations of women – it's truly an art form.

CURRY, BRICK LANE, LONDON
While working at Cafe Royal Grill Room under Marco Pierre White, on Sundays I would religiously head to Brick Lane for curry.

FISH TACOS; SAULITA, MEXICO
Surf, sand, a couple of beers, and tacos from a beach shack – sometimes I don't think you need much else

CHULETON, RESTAURANTE ALAMEDA; RIOJA, SPAIN The meat is from Galicia and the balance of beef and fat is remarkable. At Maude, we are developing dishes based on renowned wine regions of the world and the debut menu will be inspired by Rioja.

MY MUM'S ROAST PORK AND CRACKLINGS
Roast pork with a crispy skin is a very traditional meal in Australia and I insist that my mum, Lozza, prepare it for Christmas each year.

Cool the sensory overload of a Phnom Penh night market with pumpkin custard

CAMBODIA // Amid the lively action of Phnom Penh's markets, there's a good chance that you'll need a physical break, if not a sensory one. So buy a slice of pumpkin custard, pull up a tiny plastic chair and watch all the action. A slice of custard? Yep. This delicate dessert is made by steaming a coconut-flavoured custard inside a hollowed-out pumpkin known as a *kabocha*. The pumpkin is steamed whole and when it's soft and the custard contained within it firm, it's carved into thin wedges and served with shaved ice and coconut milk. Now how good does that sound?

☛ EAT IT ! *Try the Night Market (Phsar Reatrey), Preah Mohaksat Treiyani Kossamak, Phnom Penh.*

79

Pick tropical fruit with chilli salt dip – Vietnam's street food staple

VIETNAM // Guaranteed to take you right back to Vietnam's bustling city streets from the first bite, fresh tropical fruit dipped in, or sprinkled with, chilli salt is a taste of place. Vendors on street corners everywhere sell fruit with little bags of chilli salt (*muoi ot*) on the side. The salt helps to enhance the sweetness of the fruit and the chilli gives your mouth a fiery pop of flavour. Try squeezing lime into the salt before dipping in a slice of mango – the salty, sweet, sour and spicy result is the simplest representation of Vietnamese cuisine you'll ever taste.

EAT IT ! ***From street vendors all over the country.***

79

© ThaiThu / 500px

80

© Shutterstock / SueC

80

Enter your own crabby catch in an old English sandwich contest

UK // First you have to earn your crab sandwich by spending a likely fruitless but enjoyable hour or two trying to catch a crustacean off Cromer pier, where your fellow fisherfolk will range from tiny tots landing tiddlers to gnarly old Norfolk folk chatting about the Cromer and Sheringham Crab and Lobster Festival and its crab sandwich competition, held each May. So, what makes a great crab sandwich? First and foremost – fresh Cromer crab. The brown meat should be mixed with mayonnaise and spread on buttered fresh bread, then topped with the white meat, before being seasoned with lemon and salt and pepper. And that, my friends, is a winner.

EAT IT ! ***At Cromer's Crab Sandwich competition in May, or any time of year at Henry's Coffee & Tea Store, Church St, Cromer, Norfolk.***

© Getty Images / AndrisL

For the very best Belgian waffles, all roads lead to Liège

BELGIUM // If you love a good waffle (and who doesn't?) then you'll know traditional Belgian waffles are standouts for their depth, texture and the huge range of toppings you can choose from: a sprinkle of sugar, a ladling of melted chocolate, or a smothering of fresh berries with whipped cream. But if you want the best of Belgian waffles, follow your tastebuds to Liège, a city that predates the Middle Ages. There they've perfected the art of waffle making... and there's a secret weapon: pearl sugar. It's obtained by crushing blocks of white sugar, which is sifted to capture the fragments. These sweet nuggets caramelise on the waffle dough while it's baking in its extra deep iron. The result is a sweeter, crunchier waffle on the outside that leads you in to the chewy centre. Liège waffles are typically offered as plain, vanilla or cinnamon – try one where the legend began.

EAT IT ! ***Follow the aroma of cinnamon along Liège's Rue de Mineurs to Une Gaufrette Saperlipopette for fresh homemade waffles.***

82

Enjoy the formidable bounty of Copenhagen's Toverhallerne market

DENMARK // This culinary adventure is not for the small of stomach nor, for that matter, the indecisive. A selection of more than 80 food and produce stalls line a cavernous, light-filled indoor space with a towering glass and steel framework. In summer, stalls spill out on to the adjacent square, making your decisions even tougher. Come here to join local families, city workers on their lunch breaks and entranced travellers wandering the bountiful stands selling everything from meats, cheeses, seafood and fresh fruit to condiments, bread, cakes and flowers. When you've worked up an appetite, settle in to one of the restaurant stalls for a *smørrebrød* and craft beer (the microbrewery is on-site), or perhaps a confit duck roll and glass of champagne.

EAT IT ! ***Torvehallerne, Frederiksborggade 21, Copenhagen.***

© Getty Images / Raffaele Nicolussi

82

83

© Shutterstock / Phuong D. Nguyen

83

Join the crowds devouring their morning mohinga in steamy Yangon

MYANMAR // See all those people squatting on plastic chairs, noisily slurping steaming bowls of noodles? They're hunkered over Myanmar's unofficial national dish, *mohinga*, and it's about to become your favourite way to start the day in Yangon. *Mohinga* is a curried rice noodle soup made with fish stock and spices, fortified with chickpea fritters, boiled egg, fish sauce and spring onions. It's eaten in the morning before Myanmar's steamy heat reaches midday heights, and some places will sell out before lunch. However, its popularity means restaurants and food carts serve it at just about any time of the day – including the odd late-night venue serving the post-clubbing crowd.

EAT IT ! ***Wherever you see the locals getting their fix in Yangon, or pretty much anywhere in Myanmar.***

Assemble around an open wood fire for a mighty Argentinian meat feast

84

Griiled-meat greats

↓

No self-respecting Jo'burg braai (barbecue) is lit without a boerewors sausage.

 page 235

↓

Bite into a Turkish testi kebap with jaw-dropping Cappadocia as a backdrop.

 page 194

↓

Serbia's national beef meal, pljeskavica, is celebrated at an annual festival.

 page 240

ARGENTINA // Do not, under any circumstances, compliment an Argentinian on their 'BBQ'. Argentinians don't want their pure form of grilling meat over open fire to be compared with anything that is casually slapped on a gas-fired grill. *Asado* is always cooked over a wood fire, *always*: the only permissible additional fuel allowed is the odd pinecone to stoke the flames. The placement of the *parilla* (the cast-iron grill) over the hot coals is also of utmost importance, with the hottest coals being moved to the side so the dripping fat from the meat doesn't create too much smoke, which could affect the flavour.

When the temperature is right, it's time to start adding the mountains of meat. First up the larger cuts, which take longer to cook – short ribs are first, followed by flank and skirt steaks. The meat should be allowed to cook slowly and shouldn't be moved more than once. As well as being the preferred grill technique it's also the way Argentinians incorporate the social element into the *asado*; the slower the cook the more chance to drink Malbec and swap stories with friends.

Following the steaks comes the offal, the most common cut being sweetbreads known as *mollejas*, though it's not unusual to see kidneys and intestines as well. And for the final flourish, the sausages (chorizo and morcilla) and Provolone cheese. If it sounds like a lot of food, it is; there's often close to 500g of meat per person at an *asado*, so don't eat breakfast.

When the grill master has finally finished the preparation, he (and it's always a he) will serve the table to a rowdy round of applause. Drinking and gorging ensues over an evening you won't forget.

EAT IT ! ***At the classic parilla restaurant Don Julio, Guatemala 4699, 1425 CABA, Buenos Aires.***

Left: the grill master has carved and he's ready to share. Below: Argentinian asado was part of the traditional diet of cattle-rearing gauchos.

© Pablo Reinsch / pablo79 / 500px

The slower the meat cooks, the more social the asado: more chance to drink Malbec and swap stories with friends

© Lonely Planet / Andrew Montgomery

85

Grab a piece of America's favourite pie – just like mom used to make it

USA // Americans love their apple pie so much there's a whole day dedicated to this pastry sensation. National Apple Pie Day falls on 13 May each year, which is basically an invitation for everyone to indulge in one of the nation's favourite home-cooked delights. We think that this home-cooked feel is what makes a really great pie, but it also must have a gently spiced apple filling with a crumbly pie crust. For the authentic farm produce experience, Apple Annie's Orchard bakes all its pies fresh each day from apples straight off the tree. You can also pick your own to take home if you prefer your own family's recipe.

☛ EAT IT ! *At Apple Annie's Orchard, 1510 N Circle I Rd, Willcox, Arizona.*

Ping Coombes

MasterChef UK champion Ping Coombes helped popularise Malaysian cuisine at Chi Kitchen in London, as well as through her debut cookbook, Malaysia.

FRIED CHICKEN, HAT YAI, THAILAND I remember eating this as a child just across the Thai border. It's bright orange – kind of nuclear – really crispy and fragrant.

PIZZA BERBER, ATLAS MOUNTAINS, MOROCCO The owner of our hotel in the Atlas mountains made this pillowy focaccia stuffed with butter, herbs, nuts and lamb.

ROAST PIGEON, SHA TIN, HONG KONG Thai pai dong is in-between a restaurant and a street cart. It serves pigeon cut in half, with head and all – barbaric but tasty.

NOODLES, IPOH, MALAYSIA In my home town, on your birthday you're treated to a special meal. Mine was always glass noodles cooked in a clay pot, with giant river prawns.

PAELLA, LA ALBUFERA, SPAIN We walked for miles to a restaurant called La Establishment. The paella here didn't look like much but it was the best I've had. It took an hour to cook, which is what made it different.

86

Get a taste for what makes Beijing tick over a plate of steaming dumplings

CHINA // From a distance, it's easy to view Beijing through a macro lens. You see the majestic Forbidden City; ludicrously modern architecture; red flags everywhere. But up close you see the gaps between the monuments, where people actually live. Much of this life is mediated by food; in Beijing, that means *jiaozi*, the Chinese dumpling. *Jiaozi* come steamed, boiled or fried, their wheat-flour dough filled with simple food combinations, the hallmarks of quality being fresh ingredients and a wrapper that holds together under duress from chopsticks. Dipped in chilli oil or black-rice vinegar, they're chewy, filling and moreish. Enjoy them with locals among the thrum of a packed restaurant, and the real China quickly comes into focus.

EAT IT ! ***Baoyuan Jiaozi Wu is known for generously filled boiled jiaozi with brightly coloured wrappers dyed with vegetable and fruit colouring. 6 Maizidian Jie, Chaoyang District, Beijing.***

Follow your nose to the boulevard stalls selling perfect Parisian pancakes

FRANCE // So much street food is about robust flavours and fresh, local ingredients cooked quickly – trust the French to thumb their noses at the formula and shoot for restaurant-quality thin pancakes instead! In Paris, crêpes are so popular that the smell of batter on griddle from streetside stands seems to hang permanently in the air. Which is distracting. In their purest form, crêpes are buttered, sugared and rolled into tubes of sweet, faintly salty, doughy goodness. Lemon and sugar, fruit preserves and custard are also popular. As is Nutella – walk down the Champs-Élysées clutching one of those and you'll feel like the French president. Savoury crêpes, *galettes*, are made with buckwheat flour for a nutty taste. Filled with ham and Gruyère, and maybe a fried egg, they're as elegant as melty, cheesy fast food gets.

EAT IT ! ***Bretons brought crêpes to Paris, and the area around Gare Montparnasse used to be Little Brittany. That's where you need to go.***

88

Pack your pita at the flagship of a global restaurant empire

ISRAEL // From the moment you enter Israeli celebrity chef Eyal Shani's Miznon you're immersed in a cacophony of conversations, clanging pots and pans, and the shouts from chefs letting customers know their food is ready – it's like the city outside in microcosm. The energy is upbeat, the atmosphere warm, and the food shows your appetite no mercy. Shani has expanded his Miznon empire worldwide, with restaurants in Paris, New York, Melbourne and Vienna, but the original bistro on Ibn Gabirol in Tel Aviv is still the best place to get your pita fix. The pita menu is divided into four sections – meat, vegetables, seafood and dessert – but that just makes you want to come back and try the three sections you couldn't fit in the first time. Think steak with a fried egg, coriander, radish and tahini, or cauliflower florets with green onions, tomato and tahini.

EAT IT ! ***At any of the Miznon's, but best of all at the Ibn Gabirol branch in Tel Aviv, where the dish became famous.***

89

© Getty Images / Lisa Romerein

89

The po' boy, New Orleans' classic seafood sandwich, is a rich experience

USA // America is a land of sandwiches, from the humble PB&J to the man-sized party sub. But New Orleans' po' boy may well be king of them all, and eating these filled rolls here – or attempting to eat one without making a pig's ear of it while locals look on with amusement – is de rigueur. To make a perfect po' boy, start with local New Orleans French bread with a crunchy crust and a fluffy white interior. Pile on fried seafood – shrimp, oysters, catfish, crab... even nuggets of alligator. Add lettuce, tomato and a smear of mayo, and you've got yourself lunch, Creole-style. Where does the name come from? A common theory involves local restaurateurs giving free sandwiches to striking streetcar conductors ('poor boys') in the 1920s.

EAT IT ! *The half-'n-half (oysters and shrimp) po' boy at Domilise's is a local legend, but fried catfish, smoked sausage and roast beef are on offer too. 5240 Annunciation St, New Orleans.*

90

© Lonely Planet / Susan Wright

90

Go prospecting for white gold at the annual Piedmont truffle fair

ITALY // The rarity of white truffles has secured them at the top of culinary bucket lists the world over. These inauspicious-looking bulbous fungi cannot be cultivated, instead growing symbiotically at the roots of oak, beech and poplar trees, from which they're sniffed out by trained dogs in the autumn. In the absence of your own truffle hound, aficionados of the *tartufi bianchi* should visit Alba in Piedmont for the annual white truffle fair. Strolling through the marketplace while able to smell, touch, taste and buy your own earthy jewel is a sensory experience. Sit with a glass of Barolo and order up big (remembering that a tiny 10g can cost as much as €45 if it's been a dry year).

EAT IT ! *At the International Alba White Truffle festival held each autumn in Alba, Piedmont.*

91

© Travelscape Images / Alamy Stock Photo

91

91

Forage for food with indigenous people in the shadow of Australia's Uluru

AUSTRALIA // In the vast, desert centre of Australia, one of the world's iconic sights looms over the landscape – Uluru, the red rock. Drawing travellers to marvel at its inspiring presence, it is part of the region that's home to the Anangu people. As Aboriginals, the Anangu are descendants of the original inhabitants of Australia. The Aboriginals' ability to hunt and forage in one of the world's harshest environments is unrivalled, honed over generations and passed down within tribes and families. There still exists the expertise among modern generations to find food where there would seem to be none, and near Uluru, guests of the Ayers Rock Resort can join in a Bush Tucker Experience, where an indigenous guide walks participants through bushland identifying edible plants, seeds, fruits, grains and spices. You'll learn how, over thousands of years, food was found, prepared and eaten. The tour ends with you cooking and tasting some of the ingredients identified on the walk. It's an insight into the ingenuity and affinity with place at the heart of indigenous culture. And it doesn't taste half-bad.

EAT IT ! *On a walking tour, Ayers Rock Resort, Northern Territory.*

92

Cool off in Córdoba with a bowl of chilled salmorejo soup

SPAIN // Chances are, you're more familiar with salmorejo's skinnier cousin - gazpacho - but when in Córdoba, it's time to meet the hearty member of the family. This cold soup has been a staple of Córdoban cuisine for centuries; delivering fresh, punchy flavour with no bells and whistles required. Tomatoes are blended with stale bread, olive oil and perhaps a little garlic for a creamy, cooling bowlful that's a much-needed balm to the sweltering Andalusian sun. Try it the way the locals do - topped with chopped hard-boiled egg and the salty tang of serrano ham - before winding your way through the sun-splashed streets and courtyards dotted with bright flowers for a well-earned siesta.

EAT IT ! *They add a modern twist to the dish in Bodegas Campos, a warren of rooms and patios, at Calle de Lineros 32, Córdoba.*

92

Tony Singh

Tony Singh is the chef-owner of Oloroso and Tony's Table in Edinburgh, Scotland. He won ITV's Chef of the Year and co-hosted the TV show The Incredible Spice Men. His most recent cookbook is called Tasty!

LANGAR, PUNJAB, INDIA
Langar is the free communal meal — usually black lentils and roti — served in every Sikh temple around the globe, open to everyone.

PARTIN BREE, ISLE OF SKYE, SCOTLAND
Michael Smith gives you the truest taste of Scotland at his restaurant Loch Bay. My favourite is his brown native crab soup.

BÁNH MÌ, HO CHI MIN CITY, VIETNAM Every time I'm in Saigon, I head to the corner of Le Lai and Nguyen An Ninh for a Bánh mì sandwich.

TREACLE BREAD, SAT BAINS, NOTTINGHAM, UK Chef Sat Bains spends months on his flavour combos. Even the smallest things are treated with intensity, like his treacle bread.

EUCALYPTUS MARTINI, COPENHAGEN, DENMARK In the land of cool eateries, I go to Curfew Cocktail bar and Umberto Marques, who makes the best Martinis in the world.

93

Where else but Lapland for an authentic reindeer stew?

FINLAND // This classic dish from Lapland is one of those things that gets better the further north you venture. Maybe that's because the supply of reindeer becomes greater, or because the icier the outside temperature, the more this simple stew appeals. There are a few reasons a reindeer stew in northern Finland cannot be replicated elsewhere, not least because the taste of exported frozen reindeer meat does not compare to fresh. Simplicity is key: the meat should be scrumptious enough that nothing besides salt and butter is needed to enhance the flavour. A mound of stew gets dolloped over mashed potato, and across the top the typical serving is crushed, sugared lingonberry, a tart wild berry often foraged by locals.

EAT IT ! *Lapland town Rovaniemi has a renowned food scene: for starters, try upmarket Restaurant Nili, Valtakatu 20.*

© Getty Images / SolliJussila

© Images By Kenny / Alamy Stock Photo

94

Watch in awe as your Taiwanese beef noodle soup is composed

TAIWAN // Noodles are a staple food in Taiwan, and there are thousands of places to get them in Taipei, but the best genuine Taiwanese noodles you'll find will be in those restaurants serving the *dao xiao* variety, meaning knife-shaved. These are noodles shaved from a massive block of dough and flung into the beef broth in one fluid motion, the broth having been simmered for hours with bone marrow for maximum flavour. Chunks of beef, usually marbled fatty brisket, mingle with the thick broth and noodles, with a garnish of *suan cai*, a pickled Taiwanese vegetable. The result is a hearty, savoury soup packed with flavour, protein and cultural cachet. Watching the dexterity of the chefs making your dinner is almost as much fun as eating it, so grab your sides and try to bag a seat near the kitchen.

EAT IT ! *There's generally a line at Lin Dong Fang Beef Noodles, 274, Section 2, Bade Rd, Taipei, due to its popularity with locals.*

© Shutterstock / iskraphoto

97

95

Make it a halloumi-heavy meze in Beirut

LEBANON // Halloumi has been a Middle East mainstay for centuries. It's made from goat and sheep's milk, formed into wallet-sized pucks and fried till golden brown and slightly crispy on the outside, with a firm, squeaky texture within. In Lebanon, it appears on meze-covered tables, among spicy sausage, hummus, aubergine *fatteh*, *kibbeh* meatballs and more, its delicate saltiness just the appetite awakener you'll need to keep eating under the expectant eye of a generous host.

EAT IT ! *In summer, there's no better place than on the terrace at Beirut's Abd el Wahab, 51 Abdel Wahab El Inglizi St.*

96

Join a New Mexico ritual and grill those chillies

USA // The ritual begins in September as BBQs are set up roadside around Hatch, New Mexico, to start roasting the distinctive just-harvested chillies used in green chilli sauce. Locals buy up huge bags of them, which are blackened on the BBQ, skinned, then sealed in plastic and frozen to be thawed and used throughout the year. To make the sauce, the chillies are cooked with garlic, onion, cumin and pork stock. It's then applied to almost every meal served in southern New Mexico.

EAT IT ! *Whip up your own, or head to Sparky's for one of its famed green chilli burgers. 115 Franklin St, Hatch, New Mexico.*

97

The French cherry flan that's a taste of the easy life

FRANCE // Limousin's green, rolling hills and bucolic woodlands are largely untrampled by tourists, making the area a great place to recharge between major destinations. Even more so if you relax with a wickedly delicious sweet *clafoutis*. It's a Limousin speciality, made with morello cherries, stones and all, encased in a dense flan. What really makes *clafoutis* sing is the substance amygdalin, released from the stones during cooking, adding a bewitching hint of amaretto.

EAT IT ! *You'll see the same dish made with other fruit. This is called flaugnarde and is also worth sampling.*

Delve into a pan of world-famous paella in its Valencian birthplace

SPAIN // Spain's third-largest city, Valencia, tends to fly under the radar. But judging by the laidback lifestyle, locals seem fine with that. Visit in spring, when the fragrance of blossom on the orange trees mingles with the rich aroma of paella, Valencia's gift to the rest of Spain, bubbling in flat metal pans. It's a gift some Valencians regret, because they view variations from the two classic recipes – rice, chicken, rabbit, beans, tomato; or the same but with seafood subbed for the meat and beans – as sacrilege. The other essential element in paella is the toasty crust of caramelised rice that forms at the bottom of the pan. It's something so delicious that all Spaniards agree on it.

☛ EAT IT ! *At Casa Isabel, eat at a table on the edge of Valencia's big beach, Playa de Malvarrosa: Paseo Marítimo, 4 (Playa Malvarrosa).*

Catch Comoros' fresh, local fare: langouste à la vanille

COMOROS ISLANDS // Otherwise known as grilled lobsters with a vanilla sauce, this ambitious and rich flavour combination has become something of a national dish on the Comoros Islands, a small African archipelago that lies between Mozambique and Madagascar. Showcasing the best of local ingredients and cooking techniques that hark back to French colonial rule from the 19th century, the combination of fresh-out-of-the-water lobster with locally grown vanilla (the islands are one of the world's largest producers of fresh vanilla) is succulent and decadent, and unique to the Comoros.

☛ EAT IT ! *Try the busier restaurants in Moroni on the largest island, Grande Comore, Comoros Islands.*

100—199

© Lonely Planet / Julian Love

100

Break the cream tea decrees in an English country garden

UK // There may be no more English experience than politely arguing about the perfect cream tea. Is it 'scone' to rhyme with 'on' or with 'cone'? Does one apply jam then clotted cream, or vice versa? And is that strawberry jam or can one use any variety? Luckily, English cream tea is so downright decadent, so sweet and creamy, so satisfying, that even all this overthinking can't ruin it. And since it's traditionally served with toppings in separate pots, you can ruddy well make it how you want! The natural setting for enjoying oven-warm scones and a pot of tea is the garden of a stately country house. The National Trust, custodian of many beautiful properties, is renowned for exceptional cream teas... featuring a fruit scone! Is that even a thing?

EAT IT ! *The National Trust Scones blog rates Peckover House's scones as 'spectacular'. North Brink, Wisbech, Cambridgeshire.*

101

Go to Copenhagen for some winning Wienerbrød

DENMARK // The world knows them as Danish pastries but in Denmark the credit for these moreish, sticky pastry snacks goes to Viennese chefs working in Copenhagen in the 1840s. Consequently, they're known as *wienerbrød* (roughly translated as Vienna bread) throughout Denmark. Of all the *wienerbrød* around there is one you can't miss – the affectionately named *kanelsnegle*, or cinnamon snail. Danes eat them as a sweet course following breakfast or with a coffee in the afternoon; truth is, they're good at any time of the day. Copenhagen's oldest bakery, Sankt Peders Bageri, which dates back to 1652, is the place to for an authentic Danish pastry (and other golden baked goods).

EAT IT ! *Copenhagen bakery Skt Peders Bageri bakes a giant version of its best-selling snail on Wednesdays. Sankt Peders Stræde 29.*

© Anna Ivanova / 2enroute / 500px

102

Enjoy without reservation at the Viennese hotel that perfected the Sachertorte

AUSTRIA // In 19th-century Vienna, being known for a memorable torte was a big thing for a hotel. But after many cakey battles, Hotel Sacher won the war. Its owner, Eduard Sacher, spent years refining his father Franz's recipe for two perfect layers of moist chocolate cake separated by apricot jam and glazed in chocolate – the eponymous *Sachertorte*. Hotel Sacher still holds the recipe as a fiercely guarded secret and the term 'Original Sacher-Torte' as a trademark. You can buy versions all over the city, but nothing compares to the real deal, taken with coffee at the chandelier-lit Hotel Sacher. Thanks to its imperial architecture, impeccable avenues, opera houses and art galleries, Vienna is a city where everything is in its right place. Including chocolate cake.

EAT IT ! ***There are Sacher Cafés in Vienna, Salzburg, Graz and Innsbruck, but the original Hotel Sacher is where you want to go. Philharmoniker Str 4, Vienna.***

103

All aboard in the Bosphorus for Istanbul's fish sandwich

TURKEY // Are there tastier eating options in Turkey's largest city? Well, yes. Are there options more atmospheric? Probably not. Eating a fish sandwich, or *balık ekmek*, as it's known in Turkish, is the quintessential Istanbul experience. This undoubtedly has more to do with where and how the dish is prepared than its ingredients: *balık ekmek* are made on brightly coloured boats bobbing in the Bosphorus Strait. To assemble one, fillets of mackerel are griddled on the boat-bound kitchens before being inserted in a Turkish roll with lettuce, salt and a squeeze of lemon – that's it. When the pitch of the waves is just right, the simple sandwich is handed over to a diner on solid land, and eaten to a dramatic backdrop of the New Mosque and the Galata Bridge.

EAT IT ! ***At the western, 'European', end of the Galata Bridge, where several bright-coloured boats function as floating restaurants.***

103

BISMILLAHIRRAHMANIRRAHIM
LÜTFEN
DENİZE
ÇÖP ATMAYIN

Take your place in line for Shanghai's super soup dumplings, xiaolongbao

CHINA // Yes, gaze at the vaulting Shanghai skyline and wonder at the grandiose European edifices of the Bund, but promise us you'll also go hunting for the city's most significant contribution to Chinese cuisine, the soup-filled dumpling, *xiaolongbao*. They're available all over the city, but the best dumpling houses inevitably have a line out the door, especially at lunchtime, and demand you battle for a seat at a cramped table, or hover and glower at other patrons to hurry up and finish. There are several versions of *xiaolongbao*, but the classic is thin-skinned and filled with minced pork and aspic spiked with ginger and Shaoxing wine. When the dumplings are steamed, the aspic liquefies into an aromatic broth. Eating them can be messy, but biting into a steaming *xiaolongbao* and feeling that warm, delicious broth flow into your mouth – the multisensory pay-off is immense. The alternative ending is that they sell out before you get to the front of the queue, and the place closes for the day. That's just life in Shanghai.

EAT IT ! ***Nondescript shopfront. Long queue. Peerless dumplings. Jia Jia Tangbao, 90 Huanghe Rd, Huangpu Qu, Shanghai.***

104

© Lonely Planet / Matt Munro

© Lonely Planet / River Thompson

105

Get your macaron fix from a Parisian patisserie

FRANCE // Macaron bakeries have popped up everywhere, so converts can get their fix in any major city worldwide. But the best place to experience the obsession-inducing puffball of a biscuit is in Paris, perhaps after a morning of window-shopping in the Golden Triangle or real shopping along Boulevard Haussmann. The sheer number of chocolateries and patisseries that produce macarons in Paris can be overwhelming, so here's a few to get you started: Pierre Hermé offers signature flavours you're unlikely to find anywhere else, like the Ispahan, made up of raspberry, lychee and rosewater; at Ladurée there's a palate of soft pretty pastels and more traditional flavours – its signature macaron has chestnut-flavoured shells with cream, dark rum and candied chestnut pieces; at Acide, the patisserie style takes a turn for the Willy Wonka, so colours pop and flavours are on the wilder side. If none of these places satisfy your yearning than rest assured, there are more macarons in Paris than you can poke a puffed meringue at.

EAT IT ! *Pierre Hermé, 72 rue Bonaparte; Ladurée, 75 av des Champs-Élysées; and Acide, 85 rue La Boétie; all Paris.*

106

Fondue makes perfect sense in the Swiss winter

SWITZERLAND // Forget what you think you know about dodgy '70s parties – sampling fondue in a restaurant on the shores of Lake Geneva is a different proposition. Said restaurant, Buvette des Bains, is part of a 1930s lakeside public baths complex. When the winter closes in and the crowds thin, the dining cabin sparks the fire and sets about melting cheese for chilly patrons looking to escape the cold but keep the views. In a city with a reputation for professionalism and measured diplomacy, a shared fondue at Buvette des Bains is a laidback, unpretentious and sociable affair set in a stunning natural landscape. And you won't get too stuffed; the fondue here is prepared with sparkling wine, which cuts through the richness of the cheese for a lighter texture.

EAT IT ! *On the shores of Lake Geneva at La Buvette des Bains, Quai du Mont-Blanc 30, Geneva.*

Taste the sunniest season with England's summer pudding

UK // A summer pudding sings of sunshine, is packed with the abundant soft fruits of an English summer, and is the perfect end to a countryside picnic. There's something quintessentially English about a well-made summer pudding – perhaps it's the simplicity of the modest white bread mixed with strawberries, raspberries and currants (any fresh, dark berry will do) with just a slug of pouring cream as a complement. It's unfussy and seasonal, delicate and flavoursome, and just as pretty as a picture. All you need to make the scene complete is some elderflower cordial and a backdrop of lush green English countryside.

EAT IT ! ***It's a supermarket regular if cooking's not your bag – regardless, make the dining location a picnic in the country.***

108

Watch Egyptian artisans knock feteer into crowd-pleasing shape

EGYPT // It's the watching of *feteer* being made that makes the eating of it so unforgettable. Often described as Egyptian pizza because it's cooked in a wood-fired oven, this layered filo delight is also reminiscent of Malaysian *roti canai* with its stretching and folding of the pastry dough. All this expert (and speedy) kneading, slapping and folding, interspersed with the stuffing of cheese, olives and minced meat, and it's not long before you begin to fall under the spell of *feteer meshaltet*. There are restaurants serving *feteer* all over Cairo. They are hot and hectic, and the best ones are often so busy that hungry clientele stand four deep at the counter, but don't be disheartened by the crowds – just remember why you're here.

☛ EAT IT ! ***Feteer restaurants are everywhere in Cairo, but they're not commonly comfy eat-in establishments, so grab a flaky pie to go.***

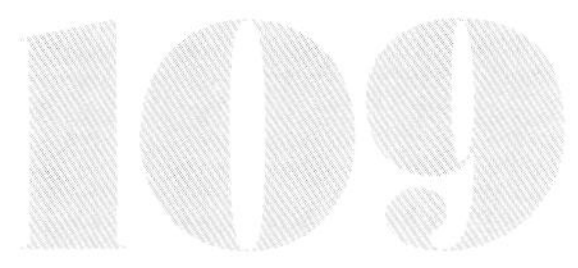

Bhel puri: India's sweet-tangy-crunchy-spicy magic

INDIA // Mumbai's Chowpatty beach at night is teeming with families, lovers, friends and tourists all eating different types of *chaats* – savoury snacks. And the snack that keeps them coming back for more is *bhel puri* – a perfect combo of crunchy puffed rice and fried chickpea-flour noodles, with a smattering of soft cooked potato chunks for texture and handfuls of spicy chillies and onions. Rich brown tamarind sauce brings sweetness and tanginess and coriander-based green chutney brightens everything up. Bought from street stalls all over western India, it's eaten from paper cones by the handful. On sweltering days – and nights – in this maelstrom of a country, it's the ultimate pick-me-up.

☛ EAT IT ! ***On Chowpatty beach, at the bhel puri stall with the longest queue – ocals know their stuff.***

Take a break from Balinese beaches with spicy gado gado

INDONESIA // If anyone's ever told you that you don't win friends with salad they haven't tasted this classic Indonesian interpretation – and they definitely haven't tried it from a classic Balinese beachside *warung* (café). Crunchy vegetables, boiled eggs, peanut sauce, fried tofu and fresh coriander – *gado gado* is the perfect end to a day that should begin with surfing and swimming on Bali's beaches. The juxtaposition of spicy sauce with crisp green beans, Chinese cabbage, carrot, cucumber and bean sprouts is typically Indonesian, and it's a salad that suits any time of the day. Drag your mates away from their sun-worshipping to pay respect to the food gods. There's no better way to begin your culinary adulation than with a bowl of *gado gado*.

☛ EAT IT ! ***With an accompanying ocean breeze at Chez Gado Gado, Jl Camplung Tanduk No 99, Seminyak.***

Sample Stockholm street food at the Nystekt Strömming van

SWEDEN // Amid the bridges, waterways, locks and, for the next few years at least, constructions sites of Slussen, Stockholm, keep your eyes peeled for a yellow fish atop an inauspicious-looking van, for it's here that you'll find Sweden's contribution to the food truck phenomenon. At Nystekt Strömming, which loosely translates as freshly fried herring, you have a choice of having these little fish fried and wrapped in flatbread, like a Swedish shawarma; fried and put inside a bun; or the classic serving, on a plate with mashed potato and crispbread, accompanied by a choice of sides like picked cucumber, red onion, sliced beetroot, dill mayonnaise or lingonberry jam. It's a taste of Stockholm that's as cheap as chips.

☛ EAT IT ! ***Nystekt Strömming, Södermalmstorg, Stokholm.***

112

Meet the bratwurst, the daddy of all hot dogs

GERMANY // A bratwurst is the perfect handheld snack in a bun from a Berlin grillwalker; a sightseeing break from a little tramside café while watching busy Berliners go about their business; or a hearty pub meal, complete with potato and red cabbage. They've been a part of Germany's culinary traditions since the early 14th century, and there's no sign of the humble sausage losing popularity any time soon. Made mostly of pork meat with a smidgen of veal, wursts are commonly spiced with nutmeg, coriander, ginger and cardamom, but there are so many regional varieties that it's impossible to tell you exactly what you'll get. If you're grabbing one on the go it will come to you in a small white roll with mustard (ketchup if you ask for it).

EAT IT ! ***Flag down a grillwalker or head to Konnopke's Imbiss at Schönhauser Allee 44B, Berlin.***

113

Feel São Paulo's pulse with a feijoada

BRAZIL // Like everything Brazilians do, their national dish is dialled up. *Feijoada* is a rich stew with black beans, salted and smoked chunks of pork and beef, collard greens or kale, and *farofa* (cassava flour), all served with rice and topped with orange slices. In some places they'll even throw in old-school pork cuts like ears, feet and tail. It's a hot-pot free-for-all – which sets the tone for pretty much any night out in São Paulo, Brazil's most food-loving, 24hr city. There are 15,000 bars in Sampa (as locals call the city) and the clock is ticking. So finish your plate of *feijoada*, down a shot of *cachaça* and get ready to drink and dance the night away, São Paulo-style.

EAT IT ! ***Head to Bolinha Restaurante, known for its local focus and very popular feijoada: Bolinha Restaurante, Av. Cidade Jardim, 53 - Jardim Europa, São Paulo.***

Mark Hix

Mark Hix is the chef-owner of Hix Soho and Hixter Bankside in London, and a food writer.

01

CLEAR SOUP WITH BAMBOO SHOOTS, HUNAN, LONDON This is a no-menu place, where they just bring a lot of small courses. All the ingredients of this soup are in the crust on the surface.

02

DANCING PRAWNS, SUSHI KEN; TOKYO They get live prawns out of the tank and once you finish them, they deep fry the shells and serve with sea salt

03

CRAB CURRY, SEAN'S PANORAMA; SYDNEY This place is an old classic and they have this Malaysian-style curry – you know they mix things up in Australia.

04

FRIED EGG WITH FOIS GRAS, EL QUIM; BARCELONA El Quim has a lot of Spanish-influenced tapas but also many things that are quite unexpected.

05

BEEF STEAK FIORENTINA, DARIO'S; PENZANO, ITALY This butcher shop is owned by this crazy guy who is always playing heavy metal – he puts on a bit of a performance. You drink wine and eat various bits of the local steak, cooked very very rare.

114

Don't rush your muffuletta, the New Orleans sandwich with a mountain of meat

USA // All we can assume is that the Sicilian immigrants to New Orleans couldn't find a way to get as much of their traditional cold meats into their meals as they could back home, so the *muffuletta* was born. Named after the sesame-crusted loaf of bread in which it's made, the *muffuletta* sandwich is a meat-lover's dream. Inside the sliced round loaf go salami, ham, coppa and mortadella, as well as provolone and mozzarella cheeses, and a marinated olive salad. And don't be too hungry when you start the preparation because experts say the best flavour comes from a sandwich that has been rested for a while to allow the olive salad to soak into the bread. You could always grab a sazarek (New Orleans' signature cocktail) and enjoy some of the French Quarter's Big Easy sounds while you wait.

EAT IT ! *Central Grocery, 923 Decatur St, New Orleans.*

114

115

Gift yourself a moreish Yuletide pairing, glühwein and stollen in Germany

GERMANY // Nothing shouts European Christmas holiday like a mug of *glühwein* and a thick slice of *stollen*. Germany's version of mulled wine, *glühwein* is a simple infusion of red wine, cloves, cinnamon and star anise; regional variations include extra shots of alcohol, sugar or fruits. The name itself translates as 'glow wine', and if you quaff enough you'll be glowing too. Throughout winter, mugs of *glühwein* are served at market stalls to keep shoppers in the Christmas spirit, which is also where you'll find *stollen*, or Christmas cake, as an edible accompaniment. Flavoured with spices such as cinnamon and cardamom, *stollen* is a fruit bread stuffed with almonds, raisins and citrus to create a taste combination in harmony with the *glühwein*.

☛ EAT IT ! ***Dresden's evocative Christmas Striezelmarkt has been enchanting patrons with glühwein and stollen since the 15th century.***

115

© Shutterstock / linerpics

116

© Lonely Planet / Susan Wright

116

Rome is the home of a classic spaghetti carbonara

ITALY // Ageless Roman comfort food, spaghetti carbonara has transitioned from being a midweek home-cooked meal to a trattoria favourite – and eating it on an unprepossessing Roman street at Da Danilo (where the location next door to a police station ensures lots of off-duty *poliziotti*) is the definitive dining experience. The basement location, trattoria decor, checked tablecloths and framed photos of happy customers with well-known faces on the walls is so classic it hardly feels real. Roman carbonara keeps it simple, forget anything like peas or onions or cream – they don't exist here. What does is a sauce made from *guanciale* (cured pork cheek), pecorino cheese, eggs (in many cases just the yolks), and a twist of black pepper.

☛ EAT IT ! ***Slurp and twirl your way through a mound of the classic carbonara at Trattoria Da Danilo, Via Petrarca 13, Rome.***

© Shutterstock / Aleksandr Shilov

117

Bánh mì and Ho Chi Minh City: a match made in heaven

VIETNAM // Bringing together two great cuisines in French and Vietnamese cooking was always going to result in some special offspring, and the sandwich superstar *bánh mì* is way up there. In the unlikely event you're unfamiliar with it, a light and crispy baguette filled with pâté, cured meats, pickled daikon, carrot, cucumber, mayonnaise, coriander and fiery red chilli offers a glorious medley of fresh, salty, crunchy, sweet, spicy and savoury flavours and textures – and is just the thing to accompany the bustling, frenetic streets of the capital, Ho Chi Minh City.

Brave the throng of locals jostling for counter space at Banh Mi Huynh Hoa; there's no queue to speak of so be prepared to shout out your order. What comes back is a classic example of the national sandwich, layer upon layer of cold meats (mostly pork), generously applied pâté, crunchy cucumber, carrot and eye-wateringly hot chilli.

EAT IT ! *Bánh Mì Huỳnh Hoa, 26 Lê Thi Riêng, Phuong Pham Ngũ Lão, Quan 1, Ho Chi Minh City.*

Dan Hunter

Dan Hunter is the chef-founder of Brae, a sustainable farm-to-table restaurant and accommodation in Victoria, Australia. He's also the author of Brae: Stories and Recipes from the Restaurant.

KAISEKI MEAL, KYOTO, JAPAN The food at Miyamasou, about an hour and a half outside Kyoto, is based on the surroundings – in winter they serve wild bear.

GRILLED TURBOT, GITARRIA, SPAIN At a famous Basque restaurant called El Carno the cooking is all done in charcoal, out on the street. The signature dish is turbot, grilled over grapevine embers.

BUFFALO MOZZARELLA, AMALFI COAST, ITALY What you do is go in and buy it before it's even cooled down, then go to a cafe and get your morning coffee, some bread, salt and olive oil, and that's your breakfast.

MAIZE, LIMA, PERU At a food festival in Lima called Mistura, all the Indians come to celebrate their indigenous ingredients. There are several thousand varieties of potato, quinoa, maize and grain dishes here.

SOUTHERN ROCK LOBSTER, AUSTRALIA In the Southern Ocean, the lobster weigh up to 5kg. It's our Christmas tradition to barbecue them over Australian timber and drink champagne.

118

Find fragrant knafeh in a Beirut backstreet

LEBANON // *Knafeh* is best enjoyed for breakfast in a street-side café in Beirut, with a strong black coffee to cut through the sweetness. Don't let the description of this as a sweet cheese dessert put you off – it's a delicate, indulgent treat. The mild mozzarella-like cheese is soaked in rose and orange-blossom syrup before being wrapped in *kataifi* pastry. The fine strands of the vermicelli-like *kataifi* wrapped around the cheese make the parcel look like a little gift – particularly once it's doused in more syrup, and sprinkled with pistachios and petals for a pretty finish.

☛ EAT IT ! ***At Amal Bohsali, Hamra, Beirut.***

Go veggie with a vada pav in Mumbai

INDIA // It's not the kind of street food that springs to mind when you think of snacking on the go in Mumbai. But what could be better than a beachside veggie burger to go? Goan-style soft white bread rolls are packed with a crispy fried potato patty with toasted green chilli pepper and chutney. Grab one from the beachside kiosk then sit and watch the couples strolling and families playing in the sand of Chowpatty beach before visiting a nearby temple to see the faithful perform their evening prayers. By which time you'll probably be ready for another *vada pav*.

☛ EAT IT ! ***On the seashore in Mumbai.***

Enjoy Korea's hotteok, the sweeter Seoul food

KOREA // Korean cuisine is renowned for its savoury bowls of rice and vegetables pimped out with fiery *kimchi*, smoky BBQd meat and stomach-filling stir fries – but there's one small, sweet treat that's equally addictive. The palm-sized pancake known as *hotteok* is sold from street carts all over South Korea. Its popularity can be attributed to the brown sugar filling which melts into a delicious mess once the whole thing has been fried on the griddle. In winter there's no better way to warm up than to eat a few when on the go.

☛ EAT IT ! ***At the tiny Sambodang hotteok stand in Seoul's Jongno-gu district.***

121

Bite into a barnacle with some Portuguese percebes

PORTUGAL // Human ingenuity in the search for food never ceases to amaze. Who, for example, was the ravenous adventurer that stumbled upon prehistoric-looking goose barnacles in the Atlantic Ocean and thought, 'Wow, those craggy bunions on that rock look tasty'? Whoever it was, though, was right. *Percebes* are considered a delicacy in Portugal, not so much because of the barnacles themselves, but because prying them off the rocks in the water is a dangerous job. Once they've been liberated from their watery resting place, they're boiled with a little salt, bay leaves and garlic and served with lemon. The best places to sample *percebes* are coastal seafood restaurants, where the respect for these craggy ocean creatures is at its highest. They taste somewhere between squid and crab, and they require some roughish handling – you need to twist the meat out of the tube shape by holding the hard shell. The coral-coloured flesh inside is your delicacy; squeeze on some lemon and devour in one bite (maybe two).

☛ EAT IT ! ***In the sea-smashed coastal towns of southern Portugal's Alentejo region.***

122

Fix eyes on your host's boerewors at a Jo'burg BBQ

SOUTH AFRICA // If you ever see a South African fire up a *braai* (BBQ), they'll soon lay a generous spiral of sausage on the grill because, as any self-respecting South African will tell you, a *braai* isn't a *braai* without *boerewors*. South Africans are serious about their sausages: spiced, hand-made *boerewors* must contain at least 90% meat, mostly beef. Be sure to pay attention to your host's *boerewors*, they're a matter of personal, and national, pride.

EAT IT ! ***In Johannesburg's Jeppestown. Pata Pata, at 286 Fox St, will give you a good starting point.***

123

Dive into an open-air assam laksa in Penang

MALAYSIA // Meet coconut cream laksa's spicy, sour cousin, *assam laksa*, a treat to eat from hawker stalls around Penang thanks to its local fish (usually mackerel). The distinctive sourness in this version of the vermicelli noodle soup comes from tamarind (*assam* in Malay), but it's the cacophony of other flavours – from sliced pineapple to ginger flower stalks – that defy reason to create an unforgettable dish. The final flourish is a teaspoon of *hae ko*, a thick, sweet fish paste.

EAT IT ! ***At open-air food markets and hawker stalls on the island of Penang.***

124

Get an appetite for all things Ecuador with llapingacho

ECUADOR // Amazon rainforest, Andean foothills, a world-heritage listed capital and the wildlife mecca of the Galapagos Islands are just a few reasons that Ecuador punches well above its weight. The same can be said for the cuisine. *Llapingachos*, thick potato pancakes, are stuffed with cheese, seared on a grill and served with a spicy peanut sauce. They make perfect street food, though you can also order them as part of a meal alongside chorizo, avocado and fried eggs.

EAT IT ! ***Find a food stall at Mercado de las Tripas (Tripe Market), in the Vicentina neighbourhood, Quito.***

123

© Lonely Planet / Austin Bush

125

Taste sweet relief with mango sticky rice on Bangkok's steamy streets

THAILAND // It's impossible to visit Bangkok and not come back with cravings for the street food you gorged on there. Exhibit A: mango sticky rice. The gelatinous texture of the rice, sweetened with coconut milk and sugar, is the perfect complement to the juicy mango. It's sold at street stalls across Bangkok, and half the fun lies in discovering your favourite place – ask around, for this is a dish that won't be signposted on TripAdvisor, and by the time it is, the vendor may have a new spot. Look out for twists such as black rice, salty coconut sauce or toasted mung beans on top for added crunch, and while the street snack is available all year long, mangoes are in season in Thailand from late March to late May, so this is the best time to sample the sweetest.

EAT IT ! *Choose one of the ubiquitous street-food stalls pretty much anywhere in Bangkok, including Sukhumvit Soi 38, Soi Sukhumvit 38, Phra Khanong, Khlong Toei, Bangkok.*

126

Kushari: dip into Cairo's melting pot

EGYPT // Whether you eat your *kushari* in the middle of the day when you have a front-row seat to the gloriously chaotic Cairo streets, or against the backdrop of an indoor fountain at spots like Abou Tarek, what you'll be eating is a culinary metaphor for Egypt itself. The revered meal is a mélange of the multicultural influences that cast their net over the land during the economic boom of the 19th century. Spices from India, pasta from Italy and Middle Eastern ingredients such as chickpeas combine with rice, lentils, tomato sauce, fried onion and chilli or garlic dressing to create a dish for the working people. Eating from a hole-in-the-wall shop on Cairo's lively streets is the best way to enjoy its hearty flavours. Egyptians are loyal to their preferred purveyor, though there are only slight variations from vendor to vendor.

EAT IT ! *From a busy street vendor, or for a more relaxed affair, Abou Tarek, at 26 El-Shaikh Marouf, Marouf, Qasr an Nile, Cairo.*

© Sarah Lawrie / wandercooks.com

© Getty Images / Carlina Teteris

127

Go large on the larb to complete a serene Laotian scene

LAOS // Vientiane isn't your average Southeast Asian city. You don't get hustled by cars or bustled by motorbikes, and its mix of French colonial architecture, Buddhist temples and colourful street markets is ripe for casual exploration on foot. The Mekong River flows to the west of the centre and when the sun sets, golden light bounces off the water. Completing the postcard setting is an array of restaurants and food carts offering Laotian classics, none better than the unofficial national dish, *larb*. It's a perfect combination of food and place, because pork *larb* is as simple and stunning as the fiery sunset. Eaten with that other local staple, sticky rice, it's filling, chilli-filled and bursting with flavour... just the high-octane fuel needed for more walking.

EAT IT ! ***Larb is sometimes prepared with raw meat, but there's risk of bacterial infection so stick with the cooked variety.***

© Shutterstock / DouglasDepies

128

Visit the Yucatán for smoky slow-cooked cochinita pibil

MEXICO // Mérida is the beautiful capital city of the Yucatán, with elegant colonial architecture and shady squares. It's here that you must come for the ultimate *cochinita pibil* – the slow-roasted shredded pork that is one of many delicious Yucatecan dishes. For some reason, the citrus hit (lime, orange and even grapefruit) has extra tang. The *achiote* marinade has a deeper, earthier and smokier flavour. And the pork seems to fall apart more effortlessly. Here, *cochinita pibil* is often a celebratory dish cooked for hours by burying a whole pig – first rubbed with an *achiote* paste of garlic, spice and orange juice – in a steamy, stone-lined pit (*cochinita* means baby pig, *pibil* means buried). They don't do that in your local Mexican chain restaurant. It's served with pickled red onion in a tortilla.

EAT IT ! ***Try it at La Chaya Maya restaurant, Calle 55, no.510, in central Mérida.***

© Shutterstock / MarinaDa

© Getty Images / Lisovskaya

129

Make like a millionaire in Moscow with caviar

RUSSIA // Caviar is one of the most exclusive, luxurious and expensive foods on the planet, with roe from the Iranian beluga fish having been known to fetch prices as astronomical as US$35,000 for just one kilo – perfect for yacht-owning oligarchs but perhaps not so accessible for mere mortals like us. In this context, a much more reasonable splurge is the caviar degustation with red pancakes from Café Pushkin in Moscow. The combination of old-world opulence and the selection of salmon caviar, vendace caviar, sturgeon caviar, beluga caviar for a smidge under US$200 (plus drinks) is a bargain. Speaking of drinks, there's champagne of course, though many Russians prefer a straight shot of Beluga vodka, to wash the decadence down.

EAT IT ! *At Café Pushkin, 26A Tverskoy Boulevard, Moscow.*

130

Declare war on your hunger at a tiny Budapest kiosk

HUNGARY // Sometimes described as Hungarian pizza, *lángos* is a deep-fried flatbread made with yogurt and sour cream or milk instead of water. It's usually served topped with sour cream, cheese and garlic butter, but there are many variations and embellishments – such as grilled sausages, chilli, peppers, tomatoes, onion – and lots of places to try them. At tiny Retró Lángos Büfé, a Communist-era kiosk in Budapest, late-night to early-morning revellers crowd around for *lángos* filled with everything from cabbage and hot dogs to the 'nuclear attack' (*atomtámadás*), featuring spicy peppers, ham, cheese, sausage and red onion. Open until 2am throughout the week and 6am on weekends, it's the best way to treat that impending hangover.

EAT IT ! *At Retró Lángos Büfé, Bajcsy Zsilinszky út, Arany János metro, Budapest.*

See why bouillabaisse is a fish stew to share in the port of Marseille

131

FRANCE // There are fish stews and then there's *bouillabaisse* – the grandfather of all great plates of the sea. From its very modest beginnings as a kind of leftovers meal for local fishermen around the port of Marseille, in southern France, it has grown in stature and popularity to become a meal favoured by French gourmands as well as fisherfolk. Like the rest of the country, Marseille's version has moved with the foodie times, replacing fish that didn't sell at market – like rockfish for example, which were too bony to offload – with more palatable scorpion fish, sea robin and European conger, though you'll sometimes also come across monkfish, turbot, bream, mullet and/or hake in it. And the seafood bonanza doesn't end there; other common seafood found in the soup includes mussels, crabs, octopus and sea urchin, and in the fancier restaurants you might see a langoustine or two, although these would never have featured in the original make-do dish. Alongside the abundance of seafood are vegetables such as leeks, celery, onion, tomato and potato, and Provençale herbs like fennel, thyme and saffron – all gently simmered in a fishy broth.

What makes eating *bouillabaisse* such a wonderful experience is the kind of culinary theatre that goes into presenting and then eating it. In Marseille, you will first be served a bowl of broth in which sit a few slices of grilled bread topped with a garlic, saffron and cayenne pepper *rouille*. The magnificent platter of seafood is served separately. Eat your broth first, followed by the fish. Then lastly ladle soup from the seafood platter over your remaining fish. And in case the general outline of excess hasn't tipped you off, when you dine on *bouillabaisse* in Marseille it is rarely ever made for less than four or five people. So you'll just have to bring your mates – or make some.

EAT IT ! ***With old or new friends at Chez Fonfon, 140 Rue du Vallon des Auffes, Marseille.***

Below: bouillabaisse fish stew began as a fishermen's meal in Marseille. Right: the seafront Endoume area of the French city.

© Lonely Planet / Myles New

© Kevin Foy / Alamy Stock Photo

132

Trace the Scotch egg's origins to a London food emporium

UK // On paper, a boiled egg wrapped in sausage meat, coated in breadcrumbs and baked or deep-fried, sounds like a greasy mass of protein that shouldn't work. But it does at London's Fortnum & Mason – as it should given that the shop claims to have invented the Scotch egg in 1738. If anticipation is part of the pleasure of a food experience, the trip through the 18th-century department store's famous hampers and loose-leaf teas on the ground floor, then down the spiral staircase into the delicatessen, serves to heighten the moment. Can the eating match the anticipation? Cutting into the firm case reveals a perfectly soft-boiled orange yolk, wrapped in a coarse, herby meat that has a robust flavour. Bite into London history!

EAT IT ! *At its spiritual home of Fortnum & Mason in London's Piccadilly. Or if you must, in the Dubai branch.*

133

Find a taste for Albania old and new with fëgesë

ALBANIA // You've spent the morning taking in Tirana's major sights of Skanderbeg Square, the Orthodox church, the National Opera House and the vast collection at the National History Museum, and now you're ready for a taste of Albania's burgeoning food scene. Effortlessly blending traditional recipes with modern cafe culture, Tirana's restaurants have a foot in the future while nodding to the past. Dishes such as the delicious *fëgesë*, a simple blend of grilled peppers, tomatoes and onions, sautéed with cottage cheese and paprika and served with bread, are centuries-old but utterly modern when delivered on the shaded terrace at Oda, accompanied, naturally, by a glass of crisp white wine.

EAT IT ! *At a truly traditional Albanian restaurant such as Oda, Rr Luigj Gurakuqi, Tirana.*

134

Clam up with fried shellfish cakes on your Rhode Island vacation

USA // New Englanders will tell you that a trip to Rhode Island only turns into a holiday once you have a paper bag full of steaming clam cakes in your hot little hands. Dispensed from takeaway windows by the half or full dozen, these fried dough balls packed with chopped clams should be eaten ASAP. Aficionados will tell you that proper New England clam cakes use the giant quahog clam but that's where everyone's agreement ends... some like their cakes neat and golf-ball-like, while others swear the best bits are the scratchings that break off from the irregularly shaped fritters; some like them dipped in a pint of creamy clam chowder, while others prefer the clear Rhode Island-style soup. There's nothing for it but to taste-test them all.

EAT IT ! *From takeaway windows and roadside restaurants across Rhode Island, New England.*

© Stan Tess / Alamy Stock Photo

© Shutterstock / Toronto-images.com

135

Don't pass up a parcel of cheesy humita in Argentina

ARGENTINA // It looks like a *tamale* but technically it's not – these little steamed parcels of seasoned corn are made with fresh corn, not the soaked, dried corn that is traditionally found in a *tamale*. The corn inside the *humita*'s husk is ground and mixed with onions, garlic, cheese, eggs and cream. Grab one from a street-stall vendor and find a shady spot to sit and unwrap your little parcel. Inside you'll find a moreish ode to corn, rich with salt and cheese, that will have you seeking out *humitas* for the rest of your stay.

EAT IT ! *From a street vendor wherever you see one.*

136

Explore the infinite possibilities of noodle at one of Tokyo's ramen joints, from hole-in-the-wall to Michelin-starred

JAPAN // It's a tribute to the complexity and sophistication of Japanese cuisine that a bowl of noodles in soup with a handful of toppings can deliver so many delicious but distinct eating experiences. Ramen, in true Japanese style, demands protocols for which ingredients and techniques go together, driven by regional variation; some ramen joints offer a range of styles, while others focus on one specific kind. And there are so many ramen joints, so many variations that it's futile to go looking for the definitive experience. Instead, do as the Japanese do: find the ramen just right for you, and eat! By virtue of its size alone, Tokyo will be your happiest hunting ground. And wherever you find your ultimate ramen – a standing-only hole-in the-wall in a narrow alley, a brightly lit food hall off a major shopping mall, or one of the city's two Michelin-starred ramen joints – slurp your noodles up quickly (to stop them getting soggy), with plenty of air (it enhances the flavour) and with plenty of noise (the sign of appreciation for the ramen chef).

EAT IT ! ***Brave the queue at Tsuta, 1 Chome-14-1 Sugamo, Toshima, Tokyo 170-0002, the 'World's First Michelin-Starred Ramen'.***

137

© YLevy / Alamy Stock Photo

137

The Argentinian appetite buster, choripán, that's big in Buenos Aires

ARGENTINA // Everyone knows that if hunger bites on the streets of Buenos Aires you head for an empanada. But what if your cravings require more than a bite-size snack? This is when your radar sends you the way of the mighty *choripán*, or *chori*. Simply put, the *choripán* is a butterflied chorizo sausage grilled on the *asado* (barbecue) and generously lathered in chimichirri and chunky onion and tomato salsa. It's then slapped inside some crusty bread and thrust into your expectant hands. Punchy, greasy and perfect for silencing a grumbling stomach.

EAT IT ! *In Buenos Aires at Chori, Thames 1653, Palermo; or Nuestra Parrilla, Bolívar 950, San Telmo.*

138

Plan for a mutton curry in modernist Chandigarh

INDIA // Several South Asian countries lay claim to this minced mutton and pea curry, but we're plumping for India's Punjab state, not least because the city of Chandigarh is such a great place in which to eat it. Laid out and designed by Le Corbusier in the 1950s in the style of Sir Ebenezer Howard's English Garden Cities and at the invitation of independent India's first prime minister, Jawaharlal Nehru, it's a beguiling example of urban planning. After a day of sightseeing the elegant modernist civic centre of Le Corbusier's Secretariat, Punjab and Haryana High Court and Legislative Assembly and, for a different perspective, the quirky Nek Chand Rock Garden, sitting down to a plate of *keema matar* will just seem, well, right.

EAT IT ! *In a Le Corbusier classic, the circular, three-storey Panjab University Students' Centre known to all as the 'Stu-C'.*

© Getty Images / Angelo DeSantis

138

© galit seligmann / Alamy Stock Photo

© Peter Tsai Photography / Alamy Stock Photo

© Shutterstock / f11photo

139

Feel the burn of chilli-doused Southern fried in a Nashville chicken shack

USA // Hold on to your cowboy hat, for this version of Southern fried chicken brings to the table more heat than hospitality. Legend has it that the dish was invented when a woman awaiting her hound dog of a husband's return from another night of philandering spiked his usual morning fried chicken with a hefty dose of cayenne pepper. To the dismay of the spurned chef, the cad actually liked it spicy, and hot fried chicken was born. Word is that this scene went down at the site of Prince's Hot Chicken, still family-owned, in Nashville's northside. Here at Prince's it's still possible to test your mettle against the spice mix designed to knock you off your chair, but be prepared to queue. We suggest medium spice if you'd like to keep your taste buds, hot will burn and extra hot, well... nice knowing you. Hot fried chicken is, in fact, found all over town and doesn't have to be a painful experience. Restaurants will often give you a head's up rating system designed to help you avoid death by chilli. And if all else fails, there's always beer.

EAT IT ! ***In varying degrees of heat at Prince's Hot Chicken Shack, 123 Ewing Dr, Nashville, Tennessee.***

140

Fish into a poke bowl in paradise on Hawaii's golden sands

USA // The first thing you'll notice in Hawaii is its beautiful geography – the crescent-shaped beaches lapped at by sparkling seas, and the verdant, mountainous interior rumbling with volcanic energy. You'll also notice the endless number of activities on hand, from surfing and snorkelling to helicopter rides and 4WD jungle tours. These islands have become one of the world's premier holiday destinations, and thanks to their diverse and unique history of settlement and immigration, Hawaiian food has also evolved to be a fascinating mix of Polynesian, European, US, Japanese, Filippino, Chinese, Portuguese and Puerto Rican influences. Out of this melting pot comes Hawaii's all-in-one super meal, the *poke* bowl. In its simplest form, a *poke* bowl is raw, cubed fish with different garnishes (like seaweed, avocado and cucumber), served on warm rice. It combines classic components with tried and tested flavours. And from the myriad influences still shaping the state's cuisine, this is one dish that's here to stay.

EAT IT ! ***Follow the locals to tiny hole-in-the-wall restaurants where you should just grab and go, to the beach.***

140

140

© Lonely Planet / Matt Munro

© Image Source / Alamy Stock Photo

141

Reach the summit of après-ski experiences with slowly melting raclette

SWITZERLAND // Lactose intolerants look away now, for here is gooey, delicious cheese in all its glory. But first you must hike, ski or snowboard in the Swiss Alps to justify this extravagance. Then park yourself in front of an open fire at a village restaurant and let the indulgence begin. Whether DIY or having it served to you, your raclette should come in a large wedge or semi-circle and be slowly toasted over an open flame. As the cheese begins to melt it should be scraped from the wedge on to a warm plate, containing cornichons, new potatoes and thin slices of ham or dried beef, then it's down to you to get all the molten cheese over as much of the other ingredients on your plate as you can before the cheese sets. Eat. Rinse and repeat.

EAT IT ! *In stunning Alpine surrounds at Restaurant Schäferstube, Riedstrasse 2, Zermatt.*

142

Warm up with a bowl of miso ramen in Sapporo

JAPAN // When winter is coming in Hokkaido, northern Japan, a bowl of steaming miso ramen is the ultimate comfort food. Chef Oku Masuhiko of Menya Saimi trained in Sapporo-style noodles at the landmark noodle shop Sumire before starting his own shop. His miso ramen always draws a crowd: it's bold but not overpowering, with dense, curly noodles and an array of toppings that include chashu pork, bamboo shoots and bean spouts. Miso ramen starts with an oily broth – Masuhiko makes his with pork bones – which is seasoned with salty miso. 'The vegetables that garnish the top are stir-fried first: this is key for Sapporo-style ramen,' says Masuhiko. His kitchen is rich with the funky aroma of pork stock, sizzling garlic and the toasted, nutty fragrance of sautéing miso. Winter doesn't stand a chance.

EAT IT ! *Menya Saimi, Misono 10-jo, Toyohira-ku, Sapporo.*

143

Get in the queue at Mr Wu to claim his famous cong you bing pancake

CHINA // In September 2016 the iconic Mr Wu hung up his pancake flipper and pulled down the shutters on his tiny takeaway window, closing a beloved business that had been running for more than 30 years. Just as Shanghai residents and scallion pancake tragics began to fear the worst, he popped up in new digs just a few blocks from his old stomping ground. Despite the new location nothing else has changed, you still need to set your alarm for first thing in the morning and contend with the same lengthy queues, but after that, the rest is all good. They're the same green-onion packed, flakey, doughy patties of deliciousness fried in a dollop of salty pork fat. Totally worth the wait, though don't turn up on a Wednesday – that's Mr Wu's one day off.

EAT IT ! *Mr Wu's A Da Cong You Bing makes 300 pancakes a day and closes on Wednesday. Shanghai, No 4, 120 Ruijin Er Lu.*

144

A taste of the Raj at London's smartest breakfast venue

UK // This decidedly un-English breakfast was brought back from India to the UK by British colonials. Once settled on English shores the Indian rice dish known as *khichari* morphed from the heavily spiced subcontinent version to the kedgeree of today – with smoked haddock, rice, parsley, boiled eggs, curry powder and cream. There are many breakfast options in Britain but you won't regret breaking with tradition and trying this surprisingly subtle dish (you can always go back to the full English tomorrow). At The Wolseley, one of London's premier breakfast establishments, the kedgeree is refined and flavourful. The rice is rich with cream and butter and mild curry spices, the haddock is lightly smoked, and the whole thing is topped with a poached egg.

EAT IT ! *In the luxurious dining room at The Wolseley, 160 Piccadilly, St James's, London.*

145

Step closer to Everest with a bowl of dal bhat

↓

NEPAL // It's a simple thing – just lentil soup and rice. But it's not what's in *dal bhat* that makes it such a special meal; it's more that it comes after a long, gruelling day of trekking towards Everest Base Camp. Stopping to rest weary limbs and to refuel on *dal bhat* is a climber's rite of passage. And this bowl of spiced lentils will sustain you through the next arduous day of climbing, bringing you one step closer to your dream of reaching the top of the world.

EAT IT ! ***At teahouses on the route to Everest, or anywhere in Nepal.***

146

Bag puffy pancake waffles with sweet sauce to go in Hong Kong

CHINA // If you've never encountered Hong Kong's iconic street food, the egg waffle, it won't be long before you spot some. Shaped like giant bubblewrap made from crispy pancake batter, the puffy waffles poke out of paper bags and are munched on by happy customers everywhere. Most street vendors sell them plain, but their popularity is such that many places have taken to inventing new flavours and accompaniments. At Oddies ice cream shop you get your waffle smothered in creamy gelato with chocolate sauce; at Hung Kee Top Quality Egg Waffle you can choose a batter made with chocolate or strawberry; and Mammy Pancake serves flavours such as seaweed and green tea. Our advice? Try them all.

☛ EAT IT ! *Oddies, 45 Gough St, Central; Hung Kee Top Quality Egg Waffle, Shop A34c, 57-87 Sau Kei Wan Rd, Sai Wan Ho; Mammy Pancake, 8-12e Carnarvon Rd, Tsim Sha Tsui; all Hong Kong.*

146

147

147

Stick to the Sofia specialists for Bulgaria's best banitsa

BULGARIA // The only guide you need to eating the *banitsa* is to avoid buying one from cheap roadside kiosks or at bus and train stations; find a cafe where you can take a load off and savour its flaky softness with a glass of *boza*, a traditional Bulgarian beverage made from boiled wheat, rye, millet and sugar. In fact it's hard to walk past a bakery in Sofia without being drawn in by the sight and smell of the wonderfully flakey pastry. A Bulgarian staple, *banitsa* is made with *sirene* cheese (similar to feta), eggs, yoghurt and oil, and is most commonly served for breakfast, though the layered filo pie can be eaten at any time of the day. Variations on the basic cheese version include spinach and cheese, spiced rice and cabbage or leeks, but our favourite is the original.

☛ EAT IT ! *Breakfast is when the banitsas are at their best so make an early start to your day and get it hot from a cafe's oven.*

Allow mapo tofu to make its mark in the Sichuan restaurant where it was first served

CHINA // Sichuan cuisine is all about the hot, mouth-numbing properties of the Sichuan pepper; the polar opposite of its mild-mannered associate, Cantonese cooking. For a baptism of fire into Sichuan food you can't go past *mapo tofu*. It's a fiery looking bowl of ground meat (usually pork but sometimes beef) mixed with *silken tofu* and a firecracker combination of fermented bean and chilli oil with Sichuan peppercorns, and a sprinkling of scallions on top. The dish got its name from the appearance of the woman who is credited with inventing the meal. Word has it that she had a distinctive pock-marked face after suffering smallpox as a child, and the dish was subsequently dubbed '*mapo*', meaning pockmarked old woman. Although it's not difficult to find excellent *mapo tofu* in Chinatowns all over the world, the best place to eat it is in the Sichuan capital of Chengu. Here is where the dish is said to originate, and those at Chen Mapo Tofu restaurant claim to be descendants of the trailblazing old lady.

EAT IT ! ***At Chen Mapo Tofu, 197 W Yulong St, LuoMaShi, Qingyang Qu, Chengdu, Sichuan, Chengdu.***

148

© Shutterstock / Rolf E. Staerk

© Shutterstock / Marcel Gussoni

149

Declare your allegiance to cassoulet atop a medieval fort in southern France

FRANCE // The medieval hilltop town of Carcassonne is the perfect place to sample one of southern France's most famous culinary achievements – the *cassoulet*. The town's ancient fortifications speak of centuries of human toil, endeavour and ingenuity, and are a fitting backdrop from which to enjoy a meal born of resourcefulness and defined by conflict. Throughout southern France the ingredients that make up a classic *cassoulet* are still hotly disputed. Up for debate is the type of meats used, whether breadcrumbs should be added to the top, and even which bean is the best. We can leave the French to their bickering, though, because most of us won't care if our *cassoulet* doesn't have the sausage from Toulouse, or the flat bean from the base of the Pyrenees, all we care about is that the meats have been slow-cooked till they've absorbed all the flavours of the stock and the flesh pulls from the bones. In Carcassonne your *cassoulet* is often served in an individual *cassole*, the traditional earthenware cooking pot.

☛ EAT IT ! ***Splurge at Restaurant La Barbacane, Place Auguste Pierre Pont, Carcassonne.***

150

Dine at Denmark's latest star purveyor of New Nordic Cuisine

DENMARK // In 2010, chef René Redzepi opened Copenhagen's multi-award winning restaurant, Noma. The philosophy behind Noma's menu, however, dates to 2004, when René, chef Claus Meyer and other Nordic food professionals developed an ethos of food gathering, preparation, cooking and eating designed to be pure, fresh and simple. Chefs were encouraged to work with seasonal produce and craft traditional meals using ingredients inspired by the regional climate, water and soil. New Nordic Cuisine was born. The latest star at the forefront of this food philosophy is Copenhagen's Geranium restaurant. Headed up by award-winning chef Rasmus Kofoed, its dishes are composed of wild and organic ingredients. Kofoed employs modern techniques with a sprinkling of molecular gastronomy to take diners to exquisite gourmet heights. Don't be deterred by its oddly juxtaposed setting at the top floor of the national football stadium; the interior is light-filled, with views over the city and nary a football strip in sight.

EAT IT ! *At Geranium, Per Henrik Lings Allé 4, 8th floor, Parken National Stadium, Copenhagen.* *See also BROR and Restaurant 108.*

© Thomas Degner / Copenhagen Media Centre

© Freya Mcomish / Copenhagen Media Centre

© Claes Bech-Poulsen

151

Mark a family Christmas in Guyana with a bowl of pepperpot stew

GUYANA // The best place to sample this dark and glistening stew, filled with things you can't recognise, is a family home at Christmas, where it will have been simmering for hours before being dished out with reverence and arguments over who wants which bit of meat (or cow heel, pig's trotter or tail, added to give a gelatinous quality). The stew commonly includes beef, mutton and pork, seasoned with cinnamon, chillies and *cassareep* sauce, made from cassava root. Credited as being handed down from the original Amerindian inhabitants of Guyana, who arrived here more than 10,000 years ago, pepperpot stew speaks volumes about the culinary history and influences that make Guyana's cuisine and culture such a unique melting pot. Eat it with some dense white bread, which soaks up the sauce nicely.

☛ EAT IT ! *No invite to a Guyanese Christmas party? Try German's Restaurant, 8 New Market & Mundy sts, Georgetown.*

152

Kick back in an Angolan beach shack with a bowl of chicken muamba

ANGOLA / The cuisines of sub-Saharan Africa receive short shrift on the world culinary stage, but you'll be scratching your head as to why after tasting Angola's spicy gift to the world, *muamba de galinha*, or chicken muamba. Under the thatched roofs of the restaurants lining the beach on Luanda Island you'll find locals and travellers alike kicking back with a beer and a bowl of this rich, fiery stew. Influenced by Portuguese flavours like chilli, garlic and tomatoes and centuries of colonisation, its red colour actually comes from the oil of the African palm tree. The chicken is marinated in the oil and cooked with okra and pumpkin and served with *funge* – a kind of porridge made with cassava or corn flour. A tasty way to while away an hour or two.

☛ EAT IT ! *At Ilha de Luanda, where there are beautiful beaches, and many restaurants where you can bliss out to this national dish.*

Monica Galetti

Monica Galetti is a veteran judge on the BBC's MasterChef: The Professionals. She also spent years as sous chef at world renowned La Gavroche and has recently opened Mere in London.

CHILLI CRAB WITH DUMPLINGS, SINGAPORE It's a street food. The first time I had it was about five years ago and I've had it every time I've been back.

SCHUER, OMAN The day before, they buy a goat in this thousand-year-old market, rub the meat in a mix of cumin and fennel, wrap it in tin foil, and cook it underground in a huge fire pit.

CEVICHE, PACIFIC ISLANDS It's actually just called raw fish where I'm from. It's different from Latin ceviche in that we use coconut milk for the marinade, as well as a bit of lime, tomato and cucumber.

HOKEY POKEY ICE CREAM, NEW ZEALAND It's a delicious vanilla-based ice cream with caramel chunks, but I now have it at my restaurant because it reminds me of home.

LEMON DRIZZLE AND STEAMED ORANGE PUDDING, MY FRIEND PRAT'S HOUSE Not many people are brave enough to cook for me, but my friends Prat and Sean make these amazing desserts.

153

Sink your teeth into jumbo cheesecake at a retro New York deli

USA // You'll be hard-pressed to find a dainty slice of cheesecake in America. Something about this iconic dessert, a mix of cream cheese, eggs, sugar and (in some versions) sour cream, baked atop a base of crushed cookies, seems to demand enormity. And where better to experience this sweet tribute to excess than in the Big Apple? At New York's old-school Jewish delis – Leo Lindemann's Lindy's deli was the first to popularise the dessert – you'll find titanic slabs of cheesecake paved with glistening strawberries, or topped with brownie chunks, or swirled with caramel. More is more, right? You can share it with a friend or two, and still have leftovers for breakfast.

EAT IT ! *Eileen's Special Cheesecake in Lower Manhattan has flavours from classic strawberry to rocky road to piña colada. 17 Cleveland Pl, New York.*

© Daniel Di Paolo

153

154

Honour the Polish pierogi at Kraków's annual festival

POLAND // You've been hiding under a rock somewhere if you've yet to come across Poland's gift to the world, the humble *pierogi*. These little dumplings, filled with minced beef, pork, veal or chicken, and sauerkraut, potatoes and cheese, are eaten all over Poland, but it's fun to come and eat them in Kraków in August, when the city hosts the annual Dumpling Festival. *Pierogi* restaurants set up stalls and compete to woo both customers and judges who award one prize for the most tasty and innovative *pierogi* and another for the crowd's favourite. Expect to find a host of flavours outside of the traditional meat and potato – 2016's winner was made with duck and apricots. It's a lot of fun, with cooking demonstrations, competitions and live music.

EAT IT ! *At the annual Dumpling Festival, Small Market Square, Kraków, Poland.*

© StockFood / Baranowski, Andre

154

A pastry-shaped breather at an Algiers breakfast

ALGERIA // The French influence in Algiers is clear in its elegant apartment buildings, wide boulevards and busy cafe culture. Join the locals in starting your day with some leisurely people-watching, a mint tea and a *makroudh*. The diamond-shaped Algerian *makroudh*, influenced by Turkish style and flavours, is a honey-doused pastry made with semolina flour and filled with dates and almond paste. It's the perfect breakfast treat before you hit the hustle and bustle of downtown Algiers.

☛ EAT IT ! ***We'd recommend Café Aroma, Bab Ezzouar, Algiers.***

156

Refine your after-hours food hit: try Icelandic lobster

ICELAND // Reykjavikians have gone and upped the ante on the rest of the world's late-night takeaway fare by by dishing out fresh lobster to their tipsy evening customers. There is one caveat: Icelandic lobster is more like langoustine, so don't expect gigantic crustaceans, but they are also sweeter and just as juicy. Choose from three: soup, lightly spiced with chilli; a simple langoustine salad; and in a sandwich with mayonnaise and crushed corn chips.

☛ EAT IT ! ***At the Lobster Hut, corner of Hverfisgata and Lækjargata, Reykjavik.***

157

The sweet Turkish orginal that's a genuine delight

TURKEY // Many Westerners are disappointed by rubbery, perfume-y mass-produced Turkish delight. But head to Turkey to try the real-deal, *lokum*, produced in the country for centuries. Here you'll find vibrantly coloured squares scented with rosewater, lemon or bitter orange, nutty versions rolled in pistachios or almonds, and nougat-like milk *lokum*. Buy it from a *lokum* vendor, and prepare for an intense toothsome hit with a Turkish coffee at the end of a meal.

☛ EAT IT ! ***Istanbul's spice bazaar has hundreds of lokum vendors.***

Prep your own pa amb tomaquet at your Catalan table

SPAIN // The simplicity of this recipe reflects the Catalan commitment to unfussy flavours and you'll find *pa amb tomaquet* (bread with tomato) and *pa ambo li* (bread with oil) served all day, as a snack or a tapa. Despite the modesty of the dish there is a strict order in which the ingredients should be combined. First garlic is rubbed on the bread, then the tomato, followed by salt and lastly olive oil. Good to know as some Catalan restaurants will supply the ingredients for you to DIY.

☛ EAT IT ! ***At tapas bars throughout Catalonia, Spain.***

Nourish your sightseeing with a Bosnian behemoth

BOSNIA // Don't be intimidated by the size of the *ćevapi* being consumed by locals, there is a more modest alternative. Start with what's known as a half serve – five pieces of sausage-shaped grilled minced meat, seasoned with garlic and served with diced onions and the pita-like bread, *somun*. You'll find the dish everywhere, so work up an appetite through a fascinating walking tour of historic Sarajevo, and make your choice when your stomach starts rumbling.

☛ EAT IT ! ***In any Old Town restaurant or takeway spot in Sarajevo.***

160

Make time for rolex, a street food classic in Uganda

UGANDA // Like its namesake, this Ugandan streetfood has all the makings of a timeless classic. An omelette fried and rolled up in a *chapati* (Indian flatbread), *rolex* is excellent food on the go, and a firm breakfast favourite on the streets of Kampala, where it's often still served in a roll or cone of newspaper. The name came about as the result of a mispronunciation. The snack was originally known as 'rolled eggs', but it sounded so much like '*rolex*' that the name stuck.

☛ EAT IT ! ***Look on street corners across Kampala for vendors flipping chapati.***

161

Uncover Fiji's underground sensation, the beachside-baked palusami

FIJI // From the comfort of your beach chair, you become aware of a tantalising smell wafting over you. This is your introduction to *palusami*, but where is the smell coming from? Underground, that's where. This little piece of island life is made up of corned beef mixed with garlic, thyme, coconut milk, onions and tomatoes, wrapped in a taro leaf. The parcel is then buried in a *lovo*, a traditional Melanesian oven that uses hot coals and embers to bake the meat underground until it is cooked. Fijians generally use tinned corned beef because it keeps better in tropical temperatures, but you could always substitute for another type of ground/minced meat back home. Roast it in a casserole dish, crack a beer, lie back and think of Fiji.

EAT IT ! ***It's best as a homecooked meal, but you won't go wrong at the Bounty Bar & Restaurant, 79 Queens Rd, Nadi.***

© Getty Images / Matteo Colombo

161

162

© GARY DOAK / Alamy Stock Photo

162

Revel in a Burns Night knees-up with its unique centrepiece, haggis

UK // On 25 January every year Scotland celebrates its national poet, Robert Burns. These Burns Night celebrations take the form of poetry readings, dancing, drinking and, most importantly, a traditional meal of haggis, neeps and tatties (swedes and potatoes). For the uninitiated, haggis is a small rugby-ball-shaped concoction of minced sheep's pluck (namely a sheep's heart, liver and lungs) mixed with onions, oatmeal, suet and spices, encased in a sheep's stomach. It sounds disgusting, looks awful and is an acquired taste. But you'll be hard-pressed to have a bad time on Burns Night thanks to Scottish hospitality and more than a little of another Scottish tradition, whisky.

EAT IT ! ***Edinburgh's Old Town pubs are your go-to-destination here – try it with your closest Scottish pals.***

163

Made only in Arbroath: savour smokies with a side-order of fresh air

UK // Haggis gets the headlines but for a less well known taste of Scotland - but one that has been protected by European Union law in the same way as champagne or prosciutto - you need to go to Arbroath on Scotland's east coast. Here, where the Atlantic crashes on the shore and an Arctic northeasterly blows, Arbroath smokies are made, the ideal antidote to the Scottish weather. Smokies are haddock (with their backbones intact) that have been traditionally cured in woodsmoke in a kiln until their skins turn bronze. The smoke and steam gives the flesh a luxurious, savoury flavour best experienced picked from the bones in the fresh air. More typically they're eaten for breakfast as the local and artisanal alternative to a kipper. However you enjoy them, they're a Scottish national treasure.

EAT IT ! *Spink & Sons has smoked haddock for five generations. In Arbroath, the Old Boatyard and the Old Brewhouse serve smokies.*

164

Sizzling snout-to-tail sisig on a steamy Filipino night

PHILIPPINES // Filipino food doesn't get a lot of play internationally compared with other Asian cuisines. And that's unfortunate, as anyone who has tasted *sisig* knows. The magic of this salty and tart pork dish is in the mix of textures – crispy fried skin, sticky cartilaginous ears, silky smooth liver. Ears? Liver? Trust us. To make the dish, pig jowls and ears are finely chopped, simmered, then fried, along with fatty bits of pork belly and unctuous liver. It's all seasoned with chillies and the tart juice of the *calamansi*, a small round citrus fruit that's green on the outside and golden on the inside, before being brought to the table with a flourish, on a sizzling cast iron plate. It's a killer complement to a cold beer on a hot Luzon night.

EAT IT ! *At Aling Lucing Sisig, in Angeles City (Cnr G Valdez and Agipito del Rosario Sts), where Lucia Cunanan, 'the Sisig Queen', made the dish famous.*

163

© Infrequent_Flyer / Alamy Stock Photo

164

© Michele Falzone / Alamy Stock Photo

© Getty Images / jackmalipan

© Lonely Planet / Mark Read

165

Run with the fresh flavours of Cambodian cuisine as found in fish amok

CAMBODIA // Situated between culinary superpowers Vietnam and Thailand, Cambodia has an unassuming cuisine of its own, often milder than its bombastic neighbours. The national dish fish *amok* is the perfect example of traditional Khmer flavours and techniques. At the heart of the dish is freshwater fish, usually catfish but sometimes snakehead fish. To prepare the meal, the fish is covered in a thick coconut sauce seasoned with fish sauce, palm sugar, eggs and a curry paste known as *kroeung*, made up of fresh chilli, galangal, turmeric, kaffir lime, garlic and lemongrass. Traditionally the fish and sauce are steamed inside a banana leaf to give the sauce a light, fluffy texture, though you're just as likely to see it being wok fried in restaurants throughout the country. The soft fish and creamy curry sauce is a gentle introduction to the spices of Southeast Asia or a welcome relief from the punchy heat found in so many of the dishes of this region.

EAT IT ! ***It's an unlikely name for a Cambodian restaurant, but The Corn delivers the goods. The Corn, 26 Preah Suramarit Blvd, Phnom Penh 12000.***

166

© Lutz Jaekel / Laif / Camera Press London

166

166

Discover why mansaf is the generous feast that all Jordanians can agree on

JORDAN // In Jordanian culture, familial or tribal disputes are traditionally settled by the meeting of elders at the home of the host family or tribe member. As a gesture of respect, the host will sacrifice a sheep and prepare *mansaf* for everyone to share; when eaten together the meal symbolises the resolution of any discord. Sample this generously heaped, aromatic plate of food and you'll see why everyone's prepared to put aside their differences and eat. Jordanian flatbread is placed on a large serving platter, and piled with rice and spiced lamb cooked in a creamy sauce, topped with toasted almonds and pine nuts. Eat only with your right hand, keeping your left tucked behind your back; break off a piece of bread and scoop up a manageable amount of the rice and lamb, putting it in your mouth in one go. Only lick your fingers clean at the end of the meal to signify you're finished. You'll be left with the feeling that there isn't anything more symbolic of respect than a plate of food prepared to be shared.

EAT IT ! ***Assuming you don't have any tribal disputes to settle, try mansaf in Jordan at the Sufra restaurant, Al Rainbow St 26, Amman.***

167

So good, it has its very own museum: Berlin's ubiquitous currywurst

GERMANY // There's an actual museum in Berlin that is dedicated to this iconic sausage snack so you know Berliners are not kidding around when it comes to the currywurst. If you haven't yet become a devotee to the steamed and fried pork sausage then you soon will be. It's the combination of tomato sauce sprinkled with curry powder that makes them such a tasty takeaway snack. And don't worry about where to find one, there are small stands dotted all across the city so you will have ample opportunity to interrupt your sightseeing and grab a plate. Most stands will cut the sausage into slices for you and throw in a side of fries.

EAT IT ! *There'll be a queue, but you know that's a good sign! Curry 36, Mehringdamm 36, 10961 Berlin, Germany*

167

168

168

Take on the Georgians in a khinkali-eating contest

GEORGIA // If you've never eaten a *khinkali*, or Georgian dumpling, before – there's a system: grab the twisted knob at the top and take a nibble to let the steam escape, then take a large bite, leaving just the knob, which you line up on your plate like trophies. It's possible to tell where your *khinkali* has come from by its stuffing. The lowland cities tend to use beef and pork, whereas the mountainous areas use lamb. But wherever you are served these doughy parcels, they'll be delicious. Beef, pork, and lamb mince is seasoned with herbs and spices and, like Chinese *xiao long bao*, cooked with a broth enclosed in it. So when you do the twist, be ready to catch that delicious broth, and the admiring looks from the locals if you manage double figures.

EAT IT ! *Just about any Georgian restaurant in the country's bigger cities will have khinkali on the menu.*

© Lonely Planet / Matt Munro

169

A croque monsieur, a classic French bistro... c'est magnifique

FRANCE // Trust France to turn a simple ham and cheese sandwich into something you'd sell your loved one for. At its most simple, the croque monsieur is a sandwich with ham, cheese (usually Gruyere or Emmental), Dijon mustard and béchamel sauce. But in the hands of Paris' bistro chefs it becomes something that makes the world melt away, so that all that matters are you and the oozing cheese. The croque monsieur at Café Trama on the Left Bank is legendary – and suitably served in a street filled with the city's trademark elegant apartment buildings. Nutty, rich Comte replaces the Gruyere, the whole thing is dusted with truffle salt, and it comes fresh from the oven with a light crust formed on the top from the baked béchamel.

EAT IT ! *At any Paris cafe, but we suggest heading for the elegant Saint-Germain-des-Prés and Café Trama, at 83 rue du Cherche-Midi.*

170

Get a glimpse of the crop of the future in a jackfruit-rich polos curry

SRI LANKA // Lots of travellers avoid jackfruit because it's often mistaken for the much stinkier but similar-looking durian. It's a shame because this monster – fruits can weigh up to 30kg – is a versatile crop that's being talked of as one that could save millions of people from starvation in the future, providing not only highly nutritious food for humans, but timber, glue, dye and leaves that can be fed to livestock. And as they know in Sri Lanka, the unripe fruit tastes quite similar to meat, which is why it's such a popular ingredient in polos, one of the numerous curries this paradise island in the Bay of Bengal is known for. Mind you, the addition of coconut milk, pungent spices and sweet fiery chillies might have something to do with it too.

EAT IT ! ***While dipping your toes in the sea at Unawatuna Beach... base yourself in the ancient and food-lover's coastal city of Galle.***

© Sandra Vungi / vegansandra.com

© Lonely Planet / Matt Munro

171

Put your hunger on hold at aperitivo time in Italy

ITALY // It takes a nation of gregarious gourmets to come up with the concept of the *aperitivo* as not just a drink whetting the appetite for dinner but also snacks accompanying that drink, thus prolonging the enjoyment and ensuring you won't be so hungry that you wolf your supper down. To make the most of this fine tradition, at around 7pm find a bar that has covered its counter in platters of antipasti, take a seat, and order your *aperitivo* – a Campari, Negroni or Aperol. Then settle in to enjoy the people-watching that's always on offer in Italy – whether a village square or St Mark's Square – and wait for your waiter to bring out your drink and personal platter. For around €9 you could eat enough to forego dinner. But mamma mia, what a thought!

EAT IT ! ***Aperitivo is at its best in northern cities like Milan, Bologna and Turin, but is widespread throughout Italy.***

© Getty Images / Masahiro Makino

172

Load up on carb-rich thukpa to help your Himalayan trek

NEPAL // This restorative noodle soup is served in the Himalayan mountains of both Nepal and Tibet, but it's in Nepal that you'll find the addition of chilli, pepper, turmeric and garam marsala, which makes the Nepali version just that little bit more moreish. There comes a point when another bowl of *dal bhat* becomes one bowl too many, and this is where *thukpa* steps in – it's equally as satisfying, and with oodles of rice noodles, lots of protein from pieces of chicken, hearty vegetables and a rich broth, will make this meal your new favourite carb load for the next day's climb.

EAT IT ! ***In restaurants around Boudhanath stupa, Kathmandu.***

173

Turn the spotlight on Bangkok's superstar soup

THAILAND // When it comes to Bangkok's best *tom yum goong*, everyone has an opinion on which restaurant reigns supreme. First, establish if you're after *nam sai*, the clear broth, or *nam khon*, with a creamy hit of evaporated milk. Creamy or clear, your soup will be spicy and sour, and rich with lemongrass, kaffir lime and chilli. A cult-like fandom exists for the soup in Bangkok, where favourites change quickly; some research will glean the social media darling of the moment.

EAT IT ! ***The creamy soup is rarer than the clear – try the former at Mit Ko Yuan, 186 Thanon Dinso, Phra Nakhon, Bangkok.***

174

Take a break for fragrant umm ali in frenetic Cairo

EGYPT // Cairo's cacophonous streets can make even hardened urbanites retreat to an air-conditioned sanctuary. Before you do, duck into a street cafe and ask for *umm ali*. What you'll be served will be the edible equivalent of a pat on the back – a sweet baklava-like dessert that is distinctly North African in flavour. How? Think puff pastry soaked in buffalo milk with honey, seasoned with cinnamon and cardamom, and baked with toasted pistachios. And... relax.

EAT IT ! ***Cairo's El Malky is a sweet choice for locals and visitors alike. 28 El Mashhad El Husseiny St, Cairo.***

Tandoori: the red-hot chicken dish of Delhi

INDIA // The enclosed restaurants of Pandara Road Market serve some of Delhi's tastiest north Indian cuisine. The food is ridiculously affordable – at Pindi, for example, a whole tandoori chicken costs about £4. The chicken, named for the tandoor oven in which it's cooked, is marinated in curd or yoghurt and masala spices, including the distinctive cayenne and red chilli powder that gives the meat its bright colour. Beware, there's no scrimping on the fiery spices here.

EAT IT ! ***Pindi is well-known for a range of chicken dishes, but its tandoori is king. Pindi, 16, Pandara Road Market, New Delhi.***

© Lonely Planet / Matt Munro

176

Come in from the Kraków cold to żurek and hot beer

POLAND // If you've been wandering Kraków's snow-covered medieval streets in winter then you'll need some warming up. Here's where you slip into one of the cafes in the Jewish Quarter and order up *żurek* and a pint of *grzane piwo*. That's sour soup and a spiced hot beer. The sour taste of the soup is balanced by salty ham, spicy sausage and potatoes, and it's served in hollowed-out bread. The accompanying hot beer provides a cinnamon, cardamom and ginger hit.

EAT IT ! ***Szynk offers traditional dishes at ul Podbrzezie 2, Kraków.***

177

Refuel on dragon beard candy in Hong Kong's malls

CHINA // Once reserved as a sweet treat for royalty, dragon beard candy now sits on food carts around Hong Kong's shopping malls, for anybody to enjoy. Made up of stretched-out, wispy threads of corn syrup, flour and sugar, these puffy little white clouds contain a sweet, nutty mixture composed of crushed peanuts and coconut shreds. They melt when exposed to heat or moisture so are the perfect on-the-run pick-me-up when Hong Kong's retail opportunities wear you down.

EAT IT ! *In any of Hong Kong's ubiquitous shopping malls – or if shopping malls aren't for you, Hong Kong airport.*

178

Meet your match with Mexico's huevos divorciados

MEXICO // Eggs are as much a part of Mexico as Mayan wonders like Chichén Itzá, and one of the best egg dishes in the country is the acrimoniously named *huevos divorciados*, or divorced eggs. Two fried eggs are separated on the plate by two sauces – green apple salsa and spicy red tomato. Far from the flavours being irreconcilable, they're very compatible – so there's hope of a reunion, though not if your dish comes with a dividing line of refried beans.

EAT IT ! *The grand Café de Tacuba will unite you with this troubled breakfast. Calle de Tacuba 28, Centro Histórico, Mexico City.*

179

Breakfast on cheesy syrniki blinis in Moscow

RUSSIA // The best way to experience these fritters is by scoring an invite into a local's home; most Russians will have their own secret recipe. Made with a tangy soft cheese called *tvorog* – similar to ricotta but with a drier texture – *syrniki blinis* are sweetened with caster sugar and vanilla, fried, dusted with icing sugar and served warm with jam and *smetana* – a kind of crème fraîche. *Syrniki* are slightly sour, delicate, and ideal accompaniments to convivial morning chat.

EAT IT ! *Home-cooked is best but cafes in the big cities will do too. Try Praga-Ast in Moscow for a glimpse into perfection.*

179

© Getty Images / antorti

© REDA &CO srl / Alamy Stock Photo

180

Picarones, Lima's late-night pick-me-up

PERU // All the best cultures put some effort into inventing a deep-fried dessert...the US has doughnuts, Spain churros, France beignets, Scotland, uh, Mars bars... Peruvians have taken up the challenge with enthusiasm and resourcefulness by pureeing sweet potato with a local squash known as *macre*, mixing it with flour, yeast and sugar, shaping it into thin doughnut-like hoops and then frying it in oil. Join Lima's late-night revellers in the Barranco looking to soak up any excess alcohol with a golden brown *picarone*, slathered in sweet *chancaca* syrup, straight from the street cart.

EAT IT ! ***In the bars of Barranco or Miraflores, or the Picarones Mary food cart in Parque de la Amistad, Santiago De Surco, Lima.***

181

Recover from last night with eggs Sardou in New Orleans

USA // If you're in town you'll be visiting the Garden District, so drop into the Commander's Palace to taste New Orlean's take on eggs Benedict. Eggs Sardou, named for the 19th-century French playwright Victorien Sardou, who travelled widely in America and was honoured by Antoine Alciatore, owner of Antoine's restaurant, with the creation. It resembles a Benedict, but in place of the spinach, Antoine's dish placed poached eggs on artichoke bottoms, and a garnish of truffles and/or ham. These days most places serve both artichoke and spinach, which is as it should be in a city that lives life to the max.

EAT IT ! ***Commander's Palace is at 1403 Washington Ave. Admire the post-Katrina restoration of the restaurant while you're there.***

BAC
NAL
12
94
Cd's 15

184

© wendy connett / Alamy Stock Photo

182

Set your watch by slow-cooked Senegalese chicken

SENEGAL // When a dish gets championed across a continent, it's doing something right. At the heart of *poulet yassa*'s appeal and intrinsic to its success is a long marinade for the chicken – some chefs claim eight hours is optimum. That marinade is made of lemon juice, chilli, mustard and onion which, soaked in to the meat, makes the flavour nuanced but mellow, with a hint of heat. In the final cook-up, in peanut oil, the onions become caramelised and the chicken tender.

EAT IT ! ***Dakar's Marché Kermel has several vendors, though the cradle of poulet yassa is Casamance, south of The Gambia.***

183

Nature's perfect fast food given a Taiwanese twist

TAIWAN // Fast food can be full of grease, sugar and saturated fats. In Taiwanese convenience stores, however, there's an old-fashioned treat that healthily holds its own against the artificial temptations: the tea egg. Warming in pots by the stores' cash registers, tea eggs are the perfect hand-held snack to go. The distinctive marbling comes from the gently cracked shell, which allows the marinade of tea, soy and Chinese five spice to permeate and flavour the egg within.

EAT IT ! ***Throughout Taiwan, at convenience stores wherever you spot a warm pot near the till.***

184

Hop off to Oaxaca to munch on grasshoppers

MEXICO // There are other places to sample Mexico's *chapulines*, or toasted grasshoppers, but the Mercado Benito Juárez, in Oaxaca's food-obsessed town, is the best. This beautiful mountain village is one of Mexico's few ecotourism destinations and the market is Oaxaca's oldest, filled with food and crafts. Grab a cup of spicy *chapulines*, cooked in garlic, lime juice and salt – the bright flavours cut through the funky richness of the grasshoppers – and explore to your heart's content.

EAT IT ! ***Mercado de Benito Juárez, Oaxaca, Centro, 68000 Oaxaca.***

185

Take a tour of Tasmania fuelled by its famous scallop pie

AUSTRALIA // Tasmania's evolution as a foodie destination is a no-brainer – it comprises large swathes of fertile farmland and, all around it, pristine ocean stuffed with delicious sea creatures. A roadtrip around the island based on cheese, cool-climate wine, whisky and gourmet food, with the odd rainforest walk and a day at Hobart's MONA art gallery, is one sophisticated holiday. But Taswegians are known for keeping things simple, hence their famous culinary invention, scallop pie – a puff pastry shell filled with whole scallops cooked in a rich curry sauce. The local scallops are plump, delicately sweet and, seeing as they're so abundant, invariably super-fresh. The creamy, mustardy sauce varies from bakery to bakery, but the seafood is always the star.

EAT IT ! *Scrap your itinerary and plan the roadtrip around pies! First stop, Exeter Bakery, where they've been perfected over more than a century. 104 Main Rd, Exeter, Tasmania.*

185

186

186

The pork, jelly, pastry staple of UK pubs and pie shops

UK // Britain's classic snack, like so many meaty treats, started life out of a household need to make food stretch a little further. Embellish pork with a pastry crust and, between filling and casing, add a layer of meat jelly and it seems more substantial. Besides providing a contrast between the soft pork and crumbly crust, the jelly preserves the freshness by filling the air gaps. Pork pie should always be eaten cold, with some pickle or mustard and ideally a pint of mellow British beer in a pub. Or opt for the traditional pie shop, where pork pies are sold alongside numerous others stuffed with various meats, vegetables and cheeses. The town of Melton Mowbray in Leicestershire is where to experience Britain's best pies – they gained Protected Geographical Indication status from the European Union in 2009.

EAT IT ! *Try Nice Pie at Gorse Farm, Old Dalby, Melton Mowbray.*

© Shutterstock / Lisovskaya Natalia

187

Dine in a 14th-century Dijon crypt, where you'll become a convert to escargot à la Bourguignonne

FRANCE // Ah snails, the great culinary divide – you either love the slimy little suckers or you don't. But if there were one snail dish to convert you it would surely be this – *escargot à la Bourguignonne* – and if there were one place for such a *volte face*, it would be in the hallowed, vaulted grandeur of La Dame d'Aquitaine in Dijon, where you'll pay €30 per person just for the privilege of sitting in the renovated 14th-century crypt. Is it worth it? We think so. For this classic French entrée from the Burgundy region, snails are harvested from the wild and are greatly prized for their plumpness and sweetness. When sautéed with outrageous amounts of butter, parsley and garlic, the meat becomes firm but not chewy, and imbued with the punchy flavours of the sauce. The dish is always served with fresh crusty French bread, which is the perfect vehicle for soaking up all the leftover garlic-infused butter. And who could resist that?

EAT IT ! ***In the vaulted grandeur of La Dame d'Aquitaine, 23 Place Bossuet, Dijon.***

188

Cool off with crazy halo-halo in hot, hot Manila

PHILIPPINES // In the depleting heat of a Filipino summer there's nothing more refreshing than the whacky, Willy Wonka-style shaved-ice dessert, halo-halo. This colourful concoction is a combo of sweet red and white beans, jackfruit, coconut, sago, tapioca, sweet plantains and *gulaman* (a type of agar jelly), covered in shaved ice and finished with sweet evaporated milk. Topped with a scoop of purple yam ice-cream, it's an ideal distraction from the tropical heat.

EAT IT ! ***At the popular Chowking chain of restaurants, all over metro Manila.***

189

Feel the heart and soul of Armenia through harissa

ARMENIA // Armenians traditionally serve this slow-cooked wheat and chicken meal on special occasions, like Easter, but as *harissa* is something of a national dish you'll be able to find it on menus in Yerevan year-round. It's time-consuming to prepare, requiring the breaking down of a whole chicken over time and constant stirring of the wheat to create the porridge-like consistency. The rich, nourishing result is a testament to Armenian resilience in the face of adversity.

EAT IT ! ***Traditional Armenian restaurants abound in Yerevan – make one of them your own.***

190

Be comforted by congee in hectic Hong Kong

CHINA // The bustle of Fa Yuen's street market – aka Sneaker St – in Hong Kong masks the degree of warm comfort coming your way. At the top of the indoor food market is Mui Kee, master of soul-warming Cantonese-style rice porridge, *congee*. Don't take our word for it, read the reviews taped to the walls. The texture of Mui Kee's *congee* is smooth, with a trace of the original rice grains for body. The pork meatball version with sliced ginger on the side is a winner.

EAT IT ! ***Climb to the 3rd level (confusingly on the 4th floor) of Fa Yuen market, Mongkok, to find Mui Kee, stall 12.***

188

191

Brigadeiro, São Paulo's handsome chocolate tribute

BRAZIL // Legend has it that this chocolate fudge ball was created in honour of a dish of a different kind – handsome Brigadier Eduardo Gomez. Eduardo was admired by a legion of female fans in the 1940s but remained perennially single. Sigh. What's a woman to do? Turn to chocolate, obviously. The resulting tribute to gorgeous Gomez is a bite-sized ball of condensed milk, butter and chocolate. Amid the modern bustle of São Paulo, they are still easily found in the city.

EAT IT ! *São Paulo's Brigadeiro Doceria & Café has branches at Av Brg Faria Lima, Rua dos Pinheiros and Rua Padre Carvalho.*

Jamón ibérico in Madrid: meat you can't beat

SPAIN // Delicate, sweet, nutty jamón ibérico is the finest ham in the world. Made from Black Iberian pigs that graze on acorn-strewn pastures, and cured for over two years, the black-hoofed legs hang like deliciously macabre chandeliers in bars and restaurants all over Spain. The meat is sliced into paper-thin, dark red sheets marbled with streaks of fat that (really do) melt in your mouth. It's served on toast with fresh tomato and olive oil, with slices of melon, or best, on its own.

EAT IT ! *Sample jamón ibérico sliced straight from the leg at Madrid's Mercado de San Miguel, Plaza de San Miguel, s/n*

Pick a paratha, any paratha, in Delhi's food alley

INDIA // Like a microcosm of Delhi itself, the narrow laneway known as Paranthe Wali Gali is a teeming, chaotic, stomach-rumbling circus dedicated to food. In this case, it's the *paratha*. There are close to 30 different restaurants and stalls to choose from, all serving this stuffed deep-fried flatbread, and every one of them is good. The cooks here work at a frightening pace; the stuffing and frying, all carried out at the front of the shops, is a blur.

EAT IT ! *Go for a trad spicy potato or experiment with cauliflower and paneer at Paranthe Wali Gali, Chandni Chowk, Delhi.*

© Lonely Planet / Matt Munro

194

Go down to the woods to source the original Black Forest cherry torte

GERMANY // The Black Forest is like something out of a fairy tale; dark wooded groves, hidden waterfalls, glacial lakes and an attraction that leads visitors, Hansel and Gretel style, to a small town in the centre of the forest in search of the *Schwarzwälder kirschtorte*, or Black Forest cherry torte. If you've spent the day hiking through the forest and marvelling at the Triberg waterfall then you'll have earned your whipped cream and kirsch-soaked layers of chocolate cake. Triberg's Café Schäefer is where the original recipe resides, with the café's current *konditormeister* (pastry chef), Claus Schaefer, possessing the recipe book once owned by Josef Keller, the mastermind behind this cake. Claus bakes to the original specifications, as set out in 1915.

EAT IT ! *Get in early and avoid busloads of tourists seeking the original and the best at Café Schäefer, Hauptstrasse 33, Triberg.*

195

Nyama choma: barbecued Kenyan meat to rival the best

KENYA // There are a number of countries worldwide vying for the title of top barbecue, but there's one contender that doesn't get quite so much press despite not scrimping on any of the passion. In Kenya, the love of *nyama choma*, which literally means 'roast meat' in Swahili, is evident at family get togethers, on the streets and at roadside shacks, at festivals and celebrations... basically pretty much at any gathering of more than a few people. Any excuse for a get together is an opportunity to get the grill going. The type of meat used is most commonly goat or beef, prepared simply with salt and oil then grilled to perfection. It's served with *kachumbari* salad (chopped tomatoes and onions) and *ugali*, which is a kind of cornmeal mash.

EAT IT ! *Forget about the other BBQs, the grill stalls in Nairobi's Kenyatta Market (Mtongwe Rd) are going to knock your socks off.*

196

Savour Sweden's shapely Christmas pepparkakor

SWEDEN // It's not Christmas in Sweden without *pepparkakor* – thin, crispy ginger snaps cut into fanciful shapes. They get their warm, toasty flavour from ginger, cinnamon, cloves and cardamom, and their sweetness from sugar and *sirap*, a liquid sweetener. Stamped into hearts, stars, people, goats and pigs (a pagan fertility symbol), they're best enjoyed with a cup of *glögg* (mulled wine) or with coffee at a daily *fika* (coffee break, a cornerstone of Swedish culture).

EAT IT ! ***Find holiday pepparkakor at Sweden's local Christmas markets. Or, yes, also at IKEA.***

197

Taramasalata: a culinary legacy of civilised Greece

GREECE // Greeks have been dipping their pitas in *taramasalata* for eons. The centuries-old blend of fresh roe (fish eggs), a little seasoning, lemon juice and olive oil has fuelled the Hellenic civilisation no doubt since the days of Sparta. If you're used to the bright pink stuff you get from the supermarket then the real deal, which is typically beige in colour, will be a creamy, tangy breath of fresh taste. You'll find homemade versions with their own twist at every taverna.

EAT IT ! ***Agistri's Taverna Moschos (Ioannou Metaxa) delivers a taramasalata that punches way above its weight.***

198

Sample the cross-cultural flavour of the Maltese

MALTA // Malta is a muddle of nearby Italy and North Africa, and Britain, its former colonists. And so it is with its cuisine, the talisman of which is lampuki pie – best eaten in someone's home, but made well in island restaurants. 'Lampuka' is the name for mahi mahi fish, the bulk of the pie filling, and while it looks influenced by pie-loving Brits, the inside is stuffed with hallmarks of Levantine (raisins, mint) and Italian food (olives, capers, tomatoes). It's a delicious cultural mix.

EAT IT ! ***Café Jubilee, a cosy, colonnaded 1920s-feel joint with three branches throughout Malta, has a fine pie selection.***

199

Top off a day of Mayan majesty with sopa de lima

MEXICO // After a day exploring the ancient Mayan ruins of Chichén Itzá you can tuck into a meal that has its roots in Mayan cuisine, in the pretty pastel-hued town of Valladolid. *Sopa de lima*, or lime soup, is classic Yucatán cuisine, with two key ingredients native to the peninsula – Yucatán lime and a hot pepper known as the *xcatic*. The soup's sweet and sour sharpness is a testament to Mayan ingenuity, though the ruins of Chichén Itzá give it a good run for its money.

EAT IT ! ***Throughout the state of Yucatán, but particularly in Valladolid.***

200–299

200

Accept a gift from the gods: Greek salad in Athens

GREECE // If you need any convincing of the greatness of Greek salad then order one in the capital of civilisation and prepare to be amazed. The first thing you notice is the generosity; lots of salty feta and a liberal sprinkling of oregano, a handful of plump Kalamata olives... all of it super fresh. Some places add capers and peppers, and the best serve it with crusty bread. Sometimes it takes going back to the source to remember why something was so great in the first place.

EAT IT ! *At Ta Karamanlidika tou Fani, Sokrates 1, Evripidou 52, Athens.*

201

Why the galette bretonne is a crêpe to crow about

FRANCE // Take your pick of picturesque towns in Brittany in which to sample the *galette bretonne*, from charming seaside Auray, to Carnac, home of the world's largest collection of Neolithic monuments, or the pretty walled town of Saint-Malo with its Roman ramparts. The locals in this northwest corner of France are fiercely proud of their take on the French crêpe, made with buckwheat flour and usually served with ham, cheese and a fried egg.

EAT IT ! *We like having our crêpe and eating it in Auray, Carnac or Saint-Malo.*

202

Romazava outside Madagascar just isn't romazava

MADAGASCAR // A juicy, leafy green, meaty stew, not dissimilar to ragu, *romazava* is often imitated outside Madagascar, but never replicated. There's the meat, for one thing: the original recipe uses *zebu*, sacred in Malagasy culture, eaten to honour the important concept of *fihavanana* (kinship), but it is tougher than beef, hence the extra-slow-cooking of this dish. Then there are the greens: Malagasy *romazava* uses anamamy, more peppery than leafy greens elsewhere.

EAT IT ! *As with most Madagascan mains, on rice; the Malagasy invitation to dinner literally translates as 'let's eat rice'.*

200

Be brave with your brew in the home of bubble tea

TAIWAN // Bubble tea may have gone global, but Taiwan is the place to try it if you're a die-hard convert. The Chun Shui Tang Teahouse prides itself on quality ingredients, fresh tapioca balls and knowledgeable staff who make more than 70 different flavours, creating at least five new ones each year. The most popular, such as lychee, mango and passion fruit, are always served, but it's worth indulging in some of the more bizarre tastes like lavender, candyfloss or avocado.

EAT IT! *Chun Shui Tang (Shinkong Mitsukoshi Dept Store), B1, No 9, Songshou Rd, Xinyi District, Taipei.*

Turn to (mopane) worms for a new fast-food fix

ZIMBABWE // As southern Zimbabweans have long seemed aware, eating insects could be key to the planet's wellbeing – bugs are high in nutrition and have less of an eco-impact than conventional sources of protein. The country's rainy season is followed by mopane worm harvest, when thousands of them are stripped from the trees and dried in the sun. The flavour depends on how they're cooked, but expect vegetal notes and a chewy texture.

EAT IT! *They're served in paper cups as a fast-food snack from local markets, and also try them at Victoria Falls' Safari Lodge.*

Find delicious fatteh flatbread in Beirut

LEBANON // Originating in the Levantine region, this is a food that transforms from the sum of its parts to something more impressive. The trick is in the texture – stale, crispy flatbread is given a new lease of life with the addition of a zingy yoghurt sauce (pimped with tahini, lemon, garlic and cumin) and warmed chickpeas. You may find cafes in Beirut that add spiced lamb, chicken or eggplant before scattering fresh parsley and lightly toasted pine nuts on top.

EAT IT ! *Seek out Al Soussi for its crunchy take on this winning dish. Chehade St, Zeideiniyye, Aicha Bakkar, Beirut.*

203

© Getty Images / RenataAphotography

206

The cream of Sicily: nibble cannoli in the sun

ITALY // In the hills behind Palermo, the tiny town of Piana degli Albanesi celebrates *cannoli*, the 'little tube', with a festival every year. The origins of Sicily's sweet, crispy treat go back to the Arabic pastry artisans who combined sugar cane and sheep's ricotta. 'It has to be sheep's ricotta,' says Davide Di Noto, of Piana degli Albanese's Pasticceria Di Noto. 'The ricotta of the Piana has an even richer flavour still, due to the altitude the sheep are grazed at, where the wild grasses and herbs are richer.'

EAT IT ! *Pasticceria Di Noto, Via Martiri Portella della Ginestra, 79, Piana degli Albanese, Sicily.*

207

Trace the postre chaja's origins to a Montevideo bakery

URUGUAY // This scrumptious cake is found across Uruguay, with many variations, but the original's recipe is a secret kept in Montevideo, so why go anywhere else? Here you'll find an outlet owned by the family of the man who created the cake over 100 years ago, Orlando Castellano. Not unlike pavlova, the *postre chaja* features layered meringue, whipped cream and sponge, and is served with peaches. The dessert gets its name from a bird that has pockets of air under its skin to aid buoyancy in water.

EAT IT ! *Postre Chaja Confiteria las Familias, 26 de Marzo 3516, Montevideo.*

208

Discover baghali ghatogh during winter in Tehran

IRAN // *Baghali ghatogh* is the dish you dream about discovering on your travels. It's the unassuming, unfamiliar bowl at the edges of the family feast laid before you. The one that stays with you and brings back all the memories when you get home. Thankfully, it is an open secret, and after trying it in a cosy restaurant in Tehran, perhaps in the shadow of the snow-topped Alborz Mountains in winter, you'll want to recreate this dish of baked eggs with turmeric, saffron, garlic and dill-scented fava beans.

EAT IT ! *Khanjoon will tick all the boxes of this ancient treasure: Aftab St, Tehran.*

© Birgit Ryningen / VWPics / Alamy Stock Photo

209

Tuck into domestic delicacy qabili palau in an Afghan family home

AFGHANISTAN // Making a good *qabili palau* is a matter of family pride in northern Afghanistan, so you can safely assume that centuries of attempts by daughter-in-laws trying to outdo the recipes of their mother-in-laws have led to a near-perfect national dish. The secret lies in the slow cooking of the rice. It must have time to absorb the flavours of the caramelised onions and stock. Lamb is the preferred meat but chicken is also popular, and it must be cooked with raisins and carrot, and, often, orange peel and pistachios. When everything is ready the richly seasoned *palau* is heaped on a plate to set in pride of place at the centre of a family feast, with fingers crossed its deliciousness doesn't start any inter-generational female feud.

☛ EAT IT ! ***As a guest at a family get-together to absorb the sense of custom, as well as the excellent food.***

210

© Shutterstock / hlphoto

Savour the fruits of the sea on Portugal's southern coast

PORTUGAL // The Algarve in Portugal's south is the country's sun-drenched playground. With beautiful beaches strung out along the dramatic coastline, the region hums with activity throughout the summer. The town of Lagos in the west is a major draw, with both its picturesque 16th-century walled old town and thriving fishing port a joy to explore on foot... which is the perfect way to build up an appetite for the regional speciality, *cataplana de marisco*. Loaded with seafood, it's served in the *cataplana*, a copper-lidded wok that's peculiar to the region. Clams, prawns, squid, lobster and whatever else is fresh from the sea on the day go into the *cataplana*, along with white wine, tomatoes and herbs, and then it's gently sautéed. It's the taste of the Med at its fish-filled finest.

☛ EAT IT ! ***At one of the beachside cafes, or better yet at the second-floor restaurant of the bustling fish market on the marina in Lagos.***

© Stephane Groleau / Alamy Stock Photo

Lose yourself in a maple sugar harvest in the forested landscape of Québec

CANADA // More than 75% of all genuine maple syrup comes from Québec, and during syrup season it's possible to visit a 'sugar shack' to see how the syrup is harvested from the maple trees. Visiting is best when the maple sap is boiled down and thickened into syrup. At Sucrerie de la Montagne, 45 minutes' drive from Montréal, this happens in February, March and April. Visiting at this time affords some special privileges, like being shown around the maple forests in a horse-drawn sleigh. You'll see one of nature's sweetest treats as it oozes from the trees before being taken to the wood-fired evaporator where the sap is turned into syrup. Back at the farmhouse a traditional Canadian feast features pancakes with maple syrup for dessert. This is followed by live music and dancing before you're shown to your log cabin for the night. In the morning you're ferried through the store. Don't pass up on buying a bottle of the real stuff – there are many imitators, but maple syrup from the source is worth its weight in gold.

EAT IT ! *At the immersive Sucrerie de la Montagne, 300 Chemin St-Georges, Rigaud, Québec.*

211

© StockFood / Hussey, Clinton

Just like the movies: fried green tomatoes at the Whistle Stop Cafe

USA // Despite fried green tomatoes originating in the northeastern states, it's now considered a classic southern dish, thanks in part to a certain popular film, which relocated the dish to the cute-as-a-button Whistle Stop Cafe in Juliette, Georgia. Though the dish can be made using under-ripe red or heirloom green tomatoes, the crucial element is that they're firm when you slice them, otherwise they'll get mushy when cooked. After being coated in egg batter and cornmeal, the tomatoes are fried in butter, creating a crunchy, savoury snack. If you're after a more substantial meal, you can get your tomatoes in a sandwich, salad or as a side. Sauces range from a simple ketchup and mayonnaise mix to a remoulade concoction injected with Cajun spice.

EAT IT ! ***At the Whistle Stop Cafe, 443 McCrackin St, in Juliette, Georgia, where the eponymous movie was filmed.***

Check out fried chicken in a Tokyo supermarket

JAPAN // There are so many great food experiences in Tokyo that it might seem strange to talk about fried chicken from a convenience store, but every now and then it's nice to have a break from mind-blowing sushi and the world's best ramen, so don't knock it till you've tried it. And it's a great way to discover the wonders of a *konbini*; the ubiquitous convenience stores that are like a microcosm of Japanese consumer culture. If you can't find what you're looking for in a *konbini* then odds are you don't need it. Of all the different *konbini* in Tokyo, the Lawson's chain gets top billing for one reason and one reason only, delicious fried chicken. There's a choice of *honetsuki* (fried chicken with the bone in), *honenashi* (boneless fried chicken) and *karaage* (chicken nuggets), and they're all good; moist on the inside, crispy on the outside. All that's left to do now is grab a coffee in a can. Snack break sorted.

EAT IT ! ***At one of the 14,000 Lawson's konbinis across Japan.***

© Shutterstock / ELBANCO04

214

A lesson in culinary simplicity: Mallorca's paletilla de cordero

SPAIN // There's a mini pilgrimage path on the Balearic island of Mallorca that culminates in, of all things, a slow-cooked shoulder of suckling lamb. The restaurant serving it at the end of the narrow, winding road is Es Verger, and behind its basic barn door lies a masterclass in simple cooking. Each morning the wood fire in the clay oven is lit to begin 3½ hours of cooking the lamb to achieve its signature softness. The meat rests on cubed potatoes, carrots and onions, and is doused in beer to retain moisture. When *paletilla de cordero* emerges from the oven, simmering and crackling, it is carved and brought to your table. The meat's texture is delicate, its flavour earthy, and the crispy skin has a salty crunch.

EAT IT ! *Work up an appetite with an invigorating 90-minute hike from Alaró to Es Verger, Camino del Castillo de Alaró, Mallorca.*

Ford Fry

James Beard-nominee Ford Fry is the Atlanta-based chef-owner of 12 restaurants across the American south, including JCT Kitchen and The Optimist.

CROISSANTS, DU PAIN ET DES IDÉES, PARIS I'm a big fan of well-made croissants so I took a $50 cab ride just to get to this place. The emulsifying of the butter was fantastic and I love the crispiness.

FRENCH FRIES, MINETTA TAVERN, NEW YORK Something about their fry process – with the stoking and the blanching – makes these fries so money.

BREAD WITH NORMANDY SALT, REPUBLIC, LOS ANGELES At this restaurant in Charlie Chaplin's old house they make this butter, hang it in a cheese cloth, and serve it with a pile of Maldon salt. Once I started eating it, I couldn't stop.

04

SHRIMP TACOS DORADO, MARISCOS JALISCO, LOS ANGELES This taco truck takes a corn tortilla with chopped up shrimp, deep fries it until crispy, then adds crunchy cabbage and avocado. I've been trying to recreate it.

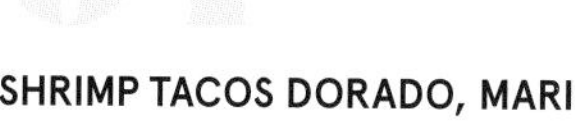

SANTA BARBARA SPOT PRAWNS, WALRUS AND THE CARPENTER, SEATTLE Whenever they're in season, this place has them. I like them just super ice-cold raw, with some extra virgin olive oil and salt.

Find lemon heaven in a tarte au citron on the Riviera

FRANCE // The last stop on the French Riviera before Italy, Menton is an unspoiled coastal idyll. Pastel houses cascade down to the water, there are beautiful landscaped gardens and the great weather is perfect for growing flavourful lemons. These are put to use in Mentonnaise tarte au citron, its pale-yellow lemon cream just firm enough to hold together, spiked with lemon juice and encased in thin, sweet pastry. Probably the world's best lemon tart.

☛ EAT IT ! *Visit in spring for Menton's Fête du Citron. There's a parade, fireworks and more tarte au citron than you can eat.*

Metemgee: a taste of the Caribbean – in Guyana

GUYANA // You'd be forgiven for thinking you'd stopped off in the Caribbean when you arrive in the South American nation of Guyana. The calypso, the colonial-style architecture, the cricket... and the food. Could it get any more Caribbean than stew with cassava, yams, plantain, okra and coconut sauce? Maybe not, but add fried fish and dumplings and you have a Guyanese national dish. Despite its multifaceted identity all you need to know is it's delicious.

☛ EAT IT ! *Pretty much anywhere and everywhere throughout Guyana.*

Enjoy a slice of Athenian life with your kourou pie

GREECE // A steady stream of locals head in and out of the century-old Ariston bakery, so you know you're on to a good thing. Inside there's a dizzying array of pastries lined up under glass cases. Don't get distracted though, you're here for *kourou* pie. Shaped in a semi-circle, the *kourou* is made with a short-crust pastry that includes yoghurt and butter, stuffed to bursting with salty feta cheese. Grab one and go sit in nearby Syntagma square to watch the world go by.

☛ EAT IT ! *Ariston Bakery, Voulis 10, Syntagma, Athens.*

© StockFood / Ekblom, Ulrika

© Shutterstock / Garsya

© StockFood / Scott, Glenn

218

Looking for a New England original? It has to be clam chowder in Boston

USA // Clam chowder is as quintessentially New England as snowy winters and dropped Rs (indeed, in local parlance the dish is pronounced chowda). It's a thick, rich stew containing staples early pioneers from Old England would have eaten in the early years, namely potatoes, celery, onions, butter and plenty of shucked clams. The result is a thick creamy soup, often made even thicker by being garnished with a handful of crushed salted crackers. The dish isn't merely a culinary staple, but a cultural one as well. New Englanders take umbrage with the idea of soups not adhering to the basic recipe being called 'New England Chowder'.

EAT IT ! *Though there are tons of places to get a great chowder in Boston, Union Oyster House, 41 Union St, is a tried and true New England culinary classic.*

Start the day with a full English breakfast

UK // Starting the day with a plate of fried food, served to you by someone you've only just met but who insists on calling you 'love', is good for the soul. And also for a hangover, it has to be said. The local British caff, with its Formica tables and laminated menus, is a window into a previous version of England – pre-globalisation, pre-digital, pre-colour-coded healthy food labelling. The canonical full English is fried bacon, fried eggs, fried tomato, fried mushrooms, buttered toast (possibly fried – can you see a pattern?), baked beans and sausages, served with a squirt of brown sauce and a mug of tea. Restaurants do posh versions but if the experience means more to you than the food, go for the greasy spoon!

EAT IT ! *London's family-run Electric Cafe at 258 Norwood Rd, is a classic caff. Or try Terry's (pictured) also in South London.*

© Daniel Di Paolo

220

More is more: chomp on a chivito in a bustling Uruguayan bar

URUGUAY // The *chivito* is Uruguay's contribution to the basic human need of putting anything tasty between two slices of bread. And boy, is it a good one; especially when sampled at a locals' bar like El Tinkal, where live music and a great atmosphere make it the place to try a dish that started with a miscommunication. An Argentinian requested goat (*chivito*), the Uruguayan didn't know what that meant so created a feast no one could refuse, and the *chivito* sandwich was born. It comprises a slice of thinly cooked beef steak, bacon and ham, an egg, olives, tomato, onions, mozzarella, lettuce and mayonnaise. Some places also pile on grilled peppers, beetroot and pickled cucumber.

EAT IT ! ***El Tinkal, Dr Emilio Frugoni 853, Montevideo.***

221

Linger loch-side with a pint and a plate of fresh langoustine

UK // The pretty little fishing village of Ullapool hugs the shores of the beautiful Lochbroom and introduces travellers to the wonders of the Summer Isles and Outer Hebrides. Despite its small size, it receives plenty of visitors eager for the stunning scenery. Fuel up loch-side with a pint and a plate of fresh langoustine, served with garlic butter or a squeeze of lemon. In summer, the outdoor tables that look out over the water are buzzing. The langoustine are straight off the boat (you can even watch the fishing vessels returning to shore) and the beer flows freely. If you're not careful, you'll find yourself here for a lot longer than you'd planned.

EAT IT ! ***The Arch Inn Restaurant, 10-11 W Shore St, Ullapool.***

© Lonely Planet / Matt Munro

222

221

How Cobb salad became the stuff of Hollywood legend

USA // Tinseltown in the 1930s was awash with classic diners filled with wannabe stars, where chefs sought to make a name for themselves. One of them was Bob Cobb, who came up with his creation after a late-night raid on the fridge. Despite the messy appearance, it works, thanks to salty blue cheese and bacon, a crunchy mix of leaves, tasty grilled chicken, the tomato sweetness, richness of boiled eggs and avocado, and a hint of garlic from the chopped chives.

EAT IT! *Head to Swingers for a great take on the Hollywood classic in a cool diner. 8020 Beverly Blvd, Los Angeles, CA.*

222

Allow khachapuri to introduce you to Georgian cuisine

GEORGIA // After seeing the cultural big-hitters of Tbilisi's Freedom Square and wandering the twisting alleys under the old town's wooden balconies, duck into Samikitno-Machakhela and choose from several varieties of *khachapuri*. This traditional Georgian bread filled with melted cheese and a just-cooked egg comes with spinach and cheese, minced lamb... and then there's the *megrelian* – cheese on cheese.

EAT IT ! *On the terrace overlooking the old town. Samikitno-Machakhela, Freedom Sq, 5/7 Pushkin St, Tbilisi.*

223

Get sweet on sandesh in classic Kolkata stores

INDIA // Bengalis are fervent about *sandesh*, as the plethora of sweet shops that fill the City of Joy's streets and markets attest. Balaram Mullick & Radharaman Mullick, dating to 1885, is one of the oldest and best places to enjoy this simple Bengali treat. Made from *chenna*, a type of whey from curdled milk with added sugar, the mixture is infused with all manner of flavours and shaped into small round or square biscuits.

EAT IT ! *Balaram Mullick & Radharaman Mullick, 2 Paddapukur Rd, Jadubabur Bazar, Bhowanipore, Kolkata.*

225

Order beer and bryndzové halušky in old Bratislava

SLOVAKIA // Tucked into a narrow, cobbled street in the shadow of Bratislava's castle is Modra Hviezda, a darkly atmospheric hole-in-the-wall restaurant. Once settled into this cosy spot, order wild boar loin and Slovakia's national dish, *bryndzové halušky*. This filling plate of potato dumplings covered in sharp-tasting sheep cheese and loaded with chunks of fried bacon is best paired with a Zámocké dark beer from the nearby castle brewery.

EAT IT ! *Make like you're a ravenous hunter returned from the chase at Modra Hviezda, Beblavého 292/14, 811 01 Bratislava.*

Match the appetite of Colombian farmers with a traditional bandeja paisa

COLOMBIA // The Paisa people of Medellín and Colombia's wider Antioquia region like to think of their most famous traditional dish, *bandeja paisa*, as the greatest meal of all time, a dish that reflects the grandeur of the mountainous terrain they inhabit and rewards the hard work of the peasant farmers who try to work it. Distinguished by the copious size and quantity of the plated items, it is an undeniable force to be reckoned with. Think you can handle it? Then here's what's coming: a heaped plate of ground meat, *chicharrón* (fried pork), chorizo, *morcilla* (blood sausage), fried egg, fried plantain, red beans cooked with pork, *arepa* (a maize bread), avocado and white rice. So... good luck with *that* gluttony.

EAT IT ! ***At any Medellín restaurant that serves traditional Colombian cuisine.***

Do as Japanese students do and enrol for a bowl of katsudon brain food

JAPAN // Press the button on the vending machine with the picture of the breaded pork chop atop a bowl of rice. Collect your ticket, descend the stairs and join the queue of mostly young Japanese students waiting for their turn to sit and tuck into this well-loved, semi-auspicious comfort dish. Auspicious? The word *katsu* has an additional meaning (on top of 'crumbed and deep-fried') – 'to be victorious'. So nervous students, hoping to pass their exams, stock up on the propitious dish. Its simplicity is another draw. The two main ingredients, crumbed pork chop and white rice, are often served with an egg and either miso soup or a broth flavoured with soy sauce, sake and green onions, which is poured over the chop.

EAT IT ! ***At Tocho, for a 32nd-floor view and a top-notch katsudon (among other local dishes). 2-8-1 Nishishinjuku, Shinjuku-ku, Tokyo.***

Gail Simmons

Gail Simmons is in her 15th season as a judge on Top Chef USA. She has also just released her first cookbook, Bringing It Home.

GRILLED CAVIAR, ASADOR ETXEBARRI, ATXONDO, SPAIN The chef here was one of the first to master this grilling technique and he grills everything. Caviar is a little bizarre, but it's more like he's smoking it.

HOKKIEN NOODLES, SINGAPORE
It usually has two different types of noodle (a thick udon and a thin vermicelli), a seafood stock, pork belly, shrimp and squid, and is finished with an Asian citrus called *kalamansi*.

BAUMKUCHEN, JAPAN
Baumkuchen is cake cooked on a spit roast over fire. You pour batter each time it comes around and you can see all the beautiful layers when you cut into it. It's actually German, but I've only ever seen it in Japan.

JERK LOBSTER, JAMAICA
Jerk rub is most common on chicken. But at the jerk shack we go to, the guy pulls spiny lobsters out of the ocean then cooks them.

PALM DESERT DATE SHAKE, PALM SPRINGS, CALIFORNIA For generations, date farmers here have made this shake, which is just vanilla ice cream, milk and blended dates.

228

Rustle up your own cha ca in the best restaurant in Hanoi

VIETNAM // There's a fierce rivalry between fans of the restaurants in Hanoi that serve this famous dill and turmeric fried-fish meal, but Cha Ca La Vong in the Old Quarter is the original and the best. Its narrow staircase leads to a modestly furnished dining room with plastic cards that outline the one and only dish on offer. Expect generous servings of vermicelli noodles piled with turmeric-marinated fish, dill, mint, coriander and green onions, topped with chopped peanuts and fresh chilli, all accompanied by a *nuac cham* dipping sauce of fish sauce, lime juice and sugar. The cook-it-yourself-at-the-table experience adds its own charm, making this one meal that is guaranteed to live on in your culinary memory.

EAT IT ! ***It gets busy at Cha Ca's home but the wait is never long. Cha Ca La Vong, 14 Cha Cá, Hàng Ðào, Hoàn Kiem, Hanoi***

Explore under the arches at London's Maltby St market

UK // There can be few places in London with such a wealth of tasty experiences in so small a space. Maltby St market extends beneath a stretch of railway track in south London. At weekends the brick arches turn from being carpenters' workshops and bric-a-brac stores to housing food stalls and restaurants, all along a narrow open-air passage. Whatever your stomach is telling you, there'll be something to eat, from sitting down to share plates at St John restaurant or Walrus and Carpenter oyster bar, to being waylaid by waffles, luxurious brownies and grilled cheese sandwiches or Grant Hawthorne's African Volcano marinated beef burger with peri-peri sauce. Try a G&T at Little Bird gin distillery to start your Saturday afternoon expedition along Bermondsey's beer mile, encompassing a series of craft breweries often housed under these arches.

EAT IT ! ***Maltby St market is a short walk from Bermondsey tube station or London Bridge.***

For a less-spicy stew, plump for home-cooked adobo in a Filipino abode

PHILIPPINES // A thick, dark stew, seasoned with only a few spices, might not be what you're expecting from Filipino cuisine; Southeast Asian food has a reputation for multi-ingredient curry pastes and dishes stacked with spices. But there's a hint in the word *adobo*, from the Spanish '*adobar*', meaning to marinate, so perhaps it's the Spanish influence that inspired this succulent dish. Or perhaps the Spanish just applied the name to the dish when they saw how it was cooked. Either way, it's a national culinary icon that every household knows how to prepare. Traditionally the meal is made with belly and shoulder of pork, marinated in vinegar, soy, garlic, ginger, bay leaf and black peppercorns, before being simmered gently. It's served with fluffy white rice. The best way to taste authentic pork *adobo* is at home, because every home cook in the Philippines is proud of their *adobo* recipe and preparation, so to taste the best, you're going to need to snag an invite to a Filipino mate's house. Failing that, any good restaurant in Manila will offer a more-than-passable version.

EAT IT ! ***Aristocrat Restaurant, 432 San Andreas St, Malate, Manila.***

Why the fiery Ethiopian combo of doro wat and injera is a feast that brings people together

ETHIOPIA // Eating in Ethiopia is a communal affair, so forget any notions of personal space. Look around while you're eating and you'll see people feeding each other. It's a custom known as *gursha* and is a sign of love and friendship. If this method of eating Ethiopian food hasn't made you feel all warm and fuzzy, just wait until you taste it.

The country's most famous culinary export is the spongy, soured bread known as *injera*. More like a porous pancake than any sourdough, it comes with just about anything you order, and is particularly delicious when it's utilised as the serving dish for *doro wat*, or spicy chicken stew. Nationally revered, *doro wat* is a heavily seasoned stew made with a *berbere* spice mix (chilli, garlic, ginger, basil, korarima, rue, ajwain, nigella and fenugreek), blended with chicken, boiled egg and onions. With your right hand, tear off a piece of *injera* and pick up some of the *wat*, then pop it in your mouth (or your neighbour's mouth, if you've forged a friendship over starters).

EAT IT ! ***Kategna is the place for doro wat; there are three different restaurant locations in Addis Ababa, one of which is at Cameroon St.***

231

© dbimages / Alamy Stock Photo

231

© Lonely Planet / Philip Lee Harvey

Enjoy the upturn in fine dining at cruising altitude

GLOBAL // We all know that complaining about airline food is de rigueur but, these days, competitive long-haul carriers are duking it out to impress frequent flyers with meals designed by renowned chefs, using fresh ingredients inspired by the carrier's local cuisine. Australia's Qantas airline works with Neil Perry to create dishes such as Chinese-style crab omelette with oyster sauce and lobster with XO spicy sauce, noodles and pak choi. So, quit your whining.

EAT IT ! ***Altitude and cabin pressure affect your taste buds – your meals are scientifically designed to compensate.***

Leipäjuusto: after dinner in the Arctic circle

FINLAND // As if Lapland's remote subarctic wilderness wasn't weird enough, being almost totally dark for months of the year, someone has just put a plate of food in front of you that looks like a triangle of toast topped with lumpy gravy and said '*nauttia jälkiruokasta*'. In Finnish, this means 'enjoy your dessert' and in this case refers to *leipäjuusto*, or bread cheese – a baked cheese with a mild, toasty flavour. It's traditionally served with cloudberry jam.

EAT IT ! ***Santa's Salmon Place's Lappish favourites include bread cheese. Santa Claus Village, Tähtikuja 96930, Rovaniemi.***

Snack on coffin bread from a noisy night-market stall

TAIWAN // Shilin night market north of Taipei is a showcase of every curbside treat you could hope to taste. Acclimatise to the colours, smells, crowds and shouting from the stall holders before you make any rash decisions, though – you can't eat it all. To start off, here's a snack that you can't pass up: a fried slab of white bread, carved out in the middle and filled with creamy chicken, seafood, offal or mushroom, topped with another slab of fried bread.

EAT IT ! ***Wander the market's basement food court to find the coffin bread stall. Shilin night market, 101 Jihe Rd, Taipei City.***

233

© Getty Images / Seagull_l

© Lonely Planet / Philip Lee Harvey

235

Summer scenery and soupe au pistou, c'est parfait

FRANCE // Sat outside with a view of lavender fields, feeling the cooling mistral breeze and sipping on a glass of crisp local rosé, you'll think you've stumbled across a cliché when you find yourself eating a bowl of this fresh vegetable soup under sunny skies in the south of France. Best eaten in high summer when the vegetable harvest is at its most abundant, *pistou*'s distinguishing features are the garlic and basil, pounded into a pesto-like paste to give the vegetables some punch. A picture of perfection.

EAT IT ! ***Near the town of Valréas in Provence, southeastern France.***

236

Cachupa: Cape Verde's hearty hotchpotch hotpot

CAPE VERDE // Cape Verdeans, residents of a gaggle of islands scattered off Africa's west coast that belonged to Portugal until the 1970s, are a mixed bag, so it seems fitting that *cachupa*, their national dish, should be an equally appealing mix. Hominy (lime-soaked puffed-up corn kernels), chorizo, pork, beans and many other secret ingredients are simmered until soft, with the flavours infused. Purportedly every island in the archipelago has its own special version, but everywhere you go, having this made for you is a treat.

EAT IT ! ***Cachupa has to have love in it, so must be home-made to be truly valued.***

237

Why harira is a blessing for any hungry belly

MOROCCO // One can imagine how good *harira*, a traditional Ramadan food, feels on the palate after a day of fasting. Lentils, chickpeas, vermicelli pasta, tomatoes, onions, coriander, spices and, often, diced lamb contribute to this rich, fragrant soup. During Ramadan, it's often served with *chebakia* (honey and sesame seed cookies). Popular across the entire Maghreb region, but perhaps most lovingly embraced by the Moroccans (it is the national soup), *harira* is also available outside of Ramadan.

EAT IT ! ***Hot bowls of harira are served in cafes in any Moroccan town or city.***

238

238

Settle for salad niçoise as you dine on the French Riviera

FRANCE // As with many meals that have taken hold of the world's culinary imagination, the original ingredients of a dish can change. So it is for this vibrant salad from the French Riviera city of Nice. Over the years, it has come to include potatoes, green beans, even rice and chicken. Now even French culinary experts can't agree on the original. Maybe that's because it's a seasonal salad, initially created to serve hungry fishermen back from their morning catch. What is largely accepted however is that this gratifying mix-up has eggs, tuna, anchovies, tomatoes, salad leaves, olives and onions. Will you even notice the absence of potatoes as you dine alfresco on the Baie des Anges in Nice with a gentle breeze blowing off the Med? We think not.

EAT IT ! *At the carnival-inspired restaurant Brasserie La Rotonde, inside Hotel Negresco, 37 Promenade des Anglais, Nice.*

© Lonely Planet / Matt Munro

© StockFood / Great Stock!

239

Tuck into tartiflette, the height of good taste in the French Alps

FRANCE // From the mountainous Savoie region comes the perfect end to a day of Alpine hiking – the rich, rewarding tartiflette. What starts as a simple potato gratin is taken to new heights through the addition of the local semi-soft, washed-rind Reblochon cheese, made with raw cows' milk and aged in mountain caves, though these days it's also aged in farmers' cellars. Its nutty flavour pairs well with potatoes, onions and chunky lardons to form the must-eat dish. It is served in almost every mountain restaurant and ski resort in the Savoie Alps, usually with a green salad and regularly with charcuterie and pickle. And the French will tell you it tastes best accompanied by a glass of crisp, dry white Savoie wine. Who are we to argue?

EAT IT ! *Restaurant Lo Sonails, Rue d'en Bas, Albiez-Montrond.*

240

Score some dulce de leche, the spread that would have won Uruguay the World Cup

URUGUAY // In 2014, the Uruguayan football team had a stash of *dulce de leche* confiscated at Brazilian customs before the start of the World Cup. Brazilian officials stated that the caramel sweet was confiscated because of its milk content, but Uruguayans believed they were being stripped of their secret weapon. The team were subsequently bundled out of the competition by Colombia at the knockout stage. Decide for yourself whether or not the sticky caramel spread has special powers. It's everywhere in Uruguay; in supermarkets, cafes, street-food stalls and restaurants, and the best way to eat it is on toast or as an indulgent addition to pancakes.

EAT IT ! *Anywhere, anytime, with whatever you want.*

© Shutterstock / AS Food Studio

Go to a country town fete for Australia's best Anzac biscuit

AUSTRALIA // Saturday morning in a small town in rural Australia and golden sunshine warms the ground and the sound of caroling magpies fills the air. Stalls line the main street and families are meandering from one to another. Country fairs and markets often celebrate a local product, for example with barrel rolling in wine-producing Rutherglen, Victoria. But there's one consistent feature: a stall run by the local Country Women's Association selling cakes, jams and Anzac biscuits. These durable biscuits, most often associated with Anzac Day in April, which marks the entry of the Australia and New Zealand Army Corps to WWI, were baked by women to send in tins to the soldiers. The biscuits are simple – oats, flour, sugar, coconut, butter and syrup – but no country fair is complete without nibbling one.

EAT IT ! ***The Country Women's Association of Mansfield, Victoria, holds monthly cake and craft stalls.***

© StockFood / Dobránska, Renáta

Grab a table at a tavern and feel Hungary's love for töltött káposzta

HUNGARY // Hungarians are so proud of their *töltött káposzta* (cabbage rolls) that there's an old saying: 'meat and cabbage are the coat of arms of Hungary'. These modest components have sustained families for generations, and the love stays strong. Almost every household has its own recipe for *töltött káposzta* and it's on menus across the country, but the common denominators are minced meat (pork and beef are popular), sauerkraut, cabbage and paprika. Some rolls add rice, onion, egg, pickled vegetables and even lardons. Most come cooked in a tomato sauce with sour cream on top. Whatever the variation, it will be everything that it's been to Hungarians for centuries – tasty, satisfying and uplifting.

EAT IT ! ***We like to tuck in to töltött káposzta at traditional tavern Csarnok Vendéglő, Hold utca 11, Budapest.***

243

Get warm inside thanks to Russia's red star, borscht

RUSSIA // Though thought of as a Russian dish, *borscht* traces its roots back to a number of spots around eastern Europe, and there are as many varieties as there are Slavic languages. The common feature is its ruby red colour, a product of its main ingredient, beetroot. It's a hearty soup, best eaten in deep winter, when its warmth and thickness (some say that until you can stand a spoon up straight in the bowl, it isn't thick enough), will set you up for the snowy environs outside.

EAT IT ! ***Travelling foodies swear by the borscht at Moscow's historic Hotel Metropol, Teatral'nyy Proyezd, 2.***

244

Make it meatballs, as do the rest of Indonesia

INDONESIA // A local take on the meatball soup you'll find throughout Southeast Asia, *bakso* is one of the most popular street foods in Indonesia. Sold in restaurants, street stalls and pedal-powered push carts, *bakso* is addiction guaranteed. The standard dish is a meaty broth stacked with firm but fluffy meatballs, thick noodles and garnish. With numerous regional variations, including fried, fishy, eggy, giant tennis-ball sized and cubed meatballs, there's a *bakso* for everyone.

EAT IT ! ***Bakso Titoti is a beacon for Jakarta's bakso lovers; the special is divine. Jln Honggowongso 42, Solo 57141.***

245

Fuel your Central Asian adventures with manti

KYRGYZSTAN // No one knows precisely where the *manti* originated. What is known is that the horsemen (and horsewomen) of Central Asia travelled long distances with supplies of these ground meat, dough-cased balls and that these epic endeavours did much to spread the food's popularity. China, Russia and even Turkey have similar delicacies, but in the 'Stans they dominate. The *manti* is consumed whole so as to retain the meaty juices that form inside.

EAT IT ! ***Start your quest for the best (and biggest) manti at Bishkek's Chaikhana Navat at 114/1 Kievskaya, Kyrgyzstan.***

243

243

© Lonely Planet / Mark Read

© Getty Images / Alan Keohane

Eat moussaka in Athens like you're one of the family

GREECE // Greek moussaka is old-school comfort food and some of the best you can eat is at someone's home, made to a family recipe passed down through generations. So if you're lucky enough to get an invite into a Greek home then take it. That said, there are plenty of options for great home-style moussaka in Athens. Two of the best, for authenticity and atmosphere, are God's Restaurant, near the Acropolis Museum, where the moussaka comes with slices of potato and courgette; and Aleka's Taverna, to the north of the Acropolis, where you can sit outside and enjoy the people-watching. Whichever you opt for, you'll find a light and creamy béchamel sauce, slices of chargrilled aubergine and a rich tomato-based minced-lamb sauce.

EAT IT ! ***At God's Restaurant, Makryianni 23; and Aleka's Taverna, Thrasivoulou 2; both in Greece's major metropolis, Athens.***

Catch that pigeon pastilla at a Marrakech market stall

MOROCCO // The surprising combination of savoury and sweet is what makes Morocco's pigeon pastilla so impossible to resist, and it forms a delicate and delightful start to a meal, or an ideal afternoon snack for visitors to Marrakech's Djemaa El Fna square. Traditionally, pigeon pastilla is a festive dish served at special occasions such as weddings or birthdays. However, it's now found in bakeries all over the country, as well as at almost every restaurant that has a traditional menu. An elegant blend of shredded pigeon, egg, roasted almonds, cinnamon and sugar makes up the filling of the pie, which is then encased in paper-thin *warqa* pastry and dusted with icing sugar.

EAT IT ! ***In the garden of restaurant Pepe Nero, 17 derb Cherkaoui, Douar Graoua, Marrakech.***

© Getty Images / Lisovskaya

Sup on Spanish history, distilled

SPAIN // As the Spanish saying goes, *'de gazpacho no hay empacho'* – you can't have enough *gazpacho*, ie, you can't have enough of a good thing. And lunching on this summery vegetable soup in an Andalucian beach-front *chiringuito* or traditional city restaurant is a very good thing indeed. Blending Roman, Moorish and Ottoman influences, some version of this cold soup has been eaten in Spain for well over 1000 years.

EAT IT ! ***At August's Gazpacho Festival in the Andalucian village of Alfarnatejo.***

Lechón as you like it in the Yucatán

MEXICO // Mexico's Yucatán Peninsula has taken to the Spanish import of *lechón al horno* with aplomb, and the oven-roasted suckling pig is the basis of multiple delicacies in the region. Whether you sample it amid the colonial architecture of Valladolid or in pastel-hued Mérida, you can eat the smoke-flavoured meat on its own, with rice and beans, in a *torta* or with French bread. Then, of course, there are tacos. Choices, choices...

EAT IT ! ***Head to Mercado Municipal Lucas de Gálvez, Mérida, for torta de lechón.***

Zimbabwe's sardine superfood

ZIMBABWE // While this little freshwater sardine can be cooked fresh or dried, the drying process actually boosts the *kapenta*'s levels of protein and calories, as well as enabling storage without refrigeration. A staple in Zimbabwe, traditionally the whole fish is shallow fried with spices and onions, then scooped up by hand with a ball of *sadza* (a kind of maize porridge). *Kapenta* is the ultimate, intensely flavoured, health snack.

EAT IT ! ***The luxurious Meikles Hotel on the corner 3rd St/Jason Moyo Ave, Harare.***

251

© Lonely Planet / Susan Wright

251

Add some orecchiette to your picturesque Pugliese vista

ITALY // The sun-drenched Italian boot-heel of Puglia is an Adriatic-facing region filled with beautiful whitewashed townships, centuries-old farmland and spectacular Mediterranean coastline. To eat here is to sample something truly special, and the dish that's the most special of the lot is Puglia's signature pasta, *orecchiette*, or 'little ears'. Despite being made with just three inexpensive ingredients (wheat flour, water and salt; no eggs because historically they were a luxury that most people couldn't afford), the pasta has a dense texture unlike any other, and when it's combined with fresh *cime di rapa*, a broccoli-like green from the turnip family, and a generous swig of olive oil, then topped with grated Pecorino Romano, it creates the best kind of seasonal, local cuisine in its purest form. Add to this the setting of a hilltop taverna in medieval Ostuni, shaded by olive trees, with a glass of Primitivo in hand, and you have the makings of a unique Italian food memory.

☛ EAT IT ! ***At the classic Taverna della Gelosia, 26 Vicolo Tommaso Andriola, Ostuni, Puglia.***

252

Big nights out in Beirut are best fuelled with shish tawook

LEBANON // Some restaurants serve *shish tawook* (also called *shish taouk*) without bread and with a side of rice and pickled vegetables, but that's a bit fancy; the best way to sample the country's favourite street food is on a summer night on the streets of Beirut. Whether you're between bars or on your way back from a beach party, it's perfect for staving off a hangover and fortifying you for the next bout of partying. Despite the Lebanese culinary scene being recognised as innovative and sophisticated, *shish tawook* is one messy, garlicky, chargrilled chicken shish kebab that incites passion in everyone from food snobs to fast-food fans. Recipes vary slightly with the addition of different spices and herbs, but by and large a *shish tawook* will comprise cubes of chicken marinated in lemon juice, garlic, yoghurt, tomato paste, pepper and salt, all folded into pita bread with lashings of garlic sauce, some fresh tomato, pickles and fries. Perhaps tone down the garlic if you're looking to make new friends.

☛ EAT IT ! ***At Tabliyit Massaad, which has seven locations across town, including the one in Gouraud St, Gemmayze, Beirut.***

© Art of Food / Alamy Stock Photo

© Getty Images / ramzihachicho

© Shutterstock / ValerioMei

Try a little tenderness with a raan biriyani in Mumbai

INDIA // Centuries ago, the purpose of a good *raan* was to take the least desirable cuts of tough meat and transform them into something not only tasty, but tender. To achieve this, nomadic chefs would first marinate then fry the meat before adding layers of rice and masala (mixed spices). The whole dish would then be slow-cooked to succulent, mouthwatering perfection. Today's cooks tend to select a choice leg of mutton to guarantee tenderness, and while the general biryani technique remains the same, the secrets of its sublime taste are often family secrets. It's best to accept you'll never know which spices should go in the marinade or how much ghee should be used to baste the meat. Just enjoy a little tenderness.

EAT IT ! ***Founded in 1970, Shalimar on Mohammad Ali Rd has become synonymous with succulent raan biryani in Mumbai.***

254

© Antonio Violi / Alamy Stock Photo

253

© Getty Images / FiledIMAGE

Your timeless chocolate treat awaits at Café Schober

SWITZERLAND // Entering Café Schober in Zurich's Old Town is like stepping into a Victorian mansion. It feels like Christmas even in July, with twinkling lights, thick red velvet cushions and gilded crown moulding. Order a slice of *apfelstrudel* or the rich, yeasted cake called *gugelhupf*, both specialities of the house, but don't neglect a cup of hot chocolate. As you'd expect from Switzerland, where locals eat an average of 25 pounds of chocolate a year, you'll get one of the finest versions in all Central Europe, with unctuous slabs of melted chocolate topped with thick, unsweetened whipped cream. Café Schober has been around since the late 1800s, and generations of Zürchers remember it as a favourite childhood treat. You'll remember it too.

EAT IT ! ***Visit during winter and you'll be treated to live music and Christmas décor, but expect to wait for a table. Napfgasse 4, Zurich.***

255

Land some suquet de peix in Catalonia

SPAIN // Inspired by the Mediterranean coast, Catalan cuisine features fish in abundance, and in *suquet de peix* (fish stew), centuries of culinary tradition are distilled into one perfect dish. *Suquet* is made with vegetables and any type of fish or seafood. What brings it to life is the *picada* sauce. Added near the end of cooking, *picada* is a uniquely Catalan combination consisting of ground nuts and bread (traditionally stale), fried in oil and added to the stock.

EAT IT ! ***With its evocative décor, Barcelona's La Taverneta, Francesc Pujols 3, is the spot to enjoy this Catalan classic.***

256

Crack a beer and a steamed crab on the East Coast

USA // In Maryland, a bounty of luscious blue crabs migrates into the Chesapeake Bay from April to November. They're steamed by the bushelful and seasoned with paprika. Though picking the buttery meat out of the shells is hard work, it's also half the fun, chatting with friends while downing bottles of icy Natty Boh (National Bohemian beer, a brewed-in-Baltimore icon). Don't ignore the 'mustard' – the rich yellowy crab guts that aficionados claim is the best bit.

EAT IT ! ***Outside Annapolis, Cantler's Riverside Inn, 458 Forest Beach Rd, is one of the best crab shacks in Maryland.***

257

Wander Havana with a bellyful of ropa vieja

CUBA // If there's a comfort food that Cubans turn to above all others, then it's the shredded beef (sometimes lamb) stew, *ropa vieja*. Central to the dish is thinly cut flank steak, tomatoes, sliced peppers and caramelised onions, but it commonly comes with black beans, yellow rice, plantains and even fried yuca. Walk off all this generous Cuban hospitality through the streets of Havana's old town, stopping every so often for a refreshing mojito or two.

EAT IT ! ***At Havana's Dona Eutemia, Callejón del Chorro No 60c, where you'll be told why the stew was named 'old clothes'.***

Nyam (eat) traditional curry goat on Jamaica

JAMAICA // If you can't wangle an invite to a family party during your Jamaican stay, grab yourself a bowl of curry goat from a roadside stall near one of Treasure Beach's coves on Jamaica's south coast. Fiery, meaty mouthfuls, a cold beer and some serious people watching is a perfect way to spend an afternoon. Curry goat is a special occasion dish here, served with a flourish at everything from birthdays and weddings to reunions and just-for-the-hell-of-it parties. Heavy with the peppery heat of the scotch bonnet, the meat is cooked slowly, until it's tender and laden with flavour. Goat is leaner than lamb, and with a gamey flavour that marries perfectly with the toasted spices of the curry, and the roasted breadfruit that accompanies the dish.

☛ EAT IT ! ***Try Strikie-T's shack in Billy's Bay, where chef Chris Bennett produces seasonal local dishes such as curry goat to his secret recipes. It's part of Treasure Beach's excellent food scene.***

258

259

Pastrmajlija: a pie so fine it's celebrated every year

MACEDONIA // Each year the city of Štip hosts a festival honouring the much-loved pizza pie, *pastrmajlija*. And any food that inspires a knees-up has got to be good. Such is the case with this baked dough pie. The name comes from the word *pastrma*, which means salted and dried meat from a lamb (although it can be made with pork). The pie is covered with cubed, salty meat topped with a couple of eggs, which cook perfectly in the oven, and spicy pickled peppers. Many restaurants, particularly in the capital Skopje, are becoming bolder with their toppings, but the original *pastrmajlija* is the finest: cheap, tasty and best shared among family and friends.

☛ EAT IT ! ***Every September in Štip or at the Pastrmajlija & Grill House, Jane Sandanski, 1000, Skopje.***

260

Join a Beirut breakfast tradition by starting mornings with manoushe

LEBANON // Nothing will remind you more of what it was like to walk the streets of Beirut at breakfast time than holding a toasty *manoushe*; the heady aroma of oregano, thyme, marjoram and sumac, brought to life by the baked, crisp flatbread, so distinctively represents mornings in the city. Locals gather around their preferred bakehouse, known as a *fern*, to catch up on gossip or chat about recent events, and eat, before starting the working day. There are *ferns* all over the city, many of them run by the same family for generations and all with their own closely guarded recipe for *manoushe*. Don't leave your *manoushe* munching too late in the day, though, as most places shut down their ovens after lunch.

EAT IT ! ***Wander at will on the streets of Beirut and you're sure to find your own fern by following your nose.***

261

Bite into nasi lemak, pandan portions of Singapore on a plate

SINGAPORE // The Lion City prides itself on efficiency. Jump on the MRT system to be anywhere on the island quickly. It's also diverse. That metro might take you to Marina Bay Sands for some rooftop swimming, to the verdant Singapore Botanic Gardens, to a gallery in the Colonial District, or to Little India, Chinatown or Arab Street. And when that sightseeing makes you hungry, the train will take you somewhere for a plate of *nasi lemak*, the Malaysian coconut-milk-infused dome of rice popular all over Singapore. And if you've got another train to catch, you can take it away, wrapped in the pandan leaves the rice was cooked in. Efficient and full of diverse flavour and texture, it's just like Singapore.

EAT IT ! ***You'll find great nasi lemak among the hawker stalls at Changi Village, and a whole lot more besides. Changi Village Rd.***

Sea views and street food: torta di ceci in Livorno

ITALY // The bustling Tuscan port city of Livorno still wears the signs of its colourful past in its mixed architectural styles and network of canals linking warehouses with the port. The waterside Terrazza Mascagni is where to break up your walking tour with a taste of the town's most popular street food, the *torta di ceci*. This thin chickpea flour pancake is cooked in large round tins on a high heat before being cut into crispy chunks and, traditionally, served in bread.

EAT IT ! *From street vendors along the Terrazza Mascagni, Livorno.*

Feast your eyes on a Cappadocian kebab sensation

TURKEY // There's nothing like a spectacle to liven your tastebuds, and central Turkey's spectacular Cappadocia can be relied on to deliver one. *Testi kebap* translates as 'pottery kebab' and is a hearty meat dish cooked in a sealed clay pot. Some versions have dough exploding from the top, but all must be cracked open to reveal the deliciousness inside. With surprise quickly followed by elation, it's not unlike encountering one of the region's famous fairy chimneys in a dish.

EAT IT ! *Sofra restaurant's testi kebap is the original and best thanks to a homemade sauce. Atatürk Cd, Avanos/Nevşehir.*

Buy the shrub and the stir fry that feeds Thailand

THAILAND // Why is *pad ka pao* one of the most popular street dishes in Bangkok and beyond? Picture this. A vendor shrouded in a haze of aromatic smoke throws minced chicken or pork with chillies and green beans into a hot wok. Then he adds a big handful of holy basil, a fragrant shrub that grows rampant across Southeast Asia. As the basil wilts, it perfumes the meat and turns a simple dish into something sublime. Served over rice with a fried egg, it's unbeatable at any time.

EAT IT ! *You'll find pad ka pao almost anywhere in Thailand you find street food, which is to say... everywhere!*

265

Let off some steam at a crawfish boil by the bayou

USA // In Louisiana's Cajun country, a crawfish boil is an event. Friends, neighbours, grandmas and second cousins twice removed all crowd into the backyard to drink beer and boil sacks of crawfish in enormous pots. These freshwater crustaceans, which look like tiny lobsters, thrive in Louisiana's muddy bayous. Once boiled and seasoned, they're placed on a picnic table covered with newspaper. Traditional accompaniments include corn, potatoes and (more) beer.

☛ EAT IT ! *Crawfish season runs from winter to late spring, so head to bayou country and make some Cajun friends.*

266

Do yourself a fava and try bean-based ta'amiya

EGYPT // Everybody knows falafel is made of chickpeas, right? Not so in Egypt, where *ta'amiya* (the local word for falafel) is made from fava beans, the flat green broad bean that's one of the world's most ancient crops. Because of this, *ta'amiya* is lighter and fluffier than chickpea falafel, its crispy exterior speckled with sesame seeds, its insides green with herbs. Egyptians claim to have invented falafel, though it doesn't really matter who did it first when you're doing it so deliciously.

☛ EAT IT ! *Mohammed Ahmed at 17 Sharia Shakor Pasha, Alexandria, is the spot for piping-hot ta'amiya with all the trimmings.*

267

Chicharrones: Cuba's double-fried delights

CUBA // On the streets of Havana, Cubans pop *chicharrones* like potato crisps. Known in other parts of the world as pork rinds or pork crackling, they're essentially skin, fat and sometimes a bit of meat from the pig's belly, deep-fried in lard. Yes, fat fried in fat – got a problem with that? Done right, the fat crisps and puffs up and the meat becomes ultra-chewy and flavourful. Throw on a liberal handful of salt and you've got one of the world's truly great snacks.

☛ EAT IT ! *Find chicharrones at street stalls and snack counters across Cuba.*

© Brett Stevens / www.superstock.com

268

Be it from a roadside stall or restaurant, Malaysian beef rendang will make your tastebuds tingle

MALAYSIA // Beef rendang, an undisputed king among curries and a meal that requires hours of preparation to bring out the tenderness and rich coconut flavour, is of Indonesian origin but is now enjoyed across Malaysia and Singapore. And what's special about eating it in Malaysia are the roadside stalls with small charcoal BBQs roasting what look like sticks of bamboo. Inside these hollowed-out tubes is sticky rice cooked in coconut milk, known as *lemang*. When you order, the stallholder will take a tube of the fragrant rice and place it on a plate or banana leaf and add a large spoonful of rendang to the side. The textural and taste combination is exceptional. If you're after a more refined rendang experience, it's served throughout Malaysia at restaurants, food courts and street stalls – just about everyone loves the intensely spicy curry sauce and melt-in-your-mouth beef (with the obvious exception of the Indian Hindu population) and it's a sound bet that wherever you choose to eat it, it will be delicious.

☛ EAT IT ! ***At makeshift roadside BBQs, usually set up at stop points on longer roads, throughout Malaysia.***

Trace wiener schnitzel to its Viennese source for an authentic Austrian experience

AUSTRIA // Wiener schnitzel is a dish that has travelled the globe and put down roots all over, making an appearance on every Austrian- or German-themed restaurant menu in the world. But why settle for a second-hand interpretation when you can have the original experience? In Vienna, at the eclectic Am Nordpol 3, they stick to tradition – more than half the plate is taken up with a breaded veal cutlet, lightly fried in vegetable oil, with a slice of lemon and a mixed-leaf salad. There are no bells and whistles, just old-school schnitzel. If you'd like to take your dining to a finer level, Skopik & Lohn makes a tasty version, served on white tablecloths, with a side salad of cucumber accompanied by dill yoghurt or classic potato salad. At either place, in fact in any restaurant in Vienna that proclaims to have the best wiener schnitzel, you'll be offered schnapps after the meal. The Viennese say it helps cut through the richness of the crumbed meat, but it also tastes great.

EAT IT ! ***Am Nordpol 3, Nordwestbahnstrasse 17, 1020 Wien; and Skopik & Lohn, Leopoldsgasse 17, 1020 Wien; both in Vienna.***

270

© Getty Images / stefanocar75

Get to the heart of the batter where the Japanese perfected tempura

JAPAN // Japan's love affair with tempura began in the 16th century when Tokyo-based Portuguese traders were seen eating deep-fried green beans as a meat substitute during the fasting known as *tempora*. Ever since, the Japanese have been busy perfecting this simple dish while applying thin layers of batter to absolutely everything from seafood to *shiitake*. The secret to truly terrific tempura is lighter-than-air batter that provides a crisp crunch with every bite. Watching a tempura chef at work is like witnessing culinary performance art.

EAT IT ! ***At Kawatatsu in Kyoto, each table gets its own chef and food is prepared fresh before you. 65 Kuzekawaharacho, Minami-Ku, Kyoto.***

For peak quinoa stew, head up to La Paz

BOLIVIA // You'd expect the world's highest capital city to offer some high-end dining, and at Gustu, helmed by Claus Meyer of Noma fame, you won't be disappointed. And what to eat in it? A surprising ancient Bolivian staple, quinoa stew, packed with vegetables, fava beans and yep, quinoa, and seasoned with bay leaves, parsley, salt and pepper. Meyer has cooked up an inventive five-star interpretation of the delicate stew, featuring kombucha, beans and miso.

EAT IT ! ***Chow down on quinoa like you've never tasted it before at Gustu, Ave Costanera 10, La Paz.***

Worship at the altar of tarta de Santiago

SPAIN // Santiago de Compostela is most famous as the end goal of the Camino de Santiago pilgrimage, but there's another thing in the Galician city worthy of veneration. The almond-based *tarta de Santiago* cakes have been around for centuries, but it was almost 100 years ago that a local patisserie added the cake's famous feature: a representation of the Cross of St James – the apostle whose remains are purportedly inside the city's cathedral – inside a dusting of icing sugar.

EAT IT ! ***Pastelería Mercedes Mora is the cake's spiritual home. Rúa do Vilar 46, Santiago de Compostela.***

Tacos al pastor: a Lebanese-inflected Mexican classic

MEXICO // *Tacos al pastor* ('shepherd-style') are an example of how immigration enriches national cuisine. Adapted from the lamb and beef *shawarma* brought to Mexico by Lebanese migrants in the 1800s, it's now pork, grilled on a vertical rotisserie, the spit often topped with a pineapple. The pork is wrapped in a corn tortilla and topped with coriander, onion, a squeeze of lime and a few chips of the roasted pineapple. In central Mexico it's hard to find a bad version.

EAT IT ! ***In Mexico City, El Huequito at Ayuntamiento 21 has been roasting tacos al pastor since 1959.***

© Lonely Planet / Justin Foulkes

274

Watch Lanzhou's lamian noodlemakers in action

CHINA // Lanzhou in northwestern China is the birthplace of the artisan hand-pulled noodle known as *lamian*, and eating it here, to the sound of the dough slapping against a hard surface while watching the noodlemakers stretch, twist, fold and pound it on to kitchen benches is special. It's hard to convey the dexterity and seriousness with which the noodlemakers apply themselves - the number of times the dough is folded determines the length and width of the noodle. It's a skilled performance with a hint of theatre that builds your anticipation for the meal ahead. The best way to enjoy these noodles is in the beef soup, Lanzhou *lamian*. It's classic Sichuan cuisine; fiery, texturally balanced and packed with powerful flavours.

☛ EAT IT ! ***The popular beef noodle restaurants are just that, popular. So be prepared to wait for a table. This goes for Mazilu Beef Noodle, Da Zhong alley 86, Lanzhou.***

Tessa Kiros

Tessa Kiros is the London-based author of 10 best-selling travel-inspired cookbooks, including Provence to Pondicherry and Falling Cloudberries.

COZIDO, SAN MIGUEL, AZORES This typical Portuguese dish is a bit heavy — it has pig's ear, blood sausage, pork belly, and chorizo for seasoning — but the one I had was cooked by the heat of the volcano. No matter what it tastes like, it's so magical.

WATERMELON AND FETA, GREECE It's a wonderful summer memory for me. Whether you're eating this on your balcony in Athens or on the beach, it's an amazing combination of sweet and salty.

WILD SALMON, LAPLAND The simplicity and the minus temperatures are what make it. The salmon up there has its own flavour.

VANILLA DUCK, LA REUNION
Vanilla grows so beautifully on this French colonial Island near Madagascar — this was the flavour that remained with me.

SARDINES, ALGARVE, PORTUGAL
We found the Sardine Festival here by chance — it's all about the rock salt, and then they just grill it and eat it with a piece of superb bread and some wonderful wine.

275

Accept no imitations, Hoi An is the home of bánh bao vac

VIETNAM // The delicate rice paper dumplings, *bánh bao vac*, are a speciality in the central Vietnamese town of Hoi An. And there are two main reasons for this, the first being that the dumplings are said to be made with water from a central well in town, and the second that the recipe is tightly held by one local family. The dumplings are made with a small portion of either pork or shrimp meat. The edges of the rice paper are comparatively large, resembling the petals of a white rose (hence their name of 'white rose dumplings'), and they're served with crispy fried garlic and a dipping sauce made with chilli and fish sauce.

EAT IT ! ***At the real-deal White Rose Restaurant, just outside the touristy part of town. 533 Hai Ba Trung, Cam Pho, Hoi An.***

Arancini: Sicily's sunny street-food stars

ITALY // Open since 1834, Palermo's Antica Focacceria San Francesco is a landmark for folksy Sicilian food, including these stuffed rice balls, coated with breadcrumbs and fried to a glorious golden-orange colour that gives these 'little oranges' their name. *Arancini* are said to have arrived in Sicily in the 10th century when the island was under Arab rule. The saffron that adds to their sunny colour would have originally arrived on ships from the east. They're eaten every December on the shortest day of the year during the Festa della Santa Lucia, the saint of light and sight who is credited with saving the island from famine in the 17th century. But you'll find them irresistible any day of the year.

EAT IT ! ***Chef Guiseppe di Mauro cooks them daily at Antica Focacceria San Francesco, on Via Alessandro Paternostro, 58, Palermo.***

© Shutterstock / Boris-B

© Lonely Planet /Susan Wright

In India, the chai stall tea break is a national pastime

INDIA // In tea-mad India you can hardly go a step without running into a chai wallah – a roadside tea vendor – hawking his wares to passers-by. Even the busiest worker has time to stop for a quick chai, made from boiled tea leaves with thick lashings of milk and sugar. With practised panache, they pour the tea from a height through a cotton strainer, then serve it in tiny glass or metal cups. Recipes vary by wallah and region – fresh ginger is a common add-in, as are cinnamon, cloves and cardamom. Some wallahs offer snacks as well as tea – toast, eggs, *vada pav* and all manner of fried morsels. Many have been hunkered down on the same patch for decades, watching India's cities grow and spin around them.

EAT IT ! ***Try a cuppa wherever you spot a wallah – the train station, the fruit market, the side of the hiking trail – in order to settle on the mix you like the best.***

Target an açaí bowl amid Belém's huge food market

BRAZIL // Belém's nine-acre Mercado Ver-O-Peso has national heritage status in Brazil, not so much for its size or 2,000+ stalls as its beguiling mix of location (facing Guajará Bay on the banks of the Amazon river) and architecture. But it's the size that will stay with you – that, and the food on offer. Amid the fish stalls of the arresting iron market and the vibrant produce, homemade sauces, livestock, and cooked foods beyond is an entire section devoted to açai berries – those oh-so-hip superfood antioxidant power-punches that form the base of *açaí na tigela*, or açai bowls. If you've never tried it then this is the place to breakfast on the mashed açai palm fruit and guaraná syrup topped with granola and banana. It should set you up for covering those nine acres.

EAT IT ! ***Beyond Belém, ask for 'ah-sigh-ee' na tigela at kiosks and juice (sucos) bars lining the beaches of Brazil's northeast coast.***

279

Try a Thai dish less travelled: khao soi soup in Chiang Mai

THAILAND // *Khao soi*, influenced by neighbouring Myanmar, is eaten all over northern Thailand but hasn't yet made the leap to restaurant menus overseas. So here's another excuse to book a holiday to Thailand to satisfy your curiosity, or craving, depending on whether you've tasted the soup before. In Chiang Mai, your *khao soi* options are vast, from simple street-side set-ups with plastic chairs to open-air cafes packed with happy diners, and even fine-dining establishments – where you're not necessarily paying for better flavours, just air-conditioned comfort. Whichever you choose, look for the busiest places as a sign that their soup is good. *Khao soi* should have a smoky, coconut flavour with notes of cardamom, ginger, cinnamon and turmeric; egg noodles and juicy tender chicken pieces; and be served with lime, chillies and pickled mustard greens.

☛ EAT IT ! ***At an open-air shophouse near the night bazaar; or Khao Soi SamerJai, Fa Ham, Mueng Chiang Mai District, Chiang Mai 50000.***

Courtesy of Giraffe Manor / The Safari Collection - thesafaricollection.com

280

Breakfast with some brass-necked friends in the suburbs of Nairobi

KENYA // Staff at this very unusual manor hotel will impress upon you the need to be at breakfast early, and not because your eggs might go cold, but because there are some very special breakfast guests who like to emerge from their forest retreat first thing to grab a bite to eat, and trust us, you won't want to miss them.

Once you've taken your seat at your window-side table, it won't be long before a surreal, Dr Dolittle-like scene starts to play out right in front of you. Slowly, from the edges of the trees, a local herd of Rothschild giraffes gracefully makes its way towards the hotel, which is situated on the outskirts of Nairobi. These impossibly grand, almost magical creatures casually make their way to your tableside window, before craning in their giant necks to wrap an enormous tongue around a sweet treat from your side plate. They then cast their gentle eyes over the strange human spectacle before them and walk off into the bush once more.

EAT IT ! ***Stick your neck out and make your way to Giraffe Manor, Gogo Falls Rd, Nairobi.***

281

Feast on a tray of takoyaki and the Tokyo avant-garde

JAPAN // Go through the looking glass to find Tokyo's epicentre of everything *kawaii* (cute) and fashion-forward in the achingly cool district of Harajuku. Along with the avant-garde display of humanity you'll find vivid street art, cosplay stores, vintage clothing shops, upscale boutiques and hipster cafes and bars. The best way to soak it all in is to buy a little cardboard tray of *takoyaki* balls from a street-food van, find somewhere to sit and watch the show unfold. These soft, golf-ball sized orbs are filled with diced octopus and covered with mayonnaise, shavings of bonito flakes and a sauce similar to Worcestershire. Eat by skewering them with a toothpick. They're a little bit weird but totally addictive. Just like Harajuku.

EAT IT ! *In Tokyo at the Gindaco Takoyaki outlet at Toshikazu Bldg, Jingumae, Shibuya; or look for signs on vans of an octopus.*

© Shutterstock / VICHAILAO

281

282

© 500px / Jeff Ehlers

282

Alaskan king crab – with mac & cheese? You know it makes sense

USA // There's something not quite right about eating one of the planet's most prized ingredients in macaroni cheese, but maybe the ludicrous excess is what makes the whole thing so delicious. Or of course, it could be the crab. The impressive quantities of juicy, soft and sweet white meat from the legs of the mighty Alaskan king crab contrasts nicely with the sharp Gruyère and Parmesan in the mac & cheese. If you're going to indulge in this exercise in excess the best place to do it is in one of Anchorage's seafood restaurants, where you're not far from the crab's home in the Bering Sea.

EAT IT ! *At Orso, 737 W 5th Ave, Anchorage, Alaska.*

Go beachside in Tobago for curried crab fusion

TRINIDAD & TOBAGO // Tobago's culinary heritage fuses traditions from around the world. Its national dish, crab and dumplings, makes use of that heritage with a curry livened up Caribbean-style with spices from India, Africa, Europe, Asia and South America. Don't leave it too late in the day to tuck in; at their beach shacks, chefs make up vats in the morning and when it's gone, so are they.

EAT IT ! ***The beach at the tip of Pigeon Point Heritage Park has great food and live music. Pigeon Point beach, Crown Point.***

Grab a crab of your own on a Darwin fishing trip

AUSTRALIA // The Darwin area is endowed with especially large specimens of delicious mud crab, and an abundant supply of them too. As commercial crab fishing is largely banned hereabouts, local, small-scale fishermen get the run of the catch. Some of these take visitors out on mud crab fishing trips: a fun experience. Netting your own then cooking it up is the way to go. Mud crabs are found during dry season (May-October).

EAT IT ! ***Catch one on a Darwin Harbour mud crab-fishing trip. Boil for 12 minutes.***

Shingara: the South Asian pastry of distinction

BANGLADESH // Most of us could be forgiven for confusing a *shingara* for a samosa. But to a Bangladeshi the differences between the two stuffed pastries is clear; a *shingara* has a heartier wrapper, a stuffing that eschews meat for potatoes, peas, cauliflower or even peanuts, and a shape that's pyramid-like. Both are seasoned with dried spices and served with a dipping sauce, but only the *shingara* functions as a light meal on its own.

EAT IT ! ***Shingara are readily available from stalls or informal restaurants.***

286

Paradise found by the sea in Tahiti with poisson cru

TAHITI // *Poisson cru* is a simple culinary masterpiece made from fresh chunks of raw tuna that have been flash marinated in lime juice to tangy, buttery-tender perfection. They're then doused in pure coconut milk and mixed with cucumbers, shredded carrots and perhaps onion and tomato. A dash of salt and pepper finishes it all off. With a view of the sea and sand between your toes, it's an addictive lunch or dinner served with white rice.

EAT IT ! ***The traditional dish is found everywhere, but try international restaurants on Tahiti for creative twists.***

287

Tread carefully with a royally hot curry in Rajasthan

INDIA // Let's be clear, *laal maas* is not for the faint-hearted. Invented in the royal kitchens of Rajasthan, the dish traditionally incorporated heat and spices to conceal the gamey taste of wild deer that went into it. These days, a leg of lamb guarantees tenderness but the wonderful mix of spices and (very) heavy hand of fiery red chillies and garlic cloves is the same. The result is a slow-cooked curry to make your eyes water with tears of pleasure and, possibly, pain.

EAT IT ! ***Jaipur's Restaurant 1135 AD serves Rajasthani dishes in a palatial setting. Nr Sheela Mata Temple, Amer Palace, Amer.***

288

Head for the source of risotto alla Milanese

ITALY // We can thank geography for gifting us the most famous risotto of them all. After rice was introduced to Italy in the Middle Ages it found perfect growing conditions in the Po Valley not far from the culinary capital of Milan. After centuries of experimentation, by the 1800s the Milanese had perfected the art of transforming their preferred carnaroli rice, sautéed in butter then added to a beefy broth infused with saffron, into the sunshine-coloured dish adored everywhere.

EAT IT ! ***For a low-key experience of authentic, homemade taste, head to Trattoria da Abele, Via Temperanza, Milan.***

289

Sample street food of impeccable taste with a lobster roll in Maine

USA // New England street food is fancy. Forget the deep fryer, or greasy cheese and processed meat, in Maine they pack their hot dog rolls with fresh lobster. Up and down the wild, rocky coast you'll find seafood shacks, takeaway stands, cookhouses and even supermarkets serving up this indulgent yet simple snack. There's never much variation in how the roll is prepared because everyone knows they're dealing with a premier ingredient that doesn't need embellishment. The standard serving is a mix of lobster meat, part tail, claw and knuckle, piled high in a toasted bun, drizzled with butter and seasoned with salt and pepper. You may get the option of mayonnaise, in the bun or on the side. Fancy for sure, but we bet you'll be back for a second roll.

EAT IT ! *At the long-standing stalwart, Red's Eats waterside food shack in the pretty town of Wiscasset, Maine.*

290

'Cos there ain't no party like a Nordic crayfish party

FINLAND, SWEDEN & NORWAY // A *kraftskiva*, otherwise known as a crayfish party, is a Nordic get together not to be missed. Maybe it's the lack of sunshine through the rest of the year, or perhaps just the sight of these little red crayfish (*rapu*) signifying summer, that sends Scandinavians a little loopy. Whatever the case, the annual *kraftskiva* is a rollicking good time of drinking, singing, dressing up and sucking the guts out of tiny crayfish. Everyone gets together around the table, wearing silly hats, slurping messily and continuously, toasting with copious amounts of *snaps* and beer. If you're unused to pulling apart small shellfish, watch your neighbour; there's no real art to it but it helps to do lots of twisting and biting. If all else fails, raise your glass.

EAT IT ! *On a warm August evening with a group of friends, a bowl of crayfish and enough alcohol to keep the toasts going.*

291

Excavate a scoop of ful medames, the dip fit for a pharoah

EGYPT // *Ful medames*, stewed spiced fava beans, is likely as old as the pyramids, and Egyptians are just as proud of their national dish as they are their glorious ruins. You can find *fūl*, as locals call it, almost anywhere, from the breakfast tables of humble homes to the finest restaurants in Cairo and Alexandria. Though recipes vary, it's often prepared with cumin, garlic, lemon juice, parsley and olive oil. Scoop it on to smoky, stone-griddled flatbread, perhaps accompanied by hard-boiled eggs and some tomato and cucumber salad. Warm and savoury, it's an exquisite way to start your day, which is probably why it's been going strong since the days of the pharaohs – some say you can even find evidence of *fūl* in excavated tombs.

☛ EAT IT ! ***Egyptian fast food chain El Tabei El Domiaty makes a worthy ful medames – there are branches all over the country.***

© Boaz Rottem - www.superstock.com

Join the foodie fanclub of British chef Yotam Ottolenghi

UK // Through his restaurants, recipe books and TV appearances, Israeli-British chef Yotam Ottolenghi has created a movement that, at its core, is about making people happy through food. Working out of a 'test-kitchen' in Camden, Ottolenghi and his team create original recipes that draw inspiration from international cuisine and the ingredients supplied to them by a network of artisan producers from the UK and Europe. Ottolenghi's online shop now sells much of this produce to a growing band of devotees who are drawn to his inventive recipes with a global outlook. If you're in London there are now four Ottolenghi restaurants to choose from, and you can order delivery. Fine dining on your doorstep, that's enough to make anyone happy.

☛ EAT IT ! ***At London's Ottolenghi Islington, 287 Upper St, which is both a deli and restaurant with a communal table.***

© Courtesy of Ottolenghi / Issy Croker

Order bò kho, a stew of Asian and French conception

VIETNAM // The French influence on Vietnamese cooking is clearest in dishes that include beef, such as pho, the famous noodle soup. More obscure is *bò kho*. It's essentially a beef stew, albeit one in which beef, carrots and potatoes are supplemented with Southeast Asian seasonings like fish sauce and lemongrass. *Bò kho* reaches its fusiony culmination via a garnish of fragrant herbs, and the fact it's usually served with rice.

☛ EAT IT ! ***Try bò kho at Lien Hoa, 15-17-19 Duong 3/2, in Dalat, where this warming comfort food feels right at home.***

Use your noodle at the finest Sanuki udon joints

JAPAN // For centuries the people of Kagawa Prefecture ate Sanuki noodles without a care in the world. Until an avalanche of media coverage in the 1980s declared theirs the ultimate noodle. Chewy and soft, Sanuki noodles are revered across Japan. Within Kagawa, there are hundreds of udon joints. The self-service restaurants are fun because you warm your noodles in hot water then choose your own side dishes and toppings.

☛ EAT IT ! ***It's so busy you'll have to hurry your meal at Hariya, but it's worth it. 587-174 Gotocho, Takamatsu, Kagawa Prefecture.***

Celebrate with pom at a Suriname birthday party

SURINAME // In Suriname they have a saying, 'there's no birthday without pom', which goes to show how highly the Surinamese value this baked chicken casserole dish with citrus and pomtajer (an indigenous root vegetable). There is some conjecture as to where the dish originated – both colonial Dutch and Jewish camps vie for first dibs. Either way, get yourself to a birthday party next time you're in Suriname.

☛ EAT IT ! ***At a local get-together (you can always pretend it's your birthday).***

© Lonely Planet / Myles New

© Lonely Planet / Matt Munro

296

Live the genuine American dream at an iconic all-day breakfast diner

USA // Everyone has an impression of what a traditional American diner is like, even if they haven't been to one. Collated from a montage of Hollywood TV shows and movies, we can all picture the archetype and imagine the scene playing out with us in it; sliding into a vinyl booth, at any time of the day or night, as a gum-chewing waitress saunters up to our table and draws the pen from behind her ear as we prepare to order from the one-page laminated menu. It's a relaxed, cheap and easy experience that Americans have refined to the point of perfection. The menus at diners are a greatest-hits collection of comfort food classics; burgers and fries, pot pies and mashed potato, bacon and eggs, waffles and pancakes, corned beef hash, meatloaf, fried chicken, lemon meringue pie and milkshakes, the list goes on. But first, coffee. That bottomless cup of Joe, poured straight from the percolator to your table. Order the coffee and take your time deciding which version of a culinary hug you want from America this morning.

EAT IT ! *Across America, from the smallest of towns to the largest of cities. In LA, we like Pann's diner at 6710 La Tijera Blvd.*

Ben Shewry

Ben Shewry is the chef-owner of Attica in Melbourne. He was also one of six chefs featured on the Netflix documentary Chef's Table.

01

MOLE, RESTAURANT QUINTONIL; MEXICO CITY It's a really passionate little place and the chef, Jorge, does a mole that's super satisfying and slightly unexpected.

02

ICE CREAM SANDWICH, LUNE; MELBOURNE They work almost like Buddhist monks when they make their pasties. Their ice cream sandwich is a laminated spiral of croissant dough, with a perfect puck of ice cream between it.

03

BORDIER BUTTER; BERGUNDY, FRANCE It's made by a guy called Jean Yves Bordier and it's better than any cheese I've eaten in my life. It's a little hard to find, but not impossible. He must have magic cows.

04

BOHEMIA BEER-BATTERED FISH TACOS, EL MOLINO CENTRAL; SONOMA The woman who runs it is a bit of a Dianne Kennedy figure for Mexican food. It's this roadside shack, where you order off a board and the ingredients are local and ethical.

05

RED MULLET TAGLIATELLE, TIPOOO; MELBOURNE This relatively new 'pasta bar' has revolutionized things a little bit down here. This dish is beautifully cooked, fresh pasta made there, with a little saffron.

Taste a world-famous winter warmer in its Hungary home

HUNGARY // Hungarian cowherds cooking humble stews over their campfires originated this dish, whose name comes from the words 'herdsmen's meat', and indulging in its warming, dense flavours in a harsh Central European winter offers a sense of how glad they must have been when they did. The slow-cooked beef stew gets its characteristic russet hue from liberal doses of paprika, made from peppers that grow on the plains of southern Hungary. Thickened with potatoes and other root vegetables, it's often served with tiny egg noodles known as *csipetke*. You'll find goulash almost everywhere, from medieval pubs to schmancy nouvelle cuisine bistros.

EAT IT ! ***Goulash is served in a small kettle at Hortobágyi Csárda, a handsome 18th-century roadside tavern in Hortobágy National Park.***

© Lonely Planet / Junichi Miyazaki

298

298

Take a bite of a perfect onigiri in Tokyo

JAPAN // Onigiri are ubiquitous in Japan, found in every convenience store. In Tokyo they're triangular, and may be spheres or ovals elsewhere in Japan. But for the best onigiri experience, you need to go to an onigiri shop, such as Yadoroku, the oldest in Tokyo, which sold its first rice ball back in 1954. A good onigiri is all about the rice: chef Yosuke Miura at Yadoroku uses fragrant Koshihikari rice from Niigata. 'If the qualities of the harvest change, I use other varieties to make sure I achieve the right stickiness and flavour,' he says. Fillings include pickled vegetables, baby anchovies and ginger in miso. Just because something is common, doesn't mean you shouldn't try to perfect it.

EAT IT ! ***Yosuke Miura's Yadoroku onigiri shop is at 3-9-10 Asakusa, Taito-ku in northeast Tokyo.***

299

Indulge in a little mee time with Malaysia's wonton ace

MALAYSIA // Outside Malaysia, you're more likely to know this dish as wonton noodles. But on the streets of George Town, Penang's unequivocal street food capital, it's all about the *wantan mee*. Essentially it's a bowl of fluffy, fresh egg noodles tossed with a dark, secret sauce, topped with wontons (small, meat-filled Chinese dumplings), *char siu* pork and a garnish of vegetables. Of course, it's usually the sauce that gets tongues and tastebuds wagging about which vendor is better: suffice to say each uses their own secret ingredients and you'll have to try them all to discover which one comes out best. While typically served with a mushroom-inspired sauce or a broth made from chicken or pork, there's also a dry version.

EAT IT ! ***Around sunset, dash to Penang's Chulia St and be ready to wait in line for some of George Town's most popular noodles.***

300–
399

300

Eat a hot dog in Iceland – they're practically healthy

ICELAND // Icelandic cuisine has some singular specialities, like boiled puffin or rancid shark, but the stalls you see everywhere are selling a more regular titbit: a hot dog or, as it's known, a *pylsa* or *pulsa*. These sausages hail from free-range sheep grazing the island's rugged terrain. There are pork and beef ones too, but again these are reared on farms in one of the world's least-polluted lands. The casing is all-natural too, purportedly guaranteeing a 'pop' as you bite.

EAT IT ! ***Even Bill Clinton has been to Reykjavik's Bœjarins Beztu Pylsur, and 'the Clinton' is as he ordered it.***

301

Take a tea break with cute wagashi in ancient Kyoto

JAPAN // *Wagashi* are delicate Japanese confections often served with tea. Exquisitely crafted pops of colour, their function is as much about aesthetics as taste. In spring, nibble *sakuramochi*, dainty parcels of pink rice cake and red bean paste in a cherry blossom leaf. In November, the month of the pig, try the little pig-shaped *inokomochi*. Or enjoy *manjū*, shaped like fruits or animals. The locals like to buy boxes of chestnut *yokan*, a thick jelly eaten in slices, for their boss.

EAT IT ! ***Kyoto's Kagizen Yoshifuza has been crafting wagashi since the Edo period. 264 Gionmachi Kitagawa.***

Binge on beer fish from Yangshou's Li river

CHINA // As the Li river meanders through the limestone beauty of Yangshuo it provides a breeding ground for freshwater carp. Only the largest are selected for Yangshuo beer fish, so generous portions are guaranteed. After frying in camellia oil, the carp is then boiled in beer from the nearby city of Guilin, along with hot peppers and fresh vegetables. As the spicy soup is reduced the fish breaks apart into morsels of white flesh that's crispy underneath from the first fry.

EAT IT ! ***Outdoors, enjoying the bright lights and people-watching at MeiJie Yangshuo. E-101 Sunshine 100 Guihua Rd.***

© Getty Images / Cheryl Chan

Dedicate your day to cacao at Quito's Salón de Chocolate

ECUADOR // Ecuador probably harvested cacao beans before anywhere else, and today produces more top-quality chocolate than any other nation. This is enough justification to celebrate the sweet stuff in a specially dedicated festival each May. Here you can learn about the entire bean to bar process, meet everyone in the industry from the growers to the sellers to the experts, as well as fellow chocoholics, and, most tantalisingly of all, line up for your chance to sample a lot of lovingly made chocolate.

EAT IT ! ***If you're not in Quito in May, try Chez Tiff in central Calle de la Ronda.***

300

© Sigurdur Jokull Olafsson / Icelandic Photo Agency / Alamy Stock Photo

304

© Getty Images / Matthew Micah Wright

304

Keep the Maori fires burning at a traditional hangi feast

NEW ZEALAND // New Zealand's Maori people traditionally cooked their food in large underground oven pits known as *hangi*. Meat and root vegetables were wrapped in flax leaf, placed on hot stones, covered with a damp cloth and buried for up to four hours (depending on the type of meat being cooked). Though the traditional method of cooking underground still occurs, it now happens only on special occasions. One of the best places to experience a *hangi* meal is at Tamaki Maori Village. At this recreated settlement you become part of a culturally immersive experience, learning about ancient rituals and traditional arts and crafts as well as what life was like as a Maori warrior and even how to perform the Haka. The highlight of the evening is the *hangi* – your hosts will explain the rituals of the cooking process as tender meat and vegetables are pulled from the ground and served around an open fire. It's a unique way to get an insight into a proud and vibrant culture, and will leave you totally sated.

EAT IT ! ***As part of a moving experience at Tamaki Maori Village, 1220 Hinemaru St, Rotorua City, Rotorua.***

305

Cocktails and local cuisine atop the Ngorongoro Crater

TANZANIA // The Ngorongoro Crater in Tanzania is the world's largest unbroken volcanic caldera. Created millions of years ago when the volcano collapsed in on itself, the floor of the caldera covers 260 sq km (100 sq miles) and is 610m (2000ft) deep. The crater floor is mostly open grassland, attracting lions, zebras, wildebeest, hyenas and the elusive black rhino. It's busy, with wildlife tours year round, but crowds won't obstruct your view when you dine at the Ngorongoro Crater Lodge, high on the southwestern rim. The menu is inspired by local ingredients and sourced from local communities – think proteins like sheep and goat – and it's expertly served, starting with sundowner cocktails. It's luxurious and extravagant, though nothing can match nature's jaw-dropping grandeur.

☛ EAT IT ! *Ngorongoro Crater Lodge, Ngorongoro Crater.*

306

Sample the Hong Kong take on classic crispy duck

CHINA // It goes by a few names, among them roast goose or Cantonese-style roast duck, and is distinct from Beijing's Peking duck dish. The Hong Kong version is most likely a derivative of the 700-year-old recipe for Peking duck, and both have that distinctive crispy skin, but in Hong Kong the inside of the duck/goose is more intensely flavoured. The roasted Hong Kong style is served as pieces with the skin on, and the tender meat is seasoned. For a Michelin-starred roast duck experience you can't go past Kam's Roast Goose in Wan Chai, but for more everyday surrounds without scrimping on the roasted crispy flavour, then go to Yat Lok, where the duck is served with a light broth and vermicelli noodles.

☛ EAT IT ! *At Kam's Roast Goose, Po Wah Centre, 226 Hennessy Rd, Wan Chai; or Yat Lok, Conwell House, 34–38 Stanley St, Central.*

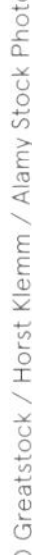

© NG K.W / Alamy Stock Photo

307

Do as bygone nomads and soldiers did, and skewer a seekh kebab in Islamabad

PAKISTAN // This staple of Tandoori cuisine was likely invented by Central Asian nomadic tribes before Turkish soldiers shared the technique as they conquered. In those days, soldiers simply used their blades to skewer meat and cook it over a campfire. The name itself derives from the Turkish 'shish', meaning sword or skewer, and 'kebab', which is meat. The classic *seekh* kebab uses minced lamb, seasoned with marinade made from freshly ground spices like ginger, garlic, coriander and cumin. The meat is then fashioned around a metal skewer into a sausage shape. Thankfully, these days the soldier's campfire has been exchanged for the charcoal flame of the tandoor. Throughout Pakistan you'll discover local differences in the marinades as well as kebabs made with every meat except pork.

☛ EAT IT ! ***Gaze down at the twinkling lights of Islamabad from the Monal restaurant terrace and imagine they're the campfires of nomads cooking the first seekh kebabs. Pirsohawa Road, Islamabad.***

308

Break down borders with a CalMex burrito

USA // Mexican food has long been favoured in the Golden State (much of which was originally part of Mexico), so it's no surprise that in a country where everything is super-sized, California would put its own large twist on this classic dish. Mission-style burritos are so overstuffed that it can take two flour tortillas to contain the portions of meat or beans, cheese, Spanish rice, vegetables and salsa. If you don't mind things messy, ask for a wet burrito, which will come smothered in a red chilli sauce with melted cheese. Though these days the burrito is almost as American as apple pie, its spicy Mexican roots still shine through, and the best place to eat one is at a no-frills Mexican *taqueria*, where you'll feel as if you've crossed the border.

☛ EAT IT ! ***There's usually a queue outside San Francisco's El Farolito, 2779 Mission St. Locals swear by its Mission-style burritos.***

© Shutterstock / Giulia M

© ABaarssen Fokke / Alamy Stock Photo

© Oleh Kosyy / 500px

309

Sniff out some Dutch musk strawberries where the wild things are

NETHERLANDS // With an aroma that draws you in from as far as 100m away, musk strawberries are impossible to pass by. Which is just as well because these somewhat smaller than regular strawberries are among the tastiest of their tribe. Often confused with popular alpine strawberries, musk strawberries (or *Fragaria moschata* if you're a scientist) explode in your mouth with a mashup flavour that's been described a mix of strawberry, raspberry and pineapple. Too delicate for mass production, these beauties can only be found in the wild.

EAT IT ! ***Hike through the revitalising Utrechtse Heuvelrug National Park, look for hedgerows and follow your nose.***

310

Make a meal of murgh makhani in its Delhi home

INDIA // Go to almost any Indian restaurant in the world and you can count on *murgh makhani* (butter chicken) being on the menu, but if you can, eat it at Old Delhi's Moti Mahal; this legendary six-generation restaurant is a retro delight. Velvety chunks of yoghurt-marinated chicken simmered in a buttery tomato gravy, *murgh makhani* is one of India's most-loved curries. Like many iconic dishes, its origins are shrouded in mystery, but most believe it was created by a Delhi restaurateur in the 1950s, based on recipes from his native Punjab. Eat it with basmati rice and tandoor-blistered rounds of naan, balancing the curry's mildness with a dab of mint chutney. Warm and creamy with a hint of toasty spices, it's the definition of comfort food.

EAT IT ! ***Around the world, but best of all at Moti Mahal, 3704 Netaji Subhash Marg, Old Delhi.***

311

Spread the love for rillettes as a classic French starter

FRANCE // What's more gloriously French than a slice of good baguette, thickly paved with a spread of meat and fat? You may be thinking pâté, but we're actually talking about *rillettes*, traditionally made with pork cooked slowly in its own fat until meltingly soft, then finely shredded. Salty and unctuous, it's often served in a small pot as a starter in the bistros of central France, perhaps with some mustard and cornichons. Though pork is traditional, you'll find *rillettes* of duck, rabbit and even seafood.

EAT IT ! *Head to the central France town of Tours for some of the country's most prolific rillettes makers.*

312

Base yourself on Nanaimo for a Canadian crunch

CANADA // Although the Nanaimo bar is adored and devoured across the whole of Canada, the nation's gift to the confectionery world should really be tasted in its birthplace on Vancouver Island, Nanaimo. Whether you've just flown over the Strait of Georgia from Vancouver's Coal Harbour on a float plane, or made the equally stunning journey here by ferry, there is no better way to remain on a travel high than to sink your teeth into this spectacularly sweet three-layered creation.

EAT IT ! *Between sips of a cappuccino at Bocca Café, savouring its chocolate top, custard-icing filling and nutty crumb base.*

313

Ackee and saltfish for a day in the Carribean sun

JAMAICA // The idyllic coastal coves of Treasure Beach are the stuff of Caribbean dreams. You spend your days beach hopping, sunbathing, swimming and snorkelling – after you've first visited Jake's restaurant for its famous ackee and saltfish. Ackee is an African fruit, most notably combined with boiled saltfish for breakfast, along with stewed peppers, tomatoes, onions and fiery scotch bonnet chillies. It's a rousing way to start a day of sun-drenched good times.

EAT IT ! *Jakes, Jakes Hotel, Calabash Bay, Treasure Beach, St Elizabeth.*

311

313

314

Sift through the weird, wonderful (and tasty) creatures of the deep at the vast Noryangjin fish market

SOUTH KOREA // The largest fish market in Seoul is a wet and hectic confluence of tons of fresh seafood, shrieking fishmongers and wide-eyed tourists, set beside the Han River. All in all, it's a hell of a lot of fun. Unlike Tokyo's Tsukiji fish market, the sellers at Noryangijin are more than happy to sell smaller quantities to individual buyers. Wander the stalls before making your selection; there are so many exotic and unusual species on show, not least of which is the *gaebul*, a type of sea worm that strikingly resembles a particular part of the male anatomy.

Most Koreans come to buy *hwe*, sliced raw fish, and the vendors are happy to help visitors out even if your Korean isn't up to much. Watch while they expertly skin, gut and slice your fish in seconds. If you'd rather have your selection cooked, take it straight to the onsite restaurants. Seafood auctions take place in the early pre-dawn hours when the freshest fish get snapped up for the day.

☛ EAT IT ! ***Noryangijin fish market, 674 Nodeul-ro, Noryangjin 1, Dongjak-gu. The restaurants are in the basement and 2nd floor.***

© Shutterstock / Nelson M S Silva

315

315

Nepalese momo, juicy dumplings from on high

NEPAL // This cartoon-sounding dumpling dish is believed to have originated in the mountains of Tibet before being shared with the world by traders. Whatever the *momo*'s origins, young Nepalese can't get enough of these juicy little critters. There is something undeniably pretty about the crescent-shaped packages, which sport ridges that allow sauces to settle in mouth-watering pools. Usually filled with fatty meat, such as pork or buffalo, succulence is the sign of good *momo*. Try them steamed and fried.

EAT IT ! ***Station, The Food Club and Sausage Park (Niva Galli, Pokhara) in Nepal.***

316

Try pap en vleis, a dish that unites all South Africa

SOUTH AFRICA // When apartheid ended, South Africa became known as the Rainbow Nation. *Pap en vleis* expresses this sentiment on a plate, representing a union of the country's black African culinary traditions and a staple of the white Afrikaners. The *pap* is a kind of porridge made from maize, which has long been an important food for the nation's poorest. The *vleis* (Afrikaans for meat) is a tasty spiced sausage made with beef and pork, known as *boerewors*. Together they are in perfect harmony.

EAT IT ! ***Mzoli, Gugulethu, Cape Town Central, serves amazing traditional food.***

317

Nigeria's prolific party food is a jollof good show

NIGERIA // Thought to have originated from the kitchens of the Wolof people, who once ruled in the region now known as Senegal and The Gambia, jollof rice has bubbled up over ensuing centuries to become a source (and sauce) of fierce pride among Nigerians, who produce more types of this tomato-rich rice party favourite than you can shake a stirring spoon at. No two jollof rice experiences are exactly the same – there's always a secret ingredient here, a secret ingredient there... the basic theme is that rice is cooked in an alluringly seasoned tomato sauce or stew.

EAT IT ! ***At any special occasion.***

© Getty Images / Johner Images

© Lonely Planet / Susan Wright

318

Suck on sweet sugarcane from a Lima street cart

PERU // For an afternoon pick-me-up in Lima, seek out a cart vendor hawking metre-long lengths of *caña de azúcar*, or sugarcane. The vendor will cut the cane fresh, using a cleaver to hack off the woody exterior before chopping the inside into cylindrical chunks. You then chomp on the fibrous cane to extract squirts of sweet, grassy juice. You could make it easier and buy the juice directly – most vendors have colourful hand-cranked presses. But that's not half as much fun.

EAT IT ! *You'll find caña de azúcar vendors all over major Peruvian cities.*

319

Tiramisù: the cloud nine of puddings

ITALY // In the walled town of Treviso, which boasts canals to rival those of Venice, a local restaurateur invented one of the world's most treasured desserts. According to the legend, Aldo Campeol's wife Ada wanted something light, sweet and refreshing and he, in turn, created tiramisù. The original 1960s recipe is for a cake consisting of sponge biscuits dipped in coffee, mascarpone cheese, sugar, cocoa powder and egg yolks. Alternative additions include sweet Marsala wine or rum.

EAT IT ! *At upmarket, cute and cosy Le Beccherie. Piazza Ancilotto 9, Treviso.*

320

Take your Swedish fika with friends and creamy semla

SWEDEN // What began as a Christian symbol for Shrove Tuesday now pops up as soon after Christmas as the *semla* fanatics can force it, festooning Swedish bakery windows in winter with plump, cream-packed, sweet buns. And how do you eat them? At *fika*, obviously. This coffee break with colleagues or friends is obligatory in many workplaces. Enter any bakery to eat your wheat bun and you'll be met with warmth and affection.

EAT IT ! *At bakeries all over Sweden and Scandinavia between Christmas and Easter.*

321

Pick a summer's day for a ploughman's lunch in rural England

UK // In life, timing is everything. Pick the right day in May, when the sun is out, the air is fragrant with blooming flowers and birds flit through the hedgerows, and if you're at The Harrow Inn in Hampshire, England, count yourself blessed. The 17th-century pub, with a doorway so low that most people need to stoop, has been run by the McCutcheon family since 1929. Its unfussy food is homemade and the ploughman's lunch is perfect for an afternoon in the garden surrounded by poppies, sweet peas and roses. A hunk of home-baked bread comes with a chunk of cheddar cheese, pickle and salad. Add a pint of local ale and settle down at a rickety table to absorb the sights and smells of an English summer. In times gone by, the ploughman's lunch would have fed a worker in the fields. These days you're at leisure to take a stroll down to the stream at the bottom of the hill.

EAT IT ! ***The Harrow Inn is between Steep and Sheet in northeast Hampshire, close to the cricket ground and tennis club.***

322

Pair the sparkling beauty of the Croatian coast with a bowl of inky black risotto

CROATIA // There was a time when the remarkable Dalmatian Coast in Croatia was a tightly held secret among the lucky few, but word got out and now pretty much everyone knows that it's the most gorgeous strip of coastline in Europe. Red-roofed villages perch in clusters along stunning white cliffs above the crystalline waters. There are countless hidden coves between small peninsulas, and hardy olive groves just back from the water's edge. It has everything, from wild parties to total privacy, and we haven't even started talking about the food. Being a Mediterranean nation, seafood abounds, and after a day of sunbathing and swimming in the cerulean sea, a glass of crisp *gemist* (white wine mixed with sparkling water) with a bowl of black risotto laden with fresh squid is food nirvana. The blackness of the risotto comes from rich, dense cuttlefish ink which is added just before serving, and the squid is tender and fresh, straight from the ocean; the light dusting of Parmesan cheese adds just the right amount of body and bite. No secrets between friends, right?

EAT IT ! ***At Konoba Matejuška, Ul Tomića stine 3, Split.***

323

Mas huni: the totally tangibly tropical taste

MALDIVES // In the Maldives, a tropical archipelago nation that is more than 90% ocean, *mas* (fish) and *huni* (shredded coconut) are the linchpins of cuisine, and *mas huni* is a popular Maldivian breakfast. It's traditionally made with cured tuna, coconut, onions, chilli and lime, served with coconut flatbread. Once, the boiling, smoking and sun-drying of the tuna was crucial for preservation; now the fish's feisty flavour is the most important consideration.

☛ EAT IT ! *At the hotel that you're staying in. Most will offer mas huni as a breakfast option.*

324

From palette to palate: London's Rex Whistler

UK // The Rex Whistler Restaurant is the culinary equivalent of a cup of tea and a good lie down for art patrons overstimulated by all the world-class pieces at Tate Britain; it is a sea of white-clothed tables encircled by a vast watercolour mural painted by inter-war artist Rex Whistler in 1927. The traditional English menu is made up of dishes such as sliced venison and terrine of seasonal game, while the wine list is one of the biggest and best in the land.

☛ EAT IT ! *At that most British of all art institutions, namely Tate Britain, Millbank, London.*

325

Elect to eat bún cha, Hanoi's presidential lunch

VIETNAM // This Hanoi dish received global attention a few years back when US President Barack Obama stopped off at Bún Cha Huong Liên between meetings. The ultimate lunchtime snack for busy Hanoians, *bún cha* comprises grilled pork (the 'cha') served on a bed of white rice (the 'bun') with herbs and dipping sauce. Mix it all together and savour the flavour. The city's narrow streets are teeming with *bún cha* bistros, each with their own variations of both meat and sauces.

☛ EAT IT ! *Bún Cha Bach Mai charcoal grills the cha on bamboo sticks. Lane 213, Bach Mai St, Hai Bà Trung District, Hanoi.*

325

326

Soak up the sake on Tokyo's drinking strip with unbeatable barbecued yakitori

JAPAN // It's not the most enticing-sounding address for a culinary experience, but scoffing *yakitori* in Piss Alley in Shinjuku is a hugely fun thing to do in Tokyo. What started as an illegal drinking den in the 1940s, Omoide Yokocho (or as it translates, Memory Lane) was given its colloquial name because this tightly packed, tiny strip of bars serving cheap drinks and *yakitori* had no WCs, so patrons had to improvise. Today the alley looks almost as it would have 70-odd years ago, which is no small feat considering it burned down in 1999. It was carefully reconstructed to remain as true to the original as possible, with one exception – there are toilets. All the bars here are virtually the same so walk along the strip until you find a spare seat. After a few beers and a sake or two the smoky aroma of all those grills will tell you it's time for some *yakitori*. Almost all the bars will have their own little charcoal grill set up to prepare these delicious skewers of BBQ chicken, and we promise that by now, they'll taste like the best thing you've ever eaten.

EAT IT ! ***At any of the bars at 1 Chome-2, Shinjuku, Tokyo. For added interest, Daikokuya has more than 150 different types of sake.***

© Shutterstock / URAIWONS

327

When in Rome... hell, snack on some suppli

ITALY // Closely related to the *arancini* balls found elsewhere in Italy, *suppli* are Rome's very own croquette version – cylinders with a chewy, cheesy twist. This deep-fried street snack consists of risotto rice in a rich tomato sauce, with either a meat or mozzarella cheese filling, soaked in egg yolk and coated in breadcrumbs. When you break it open, the cheese oozes out like a stringy web. It's this unexpected treat that gave *suppli* its name, derived from the French for 'surprise'.

EAT IT ! ***For suppli made the traditional way, stop at La Gatta Mangiona. Via Federico Ozanam 30-32, Rome.***

329

© Lonely Planet / Justin Foulkes

Indulge your inner aristo in a grand Budapest cafe

HUNGARY // Nibble a slice of *Dobos torte* at one of Budapest's grand coffee houses after a morning at the fin-de-siècle Gellért Baths. With its glossy caramel top and thin layers of sponge cake and chocolate buttercream, it speaks to the opulence of the 19th-century Austro-Hungarian empire. Created by pastry chef József Dobos, the treat was introduced to Budapest in 1885 and served to King Franz Joseph. An immediate smash, it's been a staple of high-end pastry cases ever since.

EAT IT ! ***Opulent Café Gerbeaud at Vörösmarty tér 7-8 has been serving Dobos torte to Budapest's elite for over a century.***

Count on great sauce in the land of the seven moles

MEXICO // *Mole* is so closely associated with Oaxaca that the town is known as the land of the seven *moles*, for the number of varieties it has. Best known is the chocolate, chillies, fruits, black pepper and cinnamon combo of the *mole negro*. Distinct for its deep reddish colour, its key ingredient, chocolate, is dark Oaxacan cacao, lending the sauce a sweet bitter taste. *Mole* can top many dishes from *tamales* and *enchiladas* to fried plantains; try all seven to find your chosen one.

EAT IT ! ***There are many mole stalls inside Oaxaca's Mercado 20 de Noviembre; try the ones at Comedor María Teresa.***

Crack the crust on crème brûlée in a cinematic bistro

FRANCE // As the 2001 movie *Amélie* notes, one of life's finest small pleasures is cracking the burnt sugar crust of a crème brûlée with your teaspoon. Doing it in the pretty streets of Montmartre, where much of the film is set, only adds to the pleasure as, once you've shattered the golden top, you dig into the dense but silky custard. Traditionally served in individual ramekins, it's a bistro classic, the ideal chaser to your leek tart or *steak frites*.

EAT IT ! ***Romantic Le Coupe-Chou at 11 rue de Lanneau in the Latin Quarter spikes its vanilla crème brûlée with Grand Marnier.***

331

Bust a gut for a franceshina, Porto's supersize sandwich

PORTUGAL // Should you need to replace the thousands of calories spent surfing north Portugal's wild Atlantic coast waves, a *franceshina* is the dish for you. Let us talk you through the basic components of this gut-busting sandwich from Porto and see if you believe what you're reading. Between two pieces of bread are placed ham, cured pork sausage, cooked sausage, steak, and roast beef. On top of the closed sandwich is placed a fried egg. Then the whole thing is covered in cheese, grilled, and doused in a sauce made of tomato and beer. Oh, and we forgot to mention that it's usually served with a side of fries, in case you're not already on the verge of a heart attack. Ironically this monolith of a sarnie's name means 'Little Frenchie', and if you look hard you might see some resemblance to the French Croque Madame.

EAT IT ! *Wrap your hands around this beast at Café Santiago, R. de Passos Manuel 226, Porto.*

332

Herald Oktoberfest in Munich with weisswurst and pretzels

GERMANY // A pair of plump poached veal sausages and a pretzel the size of your head, dunked in sweet mustard and washed down with an icy stein of beer. Does your stomach groan a bit just thinking of it? Well that's just breakfast. *Willkommen* to Bavaria! *Weisswurst*, a white sausage of veal and pork fat, flavoured with lemon rind, parsley and cardamom, is uncured and unsmoked, thus tradition dictates it should only be eaten before the toll of the noonday church bells for maximum freshness. The accompanying pretzels, which get their chewy golden crust from an edible lye solution, have been made in these parts since the Middle Ages. Though, no, the average Bavarian doesn't eat this breakfast every day, it's definitely the menu for kicking off proceedings at Oktoberfest.

EAT IT ! *Munich's Gaststätte Grossmarkthalle at Kochelseestr 13 opens at 7am to serve what's considered by many the best weisswurst around; wash it down with a lovely weissbier.*

Wylie Dufresne

Wylie Dufresne is the chef-owner of Du's Donuts in Manhattan, as well as a pioneer of the molecular gastronomy movement.

PIZZA, NICE SLICE; PROVIDENCE, RI Of virtually any combination my favourite is the Parallel Universe: ricotta, scallion, black pepper, bacon, mozz, olive oil and cheddar.

SUPER CAKE DOUGHNUT, CURIOSITY DOUGHNUTS; STOCKTON, NJ The super cake doughnut is the reason to go; the custard doughnut is the reason to stay.

FISH SKIN TACO, HIJA DE SANCHEZ; COPENHAGEN The lengua (beef tongue) taco is an obvious choice, but if the fish skin taco is available, that's the pro move.

THE SET MENU, SINGLE THREAD; HEALDSBURG, CA This husband and wife team meld California and Japan by tracking how Healdsburg's seasons parallel Japan's.

BABY SQUID WITH CARAMELISED ONIONS, ASADOR PORTUETXE; BASQUE COUNTRY, SPAIN It's pretty amazing to dine in a place that's 150 years older than our country.

333

Shell out on Sri Lankan fare at the Ministry of Crab

SRI LANKA // Sending Sri Lankan cuisine into the gastronomic stratosphere is celebrity chef Dharshan Munidasa's crustacean fine diner, the Ministry of Crab. Housed in a 400-year-old Dutch colonial-style building that previously functioned as a hospital, the Ministry is a homage to all things crab. The menu showcases internationally inspired dishes such as the garlic chilli crab, which cherry picks from notes of Italian and Japanese cuisine, as well as many local legends like the curry crab, which is gently sautéed in Sri Lankan curry spices. However, the best way to savour the sweet meat from these prickly creatures is to eat it chilled accompanied by a warm butter sauce. Thankfully, the restaurant isn't so fancy that you can't lick your fingers.

EAT IT ! *At Ministry of Crab, Old Dutch Hospital, Colombo.*

© Lonely Planet / Matt Munro

Go undercover for finer fare at Adelaide Central Market

AUSTRALIA // The year is 1869. Three hours before dawn, a bunch of market gardeners set up makeshift stalls along Gouger Street ready to hawk their produce to Adelaide's city slickers. Out of the darkness, hundreds of eager customers arrive. By six o'clock every stall is sold out. Such was the auspicious start to Adelaide Central Market. Now housed in a picturesque red brick building with more than 70 permanent traders, it is one of the largest undercover markets in the southern hemisphere. Catering to even the pickiest palate, it holds everything from speciality eateries to old fashioned fruit and veg stalls. As you browse the bustling aisles it will soon be clear that the traders mean it when they say their vision is to become the world's leading food and produce market.

EAT IT ! *Make a beeline for Jamu – stall 69 – and grab a 'healthier than a hipster on a health-kick' smoothie bowl to power your way around the market. Gouger St, Adelaide.*

© Southern Australia Tourist Board / Josie Withers

335

Chili con carne: the original Tex-Mex treat

USA // Despite an exotic name that hints at Spanish or Mexican roots, chili con carne – chilli with meat – is as Texan as giant belt buckles, even if it was more stolen than invented sometime in the mid 1800s in San Antonio. These days, it's the perfect Texas road trip meal, a dish that forms a flavour identity the more versions you try, everywhere from roadside diners to BBQ joints to county fairs. All of them taste incredible while wearing a 10-gallon Stetson.

EAT IT ! *Houston's oldest Tex-Mex joint, Molina's Cantina, serves up a traditional bowl with a crackers for less than $10.*

336

Roll up for Bengal's sweet rasgulla balls

INDIA // As is so often promised by sweet manufacturers, here is a treat that really will melt in your mouth. *Rasgulla* are made from semolina dough mixed with *chhena* (Indian cottage cheese), rolled into balls and then boiled in sugar syrup. When the syrup infuses the ball the result is a pale little dumpling with a delicate sweet taste. *Rasgulla* are so tasty that the governments of West Bengal and neighbouring Odisha have been arguing for decades about which state invented them.

EAT IT ! *To maximise the taste sensation, eat your rasgulla whole off the spoon, from street stalls and sweet shops across Bengal.*

337

Ratatouille: discover Provence on a plate

FRANCE // An oil paint-bright jumble of a stew, vivid with tomatoes and herbs and fresh, grassy olive oil, ratatouille sings of summer. Besides the tomatoes, typical ingredients include aubergine, courgettes, garlic, peppers, basil and thyme, which all grow lavishly in the Provençal countryside. Some versions are artfully layered, while others are more rustic jumbles. Either way, served with slices of warm grilled bread, it's an al fresco lunch par excellence.

EAT IT ! *At charming, family-run La Rossettisserie at 8 rue Mascoïnat, Nice, ratatouille is a side with any main course.*

335

337

338

© Thomas Schauer

338

© Brent Herrig

338

© Thomas Schauer

338

Join the cult of New York City's Cronut®

USA // Rain or shine, the line forms early outside Dominique Ansel's New York bakery: before 8am early. Most people are here for one thing, to tick another experience off their bucket list. They come for the Cronut®, the flaky croissant-donut spliced together by pastry genius Dominique. Is it worth the wait? Without a doubt, not least for the camaraderie of the queue, but also the sweet, cream-filled, deep-fried delight itself. You can pre-order the pastries at 11am sharp on Mondays – but where's the fun in that?

☛ EAT IT ! *Go to Dominique Ansel Bakery at 189 Spring St, New York City.*

339

Enjoy a home-cooked Kuwaiti culinary mashup

KUWAIT // Kuwaiti cuisine is a mixture of Arabic, Indian, Mediterranean and Iranian influences. Combine these with the importance that Kuwaitis place on generous hospitality and you have a food culture to rival the world's best. The pride and joy of Kuwaiti cooking is chicken *machboos*, or *machboos ala Dajaj*. Every Kuwaiti knows how to prepare this spiced meat and rice dish with a list of spices as long as your arm, and you'll find it at family celebrations and in restaurants throughout the country.

☛ EAT IT ! *If not at a Kuwaiti's home, then eat at Freej Suwaileh Salmiya, Kuwait City.*

340

Enter a chocolate factory of your dreams in Zürich

SWITZERLAND // Though the cacao plant comes from the New World, the Old World cities of Switzerland are responsible for the chocolate we love today, having turned cocoa beans into smooth bars and invented the conching machine to evenly distribute cocoa butter. Exploring its history and the array of products at the huge Confiserie Sprüngli, an institution for coffee, pastries and a galaxy of house-made chocolates, is a chocoholic's treat. You'll be in good company – the Swiss eat more chocolate than any nationality.

☛ EAT IT ! *At Confiserie Sprüngli Bahnhofstrasse 21, Zürich.*

© Mariano Garcia / Alamy Stock Photo

341

Plunge into the potted Pacific Ocean with Chile's seafood casserole, cazuela de mariscos

CHILE // Gangly Chile, spread-eagled along more than 4000km (2500 miles) of South America's Pacific seaboard, has a lot of coast. And therefore it has a lot of seafood. It makes sense, really, for this abundant seafood to converge with Chile's ultimate comfort food, the *cazuela*: a cook-up of stock-immersed fish or meat with vegetables.

Cazuela de mariscos actually translates as seafood casserole, but the heat that cooks the dish is usually from below. What matters is that white fish, and shellfish such as prawns, mussels and shrimps (often with shells left on) bubble together with onions, tomatoes and other veggies and herbs for a nice long time in a covered pot until the flavours meld. This is one to savour at weekends with the family, and an eating experience not to be rushed. Tradition dictates that the juice is slurped first, then the softened hunks of fish and vegetable.

☛ EAT IT ! ***In the Aisén and Magallanes regions, where the sea is an important livelihood, this fishy hotpot is a regular on menus.***

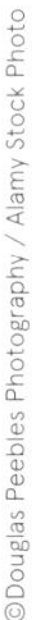
©Douglas Peebles Photography / Alamy Stock Photo

342

Get cooking with friends at a braai, the South African barbecue that demands its own national day

SOUTH AFRICA // *Braai* is not simply the South African's way of cooking meat over fire, *braai* is woven into the culture, intrinsic to their way of life. So serious are South Africans about *braai* that there's a push to incorporate National Braai Day into National Heritage Day on 24 September each year. They have a point: Heritage Day celebrates the diversity of South African culture and traditions, so what better way to do this than to get together with family and friends over an open fire with wonderful food? In Cape Town you can't swing a steak without hitting on a *braai* every weekend, but it's worth the effort to be there on Heritage/Braai Day, when the air of festive conviviality is infectious. Cape Town's beautiful setting is one of the reasons this is the place to be, but also the Capetonian's commitment to quality produce and innovative cooking means you'll get more than just a sausage slapped on the BBQ. Expect homemade *boerewors*, ostrich steaks, beer-marinated rump steaks and more. For a true South African food experience, the braai is hard to beat.

EAT IT ! ***With your mates at Wynberg Park, Wynberg, Cape Town.***

343

It's Melbourne's smashed avo on toast, mate!

AUSTRALIA // If there's one millennial dish that has gone global, it's the much-Instagrammed avocado on toast. You'll likely have a version in your local cafe. But to taste the best, go to the source: Australia. Specifically, a cafe such as Top Paddock in Richmond, Melbourne, serving avocado with peas, shallots, mint, goat's curd, chilli salt and a poached egg. Or keep it simple with The Kettle Black's half of 'seasonal' avocado with a slice of toast and local kelp salt.

EAT IT ! ***Top Paddock is at 658 Church St. The Kettle Black is at 50 Albert Rd. Both are in Melbourne.***

344

Bite into a 2000-year-old burger in Xi'an

CHINA // Sometimes called a Chinese hamburger, this sandwich actually predates the burger by two millennia or so. Originating in Shaanxi Province, *rou jia mo* consists of stewed, spiced chopped meat stuffed into flat bread similar to a pita. Topped off with coriander, it's a juicy delight, best eaten leaning over the pavement so the oils don't drip on your clothes. In non-Muslim areas, it's often made with pork (*rou*), but aficionados swear by Xi'an's beef or mutton versions.

EAT IT ! ***At night, Xi'an's Muslim Quarter is absolutely teeming with vendors hawking rou jia mo and other local treats.***

345

Fish taco: the surfers' delight in Baja California

MEXICO // It's easy to see why surfers in Baja love the deceptively simple fish taco. Fresh fish is cut into thin strips, fried and placed atop two warmed corn tortillas. Raw cabbage gives a jolt of fresh veggies while the fried fish delivers a strong crunch. The creamy sauce hides a spicy kick by mixing mayonnaise, sour cream and jalapeños. A squeeze of fresh lime gives a hint of the perfect wave – which, along a peninsula of more than 1200km (750 miles), shouldn't be too hard to find. Akaw!

EAT IT ! ***Both Ensenada and San Felipe in Baja claim to be the creators of the dish; food carts serving them abound in both spots.***

345

Elena Arzak

Elena Arzak is the chef-founder of the Michelin-starred Arzak in San Sebastián. In 2012, Restaurant magazine named her the best female chef in the world.

01

GRILLED TURBOT, GETARIA; SPAIN Aitor Arregi at Elkano does it whole on the grill with salt and a special vinaigrette, mixing with the natural gelatin to create the sauce.

02

RICE, THE MEDITERRANEAN I'm mad about all rice, from Italian risottos to the dry and soupy rice dishes of Spanish cuisine. It's a dish that seems simple but takes great skill.

03

RAW SHEEP MILK CHEESE, IDIAZABAL; BASQUE COUNTRY My favourite cheese. Each is slightly different, depending on the shepherd or where the flock is grazing.

04

IBERIAN HAM; SPAIN There is nothing like the flavour of a great Iberian ham from free range pigs who have eaten foraged acorns in the holm oak forests of western Spain.

05

SUSHI AND SASHIMI, BARCELONA Something that seems apparently simple has so many subtleties and is very delicate, and Barcelona has so many great places to eat it.

346

Bring a strong stomach for the bizarre bites at Hokitika's Wildfood Festival

NEW ZEALAND // Bring an open mouth and open mind to this annual festival of wild and weird food on the west coast of New Zealand's South Island. Held in March, Wildfoods fills the once-golden town of Hokitika (the setting for Eleanor Catton's Booker Prize-winning novel *The Luminaries*) with a cornucopia of rarely sampled flavours and textures. Amid live music and a 'feral fashion' competition, more than 50 market stalls set up for three days, dishing up everything from standard west-coast treats (whitebait fritters, game meats, a Maori *hangi*) to deep-fried pigs' ears, mountain oysters (yes, bulls' testicles), live *huhu* grubs (an NZ beetle), duck heads, or perhaps, if energy is flagging, a 'stallion protein shot', better known as horse semen.

☛ EAT IT ! ***The event is framed around Cass Sq in the centre of Hokitika, with stalls set up right along Weld St. Three campsites provide accommodation.***

347

Enjoy a happy union of fresh Costa Rican flavours in the popular casado

COSTA RICA // *Casado* means married in Spanish, and it's the perfect name for this balanced, everyday plate of food, which uses fresh Costa Rican ingredients and is served everywhere, from rustic kitchens on balmy beaches to the noisy heart of the capital, San José. It may lack fireworks but it's reliably good and usually the healthiest choice on the menu. Each *casado* contains rice, beans, plantains, salad and a tortilla, but you choose the main ingredient, usually chicken, fish, beef or pork. Spice comes from fresh tomato salsa on the side so that everyone from picky children to gourmet-leaning adults can flavour it just right.

☛ EAT IT ! ***You'll find casado in almost every restaurant in Costa Rica as well as in local homes. Each place cooks it a little differently.***

348

Sample snail porridge at Heston Blumenthal's Fat Duck

UK // Consistently voted among the world's best restaurants, The Fat Duck is nestled near the River Thames in the storybook setting of the village of Bray, from where it invites diners on a nostalgic and imaginative journey where nothing is as it seems. Imagine soup that is both hot and cold; sashimi served with a foam conjured from seafood on a bed of tapioca sand; or snail porridge. As the visual cues for each dish belie the taste, your senses soar into the unique gastronomic universe of Heston Blumenthal's creation. With just 42 daily spaces for lunch and dinner, you won't be surprised to learn that booking slots are only opened at certain times of the year, and your wait will usually run to about a four months – which will give you plenty of time to save up for the £300 meal. Without drinks.

☛ EAT IT ! ***Savour the magic of food on a genuinely mind-bending food adventure. High St, Bray, UK.***

349

Picnic in a Parisian park – and pack the quiche lorraine

FRANCE // This French classic is best eaten during a picnic on a rural French riverbank or in a Parisian park. Sit and slowly savour every mouthful; for this is a meal of such tasty parts, namely eggs and bacon, that it's hard to go wrong. Purists will tell you a true quiche lorraine doesn't have cheese and must use full cream and a pinch of nutmeg. The pastry should be flakey and there shouldn't be any onion or leek, or it becomes another quiche entirely. We say it's OK to buy a quiche lorraine with Gruyère or Emmental (many French bakeries and cafes serve it this way) but what's not OK is to rush the experience.

☛ EAT IT ! ***In a park or bucolic slice of French countryside, or if it must be indoors, at The Smiths Bakery, 12 rue de Buci, Paris.***

348

350

Chew on a chalupa in Cholula and it won't be your last

MEXICO // In Cholula, the home of the Pueblan *chalupa*, the vendors in front of Templo de Santa Monica expertly fry these moreish snacks in record time. A speciality in south-central Mexico, the deep-fried masa-dough pancakes are filled with salsa, cheese and shredded lettuce. It looks like a soggy mess, but don't judge a street snack by its cover – the *chalupa* is an explosion of spicy deliciousness and one is definitely not enough; luckily, you can get five for US$2.

EAT IT ! ***From the street vendors in Cholula, Puebla.***

351

Get to work on a bargain Hawaiian plate lunch

USA // The plate lunch's name comes from the compartmentalised plates used to serve plantation workers from mobile lunch vans in the 1930s. Almost a century on, the plate lunch has stayed true to its roots and remains a bargain. The most popular types are native specialities such as *kalua* pork, *loco moco* (hamburger patty with gravy and a fried egg) and spam *musubi* (spam and rice wrapped in nori). Honolulu's Waikiki district is a great place to find a vendor.

EAT IT ! ***From a hole-in-the-wall vendor in the Waikiki district of Honolulu, Hawaii.***

352

Kaya toast: Malaysia's back-to-basics breakfast

MALAYSIA // This breakfast staple is like a foil for all the rich and intricate seasoning of those Malaysian specialities famous for their complex spice mixes and ingredients. Kaya toast is essentially jam on toast: two slices of toasted white bread, lathered in kaya 'jam'. The jam is made with coconut milk, sugar and eggs, and is delicately sweet. It's served with very cold butter, which gently melts from the heat of the toast, and comes with a soft-boiled egg and a sugary black coffee.

EAT IT ! ***At breakfast cafes all over Kuala Lumpur.***

© John Elk III / Alamy Stock Photo

Meet the meat masters at Serbia's Grill Festival

SERBIA // Leskovac owns the meat and fire culinary formula in Serbia, with a seven-day Grill Festival and the fact that the Serbian national dish was born here. *Pljeskavica* is a ground beef (also beef and pork elsewhere) burger without a bun, served with cheese, salads and flatbread. The meat itself is spiked with onions and spices and comes from the grill caramelised and smoky. It's a study in simplicity amid the Grill Festival hubbub of local aficionados honouring the grill masters.

EAT IT ! ***At the Lescovac Grill Festival in late August/early September, or at takeaway kiosks throughout the country.***

354

Indulge in pudim, an after-dinner Brazilian treat

BRAZIL // *Pudim* is a dessert that's quintessentially Brazilian, especially when eaten with locals as part of a meal in a restaurant, bakery, cafe or, best of all, someone's home. Eggs, condensed milk, cow's milk, sugar and water combine to create a creamy pudding with a syrupy caramel sauce. Its few components makes it a favourite with home cooks, but if you don't know any, find it at eateries all over Brazil. Try it as a follow-up to your meaty *feijoada*.

EAT IT ! ***At traditional Brazilian restaurants throughout the country.***

356

© Bob Henry / Alamy Stock Photo

355

Egg hoppers, Sri Lanka's punchy pancakes

SRI LANKA // Watching roadside vendors pump out these bowl-shaped fermented pancakes is almost as much fun as eating them. The vendors pump out hoppers with speed and in hefty quantities, which is just as well, as one won't be enough. From the lacy edges to the chewy middle, the pancake hopper graces many breakfast tables, but the addition of the cracked egg in the Sri Lankan egg hopper is mostly served in the evening. Tasty versions also include a spicy coconut *sambal*, or cheese on top of the egg.

EAT IT ! ***Freshly made from small wok-like pans at roadside huts.***

356

Find Cantonese comfort in your wonton bowl

CHINA // In Hong Kong, a steamy bowl of wonton noodles is just the thing for a hangover, a broken heart or simply a late-night snack. Springy, egg-enriched noodles are drowned in a fragrant fish broth, upon which plump shrimp wontons are set to float. Everyone has preferences about the qualities that make the best soup – big wontons vs small, pure shrimp filling vs a touch of pork, etc. Slurp up your bowl and get moving – the plastic chairs of the best wonton joints are for eating on, not lingering.

EAT IT ! ***At outlets of Mak's Noodles all over Hong Kong.***

357

Try an old Havana sandwich special in a new setting

USA // The humble ham and cheese toastie as reimagined by immigrant Cuban workers in Florida with mustard, ham, pickles, Swiss cheese and, crucially, marinated roast pork. It's now popular way beyond the state, but it's still in Florida that you'll find the best ones, and chowing down on a Cuban sandwich in home-from-home communities like Tampa Bay's Ybor City, built by Cuban cigar makers who relocated here in the 1880s, will make you think you've died and gone to Havana.

EAT IT ! ***In Ybor City, or from the Zaza New Cuban Diner in Orlando; both Florida.***

358

Celebrate gulab jamun, the colourful festival food of northern India

INDIA // There's something about the tantalisingly sweet and syrupy *gulab jamun* (*gulab* meaning rose and *jamun* meaning berry) that makes it the perfect dessert to eat on the streets of northern India during festivals such as Eid, Holi, Diwali and Navratri, when they're particularly prevalent – maybe because the glistening reds and fiery oranges of these small, doughnut-like balls soaking in sugared rose water syrup make them look so, well, joyful. They are traditionally made with *khoya*, or milk solids, and can be particularly time-consuming and complex to prepare, which essentially means that you need to eat as many as you possibly can while you're on the road because you're not likely to be able to recreate the delicate signature flavours and textures at home.

EAT IT ! ***Any sweet shop you spy in northern India will serve these tasty dumplings.***

359

Dig into marrow bone on toast at St John in London

UK // It's still a dramatic sight in the austere, white-washed room: a plate of sections of roasted marrow bone, a toasted slice of rustic sourdough and a simple parsley salad. Chef Fergus Henderson, a founding father of nose-to-tail dining, opened London's St John in a dilapidated Smithfield smokehouse in 1994 and bone marrow on toast has been on the menu ever since. The devil is in the details: Henderson uses only veal marrow bones from the meat market down the street; the sourdough comes from his bakery next door, and the parsley, onion and caper salad adds bite. The dish sits beside dilled lamb tongues, crispy pig cheek with dandelion and duck hearts on toast. As Henderson has said: 'Celebrate the bone!'

EAT IT ! ***You'll usually need to book ahead to eat at St John's original Farringdon location at 26 St John St, London, though you can often slip in for a weekday lunch.***

360

Nibble on Bolivia's steaming and soupy empanada, the salteña

BOLIVIA // If there's one snack loved throughout Latin America, it is the empanada – the small parcels of toasty dough containing spiced savoury meats and vegetables are ubiquitous and impossible to resist. The Bolivian version, known as *salteña*, is a different eating experience to the Argentinian empanada because it's made using gelatin to encase the meat inside the dough. The gelatin maintains its integrity in the *salteña* while it's cool but melts into a savoury broth around the meat once the *salteña* is baked. Heed this information as it can save you from third-degree burns, or expensive laundry bills, if you bite in expecting semi-solid meat. Nibble the *salteña* from the top to allow steam to escape then slurp out the soup. When the threat of injury has passed you can enjoy the delicious parcel safely.

EAT IT ! ***Carefully – and on the street – all over the country. It's the local way.***

361

Where does a man go for ace mango? Miami, of course

USA // Burmese monks began sharing their mangoes with the world around 300BC. Since then countless cultivations have followed, but one of the planet's best emerged in Miami in 1902, when a retired US army captain planted the seedlings of the species that would bear his name, though it was his wife Florence Haden who nurtured the plants after her husband's untimely death only a year after planting. Celebrated for their flesh, fragrance and skin, Haden mangoes are the bees-knees.

☛ EAT IT ! *Miami goes mango-mad every summer; slurp one fresh while sipping on your mango margarita.*

362

See treats appear at a Papabubble candy store

JAPAN // There's something Dr Seussian about watching candies being made in a Papabubble store. Pillow-sized hunks of coloured sugar are twisted into ribbons, swirled into lollipops, snipped into lozenges. The Barcelona-based brand styles itself as a 'candy lab', with minimalist open kitchens, and sweets sold in jars and test tubes in flavours like kiwi, passionfruit and mocha. Order customised candy for events, and the staff will embed initials or images in the sugar.

☛ EAT IT ! *The futuristic glass box shop at Tokyo Station's Daimaru department store B1F 1-9-1, Marunouchi, Chiyoda-ku, Tokyo.*

363

Hit the beach in Durban with a bunny chow

SOUTH AFRICA // This odd-looking dish is thought to have come about when Durban's Indian migrant workers needed a way to carry their lunch curry to work. Some crafty cook put a curry in the hollowed-out end of a loaf of white bread and the experiment took off. Bunnies are meant to be eaten with your hands, so grab one to go and make an enjoyably messy meal of it outside, perhaps overlooking one of Durban's beautiful beaches.

☛ EAT IT ! *At CaneCutters, 53-55 Helen Joseph Rd, Bulwer, Berea, Durban.*

© Getty Images / Brett Stevens

364

Earn your fish supper in the Northern Territory by landing a battling barra

AUSTRALIA // In the ocean and rivers of Australia's Top End, a fish growing up to about 1.5m in length has become revered, both for the fierce sport of catching it and its sweetish taste. Combine catching and eating it at the Barramundi Lodge in Arnhem Land, where you can spend the day fishing and, hopefully, have your catch prepared by the chef for dinner. Known in Australia as 'barra', barramundi is to many the king of fish, headlining menus across the Northern Territory. It's so popular that much of the barra you find on plates is imported from Asian countries (where it's known as Asian sea bass), so be sure to check the provenance of the beautifully white fillet you'll find on basic pub menus as well as in the finest of restaurants.

☛ EAT IT ! *On the waterside deck of the Barramundi Lodge in Arnhem Land, Maningrida, Northern Territory.*

Don't overthink your midnight Philly cheesesteak, just get stuck in

USA // The origins of the Philly Cheesesteak, which was invented in the 1930s by a hot dog vendor who decided to cook up some sliced beef, will always be less important than the one-upmanship that surrounds this iconic hot sandwich. The 'best cheesesteak' debate rages everywhere from taxi stands to churches in the city of brotherly love, and even across Pennsylvania. Despite it being essentially the same everywhere – thinly sliced ribeye, topped with your choice of melted cheese and add-ons such as sautéed onions – there are nuances that you're better off not questioning while standing on a frigid street corner at midnight, with your sandwich in hand, surrounded by local diehards, who have thrown punches for far less.

☛ EAT IT ! *Become an instant Philly local by eating one cheesesteak at Geno's and then trying one nearby at its rival, Pat's King of Steaks (owned by the family of the man said to have invented it).*

© RosalreneBetancourt 3 / Alamy Stock Photo

366

Marry yourself to stuffed sardines while wandering the souks and shores of Morocco

MOROCCO // The idiom 'an embarrassment of riches' describes Moroccan cuisine to a tee. Meat, seafood, vegetables, pulses, nuts... it's all here. So it won't come as any surprise that food bought on the streets rivals any served in upmarket restaurants. An example is the stuffed sardine or, as they're more romantically named in Morocco, *sardines mariées* (married sardines), so-called because of the way the fillets are sandwiched together (larger fillets can be folded and stuffed). These tasty morsels are best sampled in Morocco's seaside towns where the fish are freshest, but you'll find them just about everywhere. The sardines are prepared by joining the fillets together using a layer of *chermoula*, the North African spicy sauce. They're then coated with more *chermoula* before being dusted in flour and deep-fried, served with a squeeze of lemon and a side of green chilli. Buy at least three to sustain you through a souk exploration or a break from the beach – you won't be content with just one or two.

EAT IT ! ***Buy the stuffed sardines fresh from the street-side fryers along Morocco's expansive coastline.***

366

366

© Michael Ventura / Alamy Stock Photo

© Sean Pavone / Alamy Stock Photo

367

Cool off with kokoda and beer in the Fijian heat

FIJI // This appetiser from the Fijian isles uses a meaty white fish such as Spanish mackerel or mahi mahi, marinated for a few hours in lime juice to 'cook' the *kokoda*, much like a *ceviche*. The fish is topped with chopped capsicum, onion, celery, a dash of chilli and, crucially, coconut milk, before being served in, of course, a coconut shell. Cheesy? Maybe, but it's island life at its very best; crisp and refreshing, and perfect with a cold Fiji Bitter beer on a hot, humid day.

EAT IT ! ***Nearly all menus in Fiji feature kokoda, using the catch of the day.***

368

Grab a crab cake: a classic from Chesapeake Bay

USA // Chesapeake Bay on America's mid-Atlantic coast teems with blue crabs – so plentiful that locals get creative eating them. Take crab cakes, for instance, patties of crabmeat mixed with mayonnaise and fried. Eat them on rocket salads at high-end restaurants or with saltines and lemon at Baltimore pubs. Every establishment has its own recipe, and wars have been fought over questions like 'bread crumbs or no bread crumbs?' Keep everyone happy and try both.

EAT IT ! ***The bar at Faidley's, 203 N Paca St, Baltimore, for crab cakes and cold beer.***

369

Slurp soup while liming like a true Trinidadian

TRINIDAD & TOBAGO // Popular after a party, particularly around carnival, and ideal as a portable snack while liming (the Trinidadian art of doing nothing but talking, eating and drinking with friends), corn soup can be a meal too, because of the abundance of filling ingredients. Ears of corn, pureed corn and split peas are cooked up with other delights including – crucially – dumplings. Grab a creamy, bubbling Styrofoam cupful and bring that night of liming to a close, Trini style.

EAT IT ! ***At a corn-soup stand wherever there is a celebration in Trinidad.***

370

Shojin ryori: mindfulness on the menu

JAPAN // When Chinese Buddhist monks arrived in 13th-century Japan, they brought with them thoughtful ideas about food that still resonate today. *Shojin ryori* means 'food of devotion' and is the application of Zen Buddhist principles to cuisine. It's served at temples open to the public. As well as the spiritual awareness that underpins its preparation, *shojin ryori* reflects the Zen emphasis on harmony: these delicious meals are balanced in flavour, colour and nutrition.

☛ EAT IT ! ***Dine with monks at the Buddhist temple on Mount Takao. 2177 Takao-machi, Hachioji City, Tokyo.***

371

See seswaa simmer over an open fire in Botswana

BOTSWANA // Botswana is better known for its natural assets than its cuisine. But everyone must eat and, if possible, eat well. The simplest way to do this, Botswana folks discovered, was to slow-cook meat on the bone, traditionally on a pot of bubbling water over an open fire. Salt is added to soften the meat until it is pliant enough to pummel into the finished *seswaa*. Served alongside *pap* (stiffened cornmeal), *seswaa* appears at just about any kind of occasion in the country.

☛ EAT IT ! ***The Courtyard Restaurant at handicrafts centre Botswanacraft in Gaborone usually cooks up a tasty seswaa.***

372

Mix and match to your palate's content in Bali

INDONESIA // The magic of *nasi campur* (mixed rice) is that you don't have to choose just one thing off the menu. This Balinese meal starts with a scoop of rice (hopefully from the island's paddies), and from there, you could add a few sticks of *sate lilit* (minced meat satay), some spicy soybean tempeh, stir-fried vegetables, grilled fish, hard-boiled eggs and chilli sauce, then clean your hands and dig in with your shrimp or prawn cracker. Then do it all again with different ingredients.

☛ EAT IT ! ***You'll often find the best nasi campur at the humble roadside stalls known as warungs that dot the Balinese landscape.***

372

373

Don't stop the party: Brazil's bacalhau bar food

BRAZIL // Socialising is integral to eating in Brazil, and many merry-makers do not want to break up a party with a sit-down meal. Enter the *bolinho de bacalhau*, a fried salt cod ball so time-consuming to make well that Brazilians usually have them when out. Pop one in with barely a pause in conversation, and if it is crispy outside with a creamy cod-blessed centre, served with lime and knocked back with a cold *chope* (draught beer), the evening will likely proceed swimmingly.

☛ EAT IT ! ***In many bars across almost every city in the country, from around 8pm when happy hour generally kicks off.***

374

Snack on Finnish-style tapas in Helsinki's Juuri

FINLAND // Having created the new food concept, Helsinki restaurant Ravintola Juuri has now popularised the entrée or small plate known as *sapakset* or *sapas*: Finnish tapas. The idea is to resuscitate many of the country's overlooked food traditions in a fun, modern format. Pull up a chair and welcome herring with beets and apple, burbot (a fish found in Finland's icy waters) and rainbow trout with horseradish. Modernist local hero Alvar Aalto would surely have approved.

☛ EAT IT ! ***Juuri is snugly located in central Helsinki, and is open for lunch and dinner.*** *Korkeavuorenkatu 27.*

Share a vast platter of plov in any Uzbeki town

UZBEKISTAN // For all its granular simplicity, *plov* is an obsession in Uzbekistan. Served from *kazans* (cauldrons) and dished up ubiquitously at restaurants, the dish is an amalgam of rice, carrots, onions and bits of meat, all awash in oil. Every region of the country has a distinct *plov* style, so expect a slightly different experience and flavours as you travel. *Plov* typically comes piled on a shared *lagan* (platter), from where you spoon it on to your plate.

☛ EAT IT ! ***Tashkent's Central Asian Plov Centre has plov from across the country; lunch only.*** *Cnr Abdurashidov and Ergashev.*

376

Descend a Welsh mountain for fruity bara brith

UK // This Welsh fruity favourite is a teatime sensation at quaint cafes across the country, and is just what you need after trekking in the Becon Beacons scaling one of Wales' fabulous peaks. Translated as 'speckled bread' *bara brith* is regarded by some as a cake. Whatever its genus, it's been around for centuries. The dough is made using flour, yeast and butter and can be left to rise for up to two hours. Mixed with a blend of tea, spices and dried fruit, it's then baked to moist perfection.

EAT IT ! ***Everywhere across Wales. In Camarthen, Y Pantri's version on Jacksons Lane is a succulent slice of Wales.***

377

Blaff: the day-after fish dish from French Guiana

FRENCH GUIANA // Think: the day after a party in a chilled-out, sultry island climate, and your drowsy reverie is interrupted by 'Blaff!' – the sound of a fish plunking into a pot. This is Caribbean comfort food at its best, made from fresh snapper, tuna or mackerel, marinated in lime juice with chillies and garlic. Then it's poached to make tender fish in a hangover-healing broth. It's popular throughout the region but perfected with the European influences of French Guiana.

EAT IT ! ***Small, local restaurants in Cayenne and St-Laurent-du-Maroni are your best hunting grounds.***

However you say it, gâteau aux noix is a nutty delight

FRANCE // Like most things in life, walnut cake sounds much more delicious (sexier, even) when spoken in French. Fortunately, the great taste of *gâteau aux noix* is the same whatever language you speak. For centuries, those who live in the Dordogne, southwest France, have incorporated the humble walnut into their lives. From walnut oil, which is used in this heavenly cake, to walnut wine, locals claim it's not only a taste of the earth, but the secret to health and vitality.

EAT IT ! ***Visit Moulin à huile de noix – a working walnut oil farm. Route de Saint-Céré, Les Landes, 46600 Martel.***

© Hemis / Alamy Stock Photo

© Lonely Planet / Andrew Montgomery

379

Invest in the juicy taste of oysters Rockefeller in New Orleans

USA // Based on personal experience, New Orleans is the kind of town where a stranger in a bar will buy you a drink because you remind them of an obscure indie musician from their town, and where Dr John drops in for an impromptu piano set. It's a musician's town. A foodie's town. A good-time town. And an oyster town. Fried in po' boys, raw with a dash of Tabasco, chargrilled or doused in vodka, things are done to oysters in the Big Easy, and none more famously than what's done to them at Antoine's, the 19th-century restaurant where oysters Rockefeller was invented. Drowned in a butter and herb sauce, topped with breadcrumbs and baked, the dish of native Gulf oysters was named Rockefeller by creator Jules Alciatore, 'because I know no other name rich enough for their richness'.

EAT IT ! *At Antoines, 713 Rue St Louis St. Then try the chargrilled variety at Felix's Oyster Bar, 739 Iberville St. Both New Orleans.*

© Lyudmila Zotova / Alamy Stock Photo

© Ariadne Van Zandbergen / Alamy Stock Photo

380

Fuel your South African adventures with biltong

SOUTH AFRICA // You're not likely to starve on the roads of modern-day South Africa, but setting off on a great route like the Garden Route or Limpopo's Waterburg Meander without a stash of biltong in your bag would be madness. Similar to jerky but not as sweet, this preserved produce was originally made by indigenous peoples as a way of prolonging their meat stores, and picked up enthusiastically by European colonists. Over the years the method of salting, spicing and drying has remained largely the same. The biltong you'll taste today has been spiced with black pepper, coriander, cloves, salt and vinegar, and usually the meat used is beef, as it's cheaper and easier to rear than game. That said, being Africa, biltong is also made with more exotic animals such as springbok and wildebeest, as well as chicken and fish. It's tasty and cheap, perfect for cash-poor hungry travellers.

EAT IT ! *Buy it at supermarkets to eat whenever the mood takes you or stock up if you have a long journey ahead of you.*

381

The sensational apricot harvest of northern Pakistan

PAKISTAN // In the far northern reaches of Pakistan, the locals go bananas for apricots. And for good reason, because the apricots grown in mountainous Gilgit-Pakistan are some of the sweetest, juiciest fruit you'll find. The average household has some 15 apricot trees, and families here have been cultivating the fruits for centuries, if not millennia. Find different cultivars in each village market, with fresh ones appearing from March; only dried fruit is available in winter.

EAT IT ! *Hunza Valley has been described as heaven on Earth, and is where you'll find the A+ apricots.*

382

Reignite a love for Italy at Osteria Enoteca Ai Artisti

ITALY // Tucked in the architectural heartland of romance, intimate Osteria Enoteca Ai Artisti is preserving Venice's culinary heritage. Chef Masahiro Homma's menu changes according to available local produce, but whether it's baked turbot with artichoke sauce or anchovy and Roquefort tortellini with pea cream, his sauces are a masterclass. The Japanese-born chef also only serves wines made without chemicals, so your wellbeing is as cared for as your tastebuds.

EAT IT ! *Experience the aura of Venice on the Rio De La Toletta canal. Osteria Enoteca Ai Artisti, Fondamenta della Toletta 1169/A.*

383

Find fiery balti's Birmingham birthplace

UK // The Birmingham Balti Association defines it as a fast-cooked curry dish that can be made using chicken, fish, meat or vegetables. While the association failed to secure EU protection for the name, you won't find a curry like it outside England's West Midlands. After slow-cooking the meat off the bone, baltis are then cooked over a high heat and come from the kitchen dramatically sizzling. You eat from the wok-like plate, the balti, in which the curry has been cooked.

EAT IT ! *Shabar Restaurant is one of Birmingham's oldest curry dens, with a proud history of accolades. Arden Oak Rd.*

384

Chongqing's 50,000 hotpot restaurateurs can't be wrong

CHINA // Some say the best place to view Chongqing is from a boat on the waters of the Yangtze River, especially after dark, when the Chinese megacity's forest of skyscrapers throws a neon glow into the night sky. But the real Chongqing experience is at the foot of those buildings, in the backstreets and alleys where the smell of chilli and oil hangs in the subtropical air, and locals cram into restaurants for bowls of the city's speciality, Chongqing hotpot. Chongqing was once part of Sichuan province, and it only takes a mouthful of lip-numbing broth to recognise the link to its more famous neighbour.

The dish might have been invented to combat winter chills, but it's enjoyed year-round, as if the locals take pride in staring down summer's humidity. Diners sit around their table with a bubbling, chilli- and Sichuan pepper-spiked soup at its centre, and dip ingredients in to cook. Beef, pork, fish, tofu and lotus root are staples, but culinary adventurers (or visitors who can't read Mandarin menus) might sample pig's brain and kidney, beef tripe, duck intestines and other offal.

A final layer of flavour comes via an aromatic dipping sauce of sesame oil, garlic and shallot. You can ask for your hotpot to be not too spicy – '*bu tai la*' is the magic phrase – but it'll still have plenty of kick! Locally brewed lager is a popular accompaniment, which, along with the communal, DIY nature of the dining experience, might account for the buzzing exuberance of some of these eateries. Considering the popular estimate of 50,000 hotpot restaurants in the municipality, that's a lot of chilli and pepper, a lot of dipping and a lot of buzz.

EAT IT ! ***Mang Hot Pot (Zhongxing Lu, 10 Wangyeshibao) is one of the tastiest, spiciest and liveliest hotpot restaurants in the city – in an alley in the midst of a flower market, it's a culinary adventure.***

384

385

Tackle a mouth-melting meat pie during an Aussie rules football match at Melbourne Cricket Ground

AUSTRALIA // A word of warning before you dive in... the meat inside this pastry case is as hot as molten lava, so eating what's an Australian culinary icon takes some practice and dexterity, not least because you'll be eating it alongside 90,000 roaring, jostling (hot and bothered) Aussie rules fans. So follow these instructions: buy a pie just before quarter time so you can get back to your seat while the players take a timeout – this should ensure your neighbours aren't gesticulating wildly at the players or the umpires on the field. Open the plastic bag, careful to avoid third-degree burns, and gently nibble at one of the corners to release some steam. Do not, under any circumstances, bite from the bottom. When a little time has passed, gingerly take larger bites. Don't try and catch any wayward meat with your hands, or allow it to fall on your knees, it will burn through denim. By about halfway the danger should have abated and you're free to eat like a normal human being, finishing off just as the siren sounds for the second quarter.

☛ EAT IT ! *Kiosks are located throughout the stadium and once you have your pie, you'd be mad not to grab a mouth-cooling beer.*

386

For an officially approved minced-meat meal, sign up for Helsinki vorschmack

FINLAND // There are many variations of this minced-meat meal in Eastern Europe, but the Finns' *vorschmack* perhaps sounds the most interesting (and, pace Finnish folk, least appealing), featuring as it does beef, herring, onions and anchovies – usually served with potatoes, beetroot, pickles and *smetana* (soured cream). For the best *vorschmack* in the land, book a table at the top-floor Restaurant Savoy in Helsinki. Here the dish was made famous in the early 20th century by Finland's architect of independence Marshal Mannerheim after he demanded it be included on the menu. He was so impressed with the interpretation of the dish that it never came off the menu in his lifetime, and is still just as it was in Mannerheim's day.

EAT IT ! ***In Helsinki's iconic Ravintola Savoy, Eteläesplanadi 14. Admire local hero Alvar Aalto's interior design while you're waiting.***

Kürtőskalács: Hungary's convoluted chimney cake

HUNGARY // If ever there was a contender for one of those crazy European cakes none of the amateur bakers have ever heard of on *The Great British Bake Off*, the *kürtőskalács* is it. It looks like the stovepipe/chimney its name is derived from, so the amateur bakers would need to start by wrapping one long strip of sugar-coated sweet yeast dough around a chimney-shaped mould, and basting continuously with melted butter as the golden tube turned over a charcoal spit. As that suggests, it's very hard to make, which is why it used to be a celebration cake in Hungary (and Transylvania, from where it's said to have originated in the Middle Ages). Nowadays, every bakery in Budapest has a range of varieties but find a street vendor with an original charcoal spit to taste the real thing.

EAT IT ! ***At a Christmas market. The rest of the year, from the Körösfői Kürtőskalács stand outside Budapest's Buda castle.***

388

Lahpot thoke: a plate of tea-leaf salad in Yangon

MYANMAR // There's good reason to eat *lahpet thoke* on the streets of Yangon or overlooking Inle Lake, or anywhere else in the culinary melting pot of Myanmar, and that's because you won't find the ingredients anywhere else. Usually called tea-leaf salad in English, the base of this national delicacy is pickled tea leaves mixed with peas, spices, vegetables and peanuts. Served with white rice, it's often eaten at the end of a meal. The caffeine also acts as a great pick-me-up.

EAT IT ! ***You'll find it at most Yangon restaurants, but tea shops here offer a livelier experience.***

389

Chew on salt water taffy, a Victorian-era candy crush

USA // Since the 1880s, American kids of all ages have indulged their sweet tooth with salt water taffy. A chewy candy, it originally came in molasses and chocolate flavours, quickly followed by dozens of other flavours. While salt and water are ingredients, taffys don't actually contain any saltwater – the name stems from a 19th-century marketing ploy in which a clumsy candymaker's assistant replaced tap water with salt water when boiling up the mixture for the sweets.

EAT IT ! ***Buy from Fralinger's Original Salt Water Taffy, the Atlantic City boardwalk store that made it famous.***

390

Eat éclade de moules by the Bay of Biscay

FRANCE // Along France's west coast, among the beaches that face the Bay of Biscay, you'll find *éclade de moules*, an intricate mosaic-like display of mussels in their shells. The molluscs are arranged on a plank of pine soaked in seawater before being covered in pine needles, which are then set alight. The smouldering needles give the mussels a piquant smokiness which can only be improved upon by a chunk of crusty bread with butter and a glass of white wine.

EAT IT ! ***From beachside seafood restaurants along the Bay of Biscay.***

Rowley Leigh

Rowley Leigh is a London-based chef and restaurateur, as well as an award-winning food writer.

MY FRIEND MARIGOLD'S SNIPE PUDDING; WOKING, UK A rich steamed suet pudding of steak and snipe, cooked for seven hours – it's the sort of dish that is inconceivable in a restaurant, but the essence of proper English cooking.

OYSTERS, GRILLED LANGOUSTE, BÉARNAISE SAUCE; ARCACHON BAY, FRANCE It's all about spirit of place, eating these on a brasserie terrace overlooking the oyster beds. Accompany with Château Carbonnieux – a white Bordeaux from down the road.

MUTTON BIRYANI, PESHAWAR At age 19, the combination of marijuana, very hot chillies and a realisation that we were only the white people in the neighbourhood was a sort of coming-of-age epiphany.

SOUP DUMPLINGS (XIAOLONGBAO), HONG KONG Whether you get them at the China Club or a dim sum hole-in-the-wall in North Point, I love these little dumplings, dipped in vinegar, and the intense broth that explodes in your mouth.

PERCEBES, MADRID These northern Iberian barnacle clams (below) are sweet, rich and the ultimate umami.

© Shutterstock/JM Travel Photography

391

Got the munchies in Montréal? There's a Québécois fix for that – the cheesy chips-and-gravy dish, poutine

CANADA // If you think the USA holds all the cards when it comes to stoner food then you haven't eaten Québécois poutine. The origins of this much-loved cure for the munchies are generally attributed to a truck driver looking for a satisfying meal to go. The result? A plate of fries topped with cheese curd, covered in gravy. From these humble beginnings the poutine has exploded in popularity to the point that there's now an annual festival held in its honour in Montréal.

In the snow-bound city, the love of poutine is understandable. But it's not just Québec that has fallen for the greasy fries – poutine pops up on menus around the country.

If you're new to the dish then start at Montréal La Banquise, where there are more than 30 different varieties to choose from. It's not just La Banquise that's taken the dish and run with it. It has evolved to include BBQ pork poutine, fried shrimp and lobster poutine, mushroom poutine and even upmarket combinations featuring confit duck and and other luxuries. Or how about a poutine where the cheese curd is fried before adding it to the fries? There is no end to the inventiveness where Québec's carbohydrates are concerned.

EAT IT ! *At La Banquise, 994 Rue Rachel E, Montréal, Québec.*

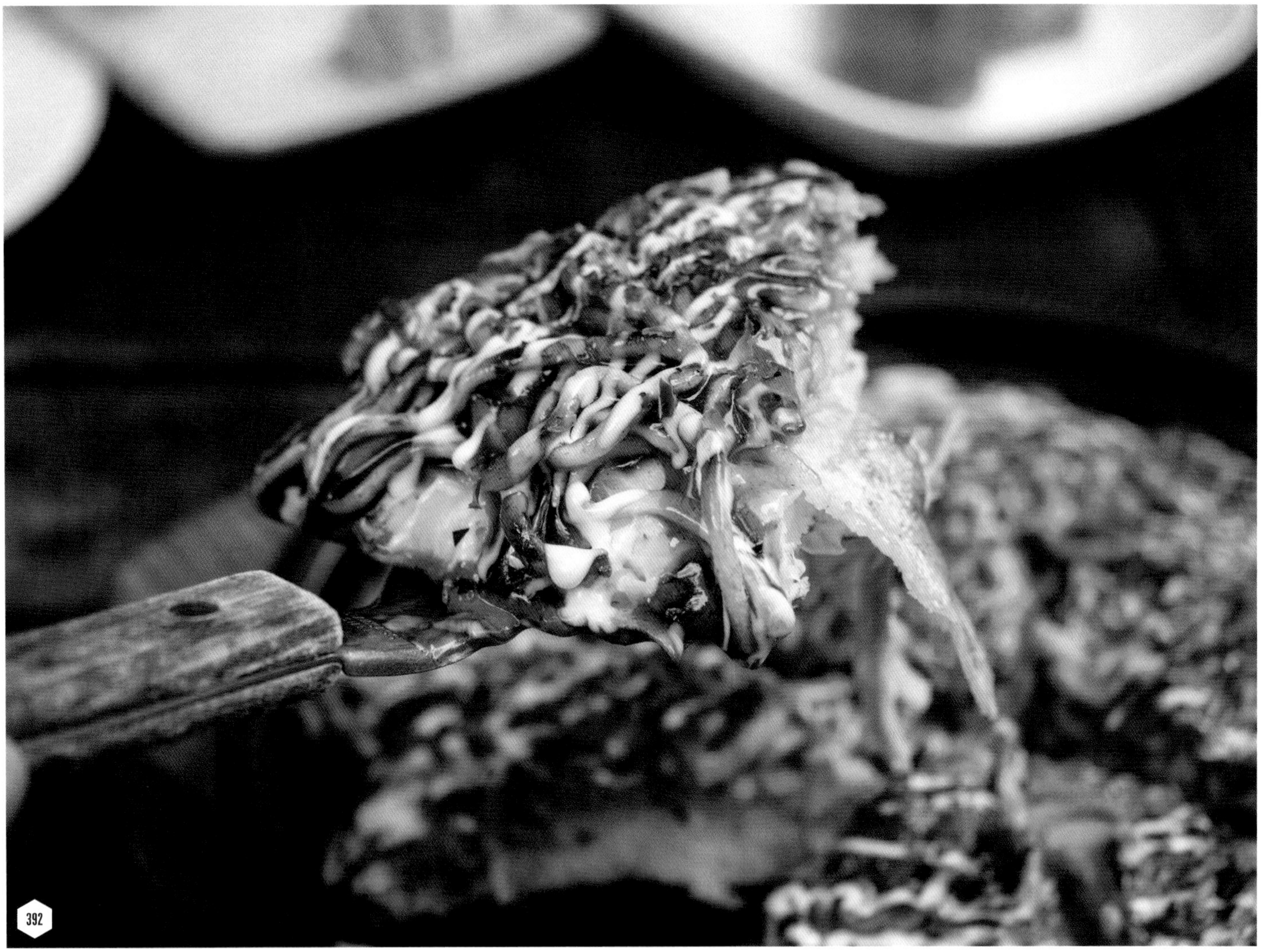

© Getty Images / artran

392

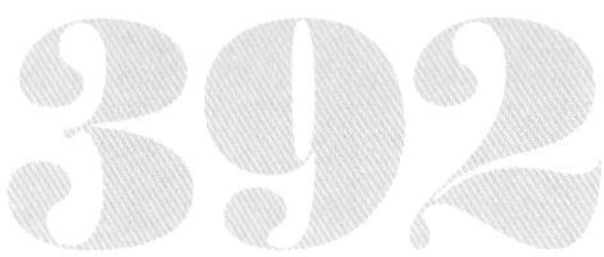

In Osaka and Hiroshima, the masters of refinement make messy with grilled okonomiyaki

JAPAN // Is it a pancake? Is it a fritter? Is it a griddle cake? It can be all or none of these things as *okonomiyaki* is named after the Japanese word *okonomi*, meaning 'what you like', and 'yaki', meaning grill. So, it's just that: stuff you like, grilled. Japanese cuisine is famed for its freshness, texture and delicate presentation so it's a surprise to find the scruffy-looking *okonomiyaki* topping many people's list of favourite Japanese snacks. The most common version is from Osaka, where the dish originated, and is made up of a mixed batter with flour, egg, dashi, *nagaimo* (a type of yam), cabbage, spring onion, pork belly, seafood and mochi cheese. The mixture is fried on the grill and topped with a sweet sauce, bonito flakes, mayonnaise and pickled ginger. You'll find this everywhere in Japan but for something a bit different try the version from Hiroshima. Here, the cabbage, pork and seafood is layered and topped with udon noodles, a fried egg and the *okonomiyaki* sauce. A delicious twist on a seasoned favourite.

☛ EAT IT ! *At Okonomiyaki Kiji, Kita, Oyodonaka, 1 Chome-1-90, Osaka; Nagata-ya, Naka Ward, Otemachi, 1 Chome-7-19, Hiroshima.*

© Getty Images / BirgerNiss

393

Live la vida buena in Los Angeles and go veggie with your tacos

USA // Perhaps no dish is as associated with Mexican American culture as the taco, and though never considered a health food, your basic street-truck taco is actually surprisingly healthy. Add to the mix vegetarian and vegan options and the humble taco actually comes close to artisanal market salad bar levels of healthiness… which, of course, is what you'd expect to find in LA. A vegetarian taco's protein usually comes from black beans, pinto beans, or even tofu, while the veggie element will usually be a combination of crisp lettuce and a spicy salsa made with tomatoes, onions, chillies and garlic, sometimes served with creamy, tangy guacamole. Holding it all together is an outer shell made from crisp corn, or a softer shell made from flour.

EAT IT ! *Danny Trejo's LA-based Trejo's Tacos, 1048 South La Brea Ave, is boldly creative when it comes to vegan options.*

393

394

394

Find your stomach for an ancient Peruvian foodstuff – cuy, or whole guinea pig

PERU // In Peru, the guinea pig is serious culinary business – *cuy* has been part of the Andean diet for more than 5000 years, is celebrated as healthy and tasty, and gourmet ones are fed exclusively on an alfalfa diet to ensure the meat is tender. The common way you'll see the *cuy* prepared is flattened under stones and then fried or roasted over hot coals or a spit. In both cases the animal is cooked whole, with the head and tiny feet left intact – which does makes the experience of eating one a bit challenging, if you're not one for looking your lunch in the eye (or teeth). It tastes great though, like a cross between chicken and rabbit.

EAT IT ! *Get past the macabre presentation to discover tender meat and crispy skin at Kusikuy, Calle Amargura 140, Cusco.*

395

Bites on the bullet: ekiben bento boxes

↓

JAPAN // In many countries, train station food means soggy sandwiches. In Japan? How about a geometric grid of bite-sized morsels. This is the *ekiben*, a type of bento box made for passengers on Japan's ultra-high-speed Shinkansen trains. As you zoom through the countryside and cities, you'll marvel over these mini culinary artworks. Every piece reflects Japan's love of craftsmanship and each region has its own speciality, changing with the seasons.

EAT IT !
Before catching your train, head to Tokyo Station's Ekibenya Matsuri for your ekiben.

The Olot eatery that elevated a Catalan classic

SPAIN // Across Catalan country, locals eat *xato*, the tomato-based sauce with almond and roasted hazelnut, for breakfast, lunch and dinner; spread over a warm *bocadillo*, a salad or local fish. But it's in Olot, the provincial capital of Girona, that chef Fina Puigdevall created its perfect fine dining accompaniment: homemade buckwheat bread stuffed with a fresh seafood salad. Ask for the *Xato con Panecillo de Alforfón*.

☛ EAT IT ! *Run from the family homestead, Restaurant Les Cols aims to transform ultra-local produce into gourmet masterpieces. Mas les Cols, Ctra De la Canya, Olot, Girona.*

397

Make a date for your dairy: New England ice cream

USA // For kids (and sugar-loving adults) in New England, summer means one thing: the opening of the seasonal ice-cream shops. From the meadows of Vermont to the coast of Maine, the region is dotted with small, family-run farms, stands and 'dairy bars' selling ice-cream homemade using the milk of local cows. Flavours include maple walnut, black raspberry, Indian pudding and Grape-Nuts – yes, ice cream loaded with nubbly bits of Grape-Nuts cereal.

☛ EAT IT ! *Kimball Farm has been scooping since 1939, with four locations in Massachusetts and New Hampshire.*

Eat like The King with a Belgian mitraillette

BELGIUM // *Friteries* across Belgium have made the nation's answer to the Elvis sandwich their own – note that the *mitraillette* is not for a first date nor any situation that demands a modicum of decorum. Two things are constant: the sliced white baguette and mountain of fries. Then it's a free for all; add your choice of fried meat, then cover in sauce. You can always add some token salad items if you feel guilty. As Elvis would say, thank you very much.

☛ EAT IT ! *Enjoy this late-night indulgence at Fritland, Rue Henri Maus 49, Brussels.*

399

Roast meats in Hong Kong: vegetarians take cover!

CHINA // Mistaking a traditional Hong Kong roast meat joint for any other type of eatery is nearly impossible. If the sight of whole amber ducks, golden chickens and long slabs of pork, each hanging in the window and dripping with their own fat, doesn't clue you into the carnivorous feast to come, their combined aroma wafting through the doors definitely will. Though everyone has their preference, the serious HK BBQ aficionado will go for a mixed platter containing slices of all three for a tasty barnyard reunion served over white rice with a token dash of green vegetables. Hong Kong-style roast duck differs from its Beijing counterpart in cooking method, so expect a higher fat content, crispy skin and definitely no thin pancakes. The chicken should be light and moist, and the pork deliciously marbled and fatty.

EAT IT ! *Lung Kee Restaurant, 5 Gage St, Central, in Hong Kong is the place to go for this traditional HK feast.*

400–500

400

Pick up America's top hot dog in Motor City

USA // Ain't no boardwalk or Atlantic views on Detroit's Coney Island, but there is a good reason to visit, and that's to sample one of the best hot dogs in the country. This Coney Island classic doesn't settle for mustard and ketchup or even onions and cheese. Instead it comes lathered in ground beef chilli, with chopped onions and mustard. The credit for its invention probably goes to Greek immigrants who hit on the idea when moving through Coney Island to settle in Detroit.

EAT IT ! ***Try one of these shirt-stainers at the long-standing Lafayette Coney Island, 118 W Lafayette Blvd, Detroit, Michigan.***

401

Spam in Japan? It's got to be goya champuru

JAPAN // A *champuru* is an Okinawan dish of stir-fried tofu, vegetables, egg and meat or fish. The two distinguishing ingredients that make *goya champuru* stand out are the bitter melon called *goya*, and Spam. American GIs stationed in Okinawa during WWII were issued Spam as part of their rations, and by the time they left, the locals were hooked on the tinned meat. It's a dish tied so closely to Okinawa that you won't find a re-creation as tasty anywhere else.

EAT IT ! ***The southern island is your goal – make your way to Yunangi, 3-3-3 Kumoji, Naha 900-0015, Okinawa Prefecture.***

402

Binge on Moreton Bay bugs in Brisbane

AUSTRALIA // These strange, flat-headed lobsters might not appear appetising when pulled from the ocean at Moreton Bay, near Brisbane, but split them in half lengthwise, place them on a barbecue (shell-side down) for a few minutes, crack open a cold beer, and you're on your way towards Aussie food nirvana. To serve, slather the bugs in warmed butter and a squeeze of half a lemon and pick out the sweet, fleshy tails. Best enjoyed with mates at a beach or backyard barbie.

EAT IT ! ***Gambaro Seafood Restaurant, 33 Caxton St, Brisbane, serves a $60 plate of barbecued bugs.***

401

403

Savour tamales in a Mexican restaurant

MEXICO // There's nothing better to unwrap than freshly cooked *tamales*, a dish that embraced the slow cooking movement before the phrase was coined. Prior to assembling the package, the outer wrapping of corn husk must be soaked overnight to make it pliable. In the morning the husks are stuffed with *tamale* dough and meat, and the ends tied together with thin strips of husks before being steamed. Unwrapping the *tamale* reveals delicious soft pork or chicken.

☛ EAT IT ! ***A staple of Mexican restaurants throughout North America, it's also a snack sold by street vendors in Central America.***

404

Perk up your day in Penang with roti canai

MALAYSIA // Greet the morning in Malaysia with *roti canai*, a flaky, ghee-enriched pancake usually served with a bowl of curry or lentils. It's a speciality of street and hawker centre (outdoor food court) vendors, who spread the batter on hot griddles so quickly their hands blur. If you're not a morning curry person, order a sweet roti with bananas, durian or a drizzle of sticky condensed milk. Look for the *mamak* (Muslim Indian) stall with the longest line.

☛ EAT IT ! ***Head to the Little India quarter in George Town, on the Malaysian island of Penang, for primo roti canai.***

405

Fall for biang biang noodles in Xi'an

CHINA // *Biang biang* noodles are wider and thicker than any other. To get the noodle to its required length, chefs employ a fascinating technique of pulling and stretching. Watch them do it in Xi'an's eclectic Muslim Quarter and learn why they're called *biang biang* – it refers to the sound of the noodle slapping against the counter as it's being made. A typical dish consists of just one noodle served with hot chillies or peppers and a soy-themed sauce.

☛ EAT IT ! ***At the cafes and from the stalls and hawkers around Huimin St, Xi'an.***

406

Get the low-down on lox bagels at Russ & Daughters in NYC

USA // What makes a New York bagel genuine? Two words: preparation and water. Bagel-making takes time, from kneading to lengthy pre-bake proofing to allow the dough to rise and ferment, to boiling in seasoned water then baking. As for water, as anyone who loves true NYC bagels or pizza will tell you, NYC H20 is key thanks to the mineral content in local water. This creates the bagel's slightly crusty exterior and soft, doughy interior. Where lox is concerned, nothing less than thinly sliced Nova smoked salmon will do. Add a schmear of cream cheese, tomato, onions and capers, and the result is a mixture of salty, sweet and sour flavours that perfectly represents the infinite cultural variety of the Big Apple.

For the real deal, head to the Lower East Side's Russ & Daughters; the quintessential NY deli has been serving lox bagels here since 1920. Don't be dissuaded by the brusque service: grab your bagel and take a bite on New York's mean streets.

EAT IT ! *At historical and culinary institution Russ & Daughters 179 E Houston, New York.*

407

Wallaby tail soup, Melbourne's multicultural hit

AUSTRALIA // Night-time in Melbourne's Chinatown and neon signs reflect in puddles along the laneways. On Market Lane, Flower Drum has served food for over 40 years. One of its classic dishes sums up the entwining of foreign cuisines with modern Australia. Flower Drum's double-boiled wallaby tail soup features a mound of Flinders Island wallaby tail circled by a rich broth, with goji berries, ginger and wild yam: Australian resources and Cantonese know-how.

EAT IT ! *Flower Drum restaurant is at 17 Market Lane, Melbourne.*

408

In Guinea-Bissau? Refresh yourself with cashew fruit

GUINEA-BISSAU // The weird thing about cashew nuts is that they grow alongside a larger fruit, sometimes known as the cashew apple. This fruit is edible but it goes off in one day, so you've probably never heard of it, yet alone seen one in a supermarket. But if you're in Guinea-Bissau, the tropical West African nation celebrated for its cashews, you'll come across them everywhere. Locals drink their juice for refreshment but it's also a desiccant that dries your mouth.

EAT IT ! *Ask local villagers for a taste of the fruit, and wash it down with some cashew beer.*

409

Share pizza with Hollywood stars at LA's Spago

USA // Lights, camera, action! As one of a handful of restaurants in Los Angeles to be awarded two Michelin stars, Spago has the culinary credentials to justify its popularity with Hollywood's elite. Since opening on Sunset Strip in 1982, chef Wolfgang Puck's innovative eatery has been a beacon for movie icons, music stars and movers and shakers in the City of Angels. The alluringly unpretentious fine-dining menu includes Spago's signature smoked salmon pizza.

EAT IT ! *If you can get a reservation, Spago Beverly Hills is absolutely the place to be. 176 N Canon Drive, Beverly Hills, CA.*

410

Discover a locally focused food culture in the Faroes

FAROE ISLANDS // Being remote and at the mercy of wild weather conditions, the Faroese people have learned to be imaginative and resourceful when it comes to food. There's a strong ethos concerned with supporting local producers and foraging for unique ingredients. In 2017, the Faroe Islands received its first Michelin star, awarded to Koks restaurant for its innovative 17-course tasting menu designed around local produce. The restaurant, which in April 2018 relocated to an 18th-century lakeside farmhouse in the wild valley of Leynavatn, employs an experienced staff of foragers, divers, fisher people and farmers to help craft a unique menu based around the Islands' sometimes brutal seasons. The whole experience is a testament to tenacity, taste and pride of place.

☛ EAT IT ! ***Kok's Restaurant is a 20-minute drive from the capital, Tórshavn. Frammi vio Gjónna, Leynavatn, Faroe Islands.***

Learn the art of prepping Korean kimchi, the country's ubiquitous foodstuff

SOUTH KOREA // In South Korea, *kimchi*, the chilli-infused, fermented cabbage mixture, is an obsession; there are hundreds of varieties, thousands of family recipes and nary a table that doesn't sport a jar so that the condiment can be added to anything and everything. The traditional *kimchi* preparation process is labour-intensive but often shared among female family members as part of a communal prepping session. It's an invaluable lesson if you're lucky enough to be involved. When the cabbage and radish have been cleaned and salted, the individual leaves are coated in a thick spicy chilli paste that includes garlic, ginger and *aekjeot* (fermented fish sauce). When completely covered, the vegetables are packed into a jar and sealed to start the fermentation process. *Kimchi* jars were once buried in the ground over winter to keep cool, and defrosted during summer, but these days a refrigerator does the trick. Once suitably fermented, anything from three days to a year later, it's ready for your table.

EAT IT ! ***From any and every South Korean table, whether at home or out, as an accompaniment to pretty much everything.***

411

412

Eat at Ulo with a view of the greatest show on ice

GREENLAND // Few sights are as striking as Ilulissat's glacial ice fjord. View it from a table at Restaurant Ulo, in the Hotel Arctic. If you can take your eyes off the giant floating ice sculptures, you'll see that the food in front of you reflects the exceptional surrounds. Priding itself on traditional cooking, Ulo showcases unusual Greenland fare such as sustainably caught Atlantic wolf-fish, cured reindeer and Arctic Labrador tea, simply prepared to let the ingredients shine.

☛ EAT IT ! ***With a view at Restaurant Ulo, Hotel Arctic, Ilulissat.***

413

Be an early bird at Marché Bastille to catch a poulet roti

FRANCE // At Bastille Market in Paris, the juicy spatchcocked birds slowly turning on the rotisserie lure unsuspecting market goers close with the aroma of crispy chicken skin, and a hint of citrus and ginger marinade in the air. Once they're close enough to see the barbecuing birds then... wham, it's too late to resist. The chickens are almost caramel in colour and, for flightless birds, they sure do move quickly – most are sold by 10am.

☛ EAT IT ! ***From Catherine the Chicken Lady in Marché Bastille, 8 boulevard Richard Lenoir, Paris.***

414

Tour Tallinn and break for Baojaam's fusion

ESTONIA / Fusion cuisine doesn't always win but Mihkel Rand, Tallinn-based recipient of Estonia's Best Chef Award, has hit the jackpot by merging Nordic ingredients and Chinese *bao* at his tiny market stall Baojaam. There's a small menu of fluffy *bao* with fillings such as crispy crumbed chicken and coriander, *char sui* pork, octopus and cucumber, and flank steak with paprika and walnuts, which all sell like hot cakes. Grab one and explore the rest of the market.

☛ EAT IT ! ***At Baojaam, which is inside the Balti Jaam Turg market hall in the Estonian capital, Tallinn.***

© Lonely Planet / Lottie Davies

© Shutterstock / lembi

115

Chase cicchetti in Venice

↓

ITALY // Venetians may share their city with millions of visitors but they keep some treats for themselves. One such are *cicchetti*, the bite-sized morsels served in the locals' *bacari* (bars). Take a vaporetto to Cannaregio, an off-the-beaten path neighbourhood and seek out a *bacaro* like Ai Divini, with its secluded courtyard opening on to the canal. Here, try *cicchetti* such as salt cod on *crostini* or the various cheeses.

☛ EAT IT !
Ai Divini is at Cannaregio 5905 in Venice.

416

Enjoy every shade of tlacoyo in Mexico City

MEXICO // Market vendors in Mexico City use a covered basket to keep these torpedo-shaped tortillas warm and fresh. Stuffed inside are tasty fillings like refried black beans, cheese and chicharrons. Traditional *tlacoyos* are served with a splash of salsa, but vendors in Mexico City also pile on fresh chillies, cheese and green *pasilla*. The maize missiles come in yellow, orange and blue due to different coloured kernels in the cornmeal.

EAT IT ! ***Discover the tlacoyos of your dreams on the street above Chilpancingo Metro station. Hipódromo, Mexico City.***

417

Honour an empanada in Argentina

ARGENTINA // Doesn't empanada sound more appealing than pasty? Even its translation – 'wrapped in bread' – is alluring. In Argentina, there are fierce debates about what the ingredients should be, and in the northern province town of Salta the humble snack even has its own celebration day on 4 April. So where better to try it than in this lively city ringed by Andean peaks, red-rock valleys and vineyards?

EAT IT ! ***At one of the bars and cafes surrounding the Plaza 9 de Julio, Salta's main square and the town's heartbeat.***

418

Chill out in the Polish sun with a bowl of chlodnik

POLAND // In a country that endures bitter winters, where sub-zero temperatures are recorded for half the year, Poles make the most of the warm weather when it arrives. One dish that embodies this celebration of summer is the chilled, tangy beetroot soup, *chlodnik*. Its refreshingly sweet and sour flavours are perfect for a summer lunch. It's often bolstered with cucumber, radish, Swiss chard, dill and half a hard-boiled egg.

EAT IT ! ***At restaurants in Kraków that specialise in traditional cuisine.***

419

Go straight to the home of Kobe beef to choose from grilled or seared

JAPAN // Famous for its concentrated marbling of fat, Kobe beef has a worldwide reputation for incomparable tenderness and an almost-melting texture when cooked. The air of exclusivity around this breed of beef has been cultivated not least by the fact that it wasn't even exported until 2012. It's safe to say that one of the best places to sample the meat is in its home city. Kobe beef is best grilled over charcoal, *yakiniku*, or seared on an iron cooktop, *teppanyaki*. To get the softest texture, the meat is seared quickly, allowing the heat to melt the ribbons of fat, though some chefs cook it for longer to retain some structure. Most restaurants in Kobe serving the beef will offer different cuts and a choice of marinades and side dishes.

EAT IT ! *Kobe Nikusho Ichiya offers a relatively affordable chance to indulge in this generally expensive delicacy. Shimabun Bldg, BB Plaza annex, 4-2-7 Iwaya Nakamachi, Kobe Nada Ward, Hyogo.*

419

420

420

Gỏi cuốn to get you started in Vietnam

VIETNAM // It's virtually impossible to eat a bad meal in Ho Chi Minh City, where it can feel like every street is lined with either air-conditioned restaurants with throngs of happy diners sitting in cool comfort or food carts thronged with plastic stools street-side. Or both. Where to begin? Here's a tip: pick a place with satisfied-looking clientele and order some *goi cuon*. Everybody's favourite, these cold, fresh (not fried) rice-paper rolls are filled with vermicelli noodles, pork, prawn, lettuce, and herbs like basil and mint, and eaten with an accompanying nutty hoisin sauce and minced chilli. Dip in and enjoy.

EAT IT ! *At any busy restaurant in Ho Chi Minh City, where goi cuon are the quintessential Vietnamese starter.*

Pick up a slice of pizza, day or night, in New York City

USA // It's not the most authentic pizza you'll ever taste but it's a taste of authentic New York. We're not after a traditional-style, wood-fired piece of pizza in the Big Apple (though it's there if you want it; well, what isn't?), instead the pizza experience in NYC is all about giant slices, crisp on the crust but gooey and pliable enough towards the middle so that it can be folded in half and eaten on the go. Cutlery? Pfft. It all began at Lombardi's in Little Italy, Manhattan, in 1905 when Italian immigrant Gennaro Lombardi began selling slices of margarita from his deli. It didn't take long for wily New Yorkers to cotton on to one of the world's greatest foods, especially as it was good to go. It's still possible to grab a slice of history (and pie) from Lombardi's in NY's Nolita neighbourhood. Though many argue that Joe's, in Greenwich Village, has original New York style to rival the trailblazer.

EAT IT ! ***With your hands at Lombardi's, 32 Spring St; or Joe's, 7 Carmine St; both New York.***

© Jamie Mason / Alamy Stock Photo

© Ted Pink / Alamy Stock Photo

© peeterv / Getty Images

Make time for roadside akara amid Lagos' bustle

NIGERIA // Lagos, the capital city of Africa's most populous nation, is a heaving metropolis that's not for the faint-hearted. The streets can feel like a seething mass of traffic and people, and as a result many visitors stick to the tourist spots for sightseeing and hotel restaurants for dining, but we think you should brave the crowds and seek out a street vendor selling one of Nigeria's favourite snacks, *akara*. Made from crushed black-eyed beans mixed with chilli peppers, onion and salt, the rough-hewn balls are fried in palm oil. The taste can vary slightly from vendor to vendor; competition for business means they add secret ingredients like crayfish or yams to boost their popularity.

EAT IT ! ***Vendors cry out 'àkàrà-je!', which effectively means 'Come and get your akara!' in the Yoruba language.***

© Adrian Danciu

Andrew Zimmern

Andrew Zimmern is the creator and host of the long-running Bizarre Foods TV series.

POLLO AL CARBON, EL ALJIBE, HAVANA, CUBA This restaurant went so far downhill as a government-run eatery that the Castro regime invited the original owners back. The roast chicken has a lemony 'gravy' served with rice, beans and caramel sweet plantains.

ANYTHING AT BADJAO SEAFOOD HOUSE, PALAWAN, PHILIPPINES Fishing boats sink under the weight of clams, shrimp and lobster, as they manoeuvre underneath the restaurant to deliver their haul.

GRILLED STEAK, BAZAAR MEAT, LAS VEGAS I had a lot of opinions on where to get the best steak on Earth. Then I went to José Andrés' spot in Vegas and everything went topsy-turvy on me.

SHENG JIAN BAO, DA HU CHUN, SHANGHAI, CHINA All morning, the cooks here roll and shape dough into perfect discs, filling them with impeccably seasoned ground pork, whole shrimp, even clams.

MARINARA PIE, PIZZERIA BIANCO, PHOENIX, ARIZONA I've eaten at every pie shop and slice joint from Naples to New York City. But, proverbially with a gun to my head, I would take Bianco's over anyone else's.

©Shutterstock / Maksim Toome

423

Pig out on pork knuckle, sauerkraut and Bavarian beer

GERMANY // To the uninitiated, *schweinshaxe* – German pork knuckle – is slightly terrifying to gaze upon. It looks like food for a Viking, or an ogre; a veritable barrel of meat, covered in thick, ruddy skin, with a bone sticking out of the top like a handle. Yup, this is how they roll in Bavaria. Pork knuckle (AKA ham hock) is the lower portion of a pig's leg, slow-roasted until the skin is crunchy and the meat ready to slide off the bone. It's plunked on a plate atop a big ol' pile of sauerkraut and roast potatoes and served at the medieval taverns and beer halls of Bavaria along with stein after stein of frothy beer. It'll give you the energy, and drinking tolerance, of a 16th-century German peasant.

☛ EAT IT ! ***Fortify yourself with schweinshaxe and sauerkraut for a night of drinking at the Hofbräuhaus, Munich's venerable, kitschy and much-visited beer hall.***

© Shutterstock / Kzenon

© Getty Images / Richard Ernest Yap

424

Gimbap, South Korea's fish-free sushi substitute, is on a roll

SOUTH KOREA // Do you love the look of sushi but have never been sure about the raw fish? Welcome to the *gimbap*. This South Korean snack and picnic staple eschews the fish in favour of some equally delicious ingredients such as *bulgogi* (beef marinated in soy sauce, onion, garlic and sesame oil), omelette and fresh vegetables rolled up in dried seaweed (*gim*) and rice (*bap*). That's not all, as the fillings for *gimbap* have been becoming increasingly adventurous recently, comprising combinations like black rice and *kimchi*, or deodeok root with *chwinamul* (a leafy mountain vegetable). Basically, anything goes.

EAT IT ! *As part of a picnic after working up an appetite on a cycle ride in Seoul's Yeouido Hangang Park.*

© Getty Images / AmaliaEka

425

Breakfast on a bag of black rice pudding before the tourists wake up

INDONESIA // Ubud is the cool-climate ying to Bali's beach-life yang, a relief from the party vibe closer to shore. Up here in the mountains it's cooler and life is lived without having to dodge surfboards on the backs of motorbikes. Visitors come for the arts and crafts, the ancient sites, the rainforests and rice paddies... and the food. Start your day in Ubud by visiting a market for breakfast. Look for the small stalls with glossy black rice in cooking pots. This sweet, slightly salty bowl (or bag, if you're walking and eating) comes with slices of banana and coconut cream and will keep you going till lunchtime.

EAT IT ! *At the Ubud morning market, preferably before 9am, as after that it fills up with touristy fare.*

126

Stop for flódni in Budapest's Jewish Quarter

HUNGARY // This Hungarian-Jewish sweet layered cake features five cake layers interspersed with flaky pastry and four layers of filling: stewed apple, walnut paste, poppy seed and plum jam. The original recipe has been around since medieval times but has been made famous in Hungary more recently by local chef Raj Ráchel. Her *flódni* is one of the most sought-after in the country but it's not the only example – any traditional Jewish bakery worth its sugar will serve *flódni*.

EAT IT ! *At Café Noe, Wesselényi utca 13, Budapest.*

127

Taco rice: a taste of home for GIs based in Japan

JAPAN // Okinawa has been catering to American palates since US army bases were established there in the wake of WWII. Taco rice simply fused the island's rice with the minced beef, shredded cheese, salad and salsa desired by homesick GIs who'd grown up with Tex-Mex food. To achieve the familiar flavour, chefs originally used a blend of sake with soy and mirin sauce. Not surprisingly, the fusion has been a hit since the 1950s and is now served on the Japanese mainland.

EAT IT ! *Olive Batake's menu celebrates traditional Okinawa cuisine. 4-12-5 Awase.*

128

Take away Taiwan's flaky pineapple cake

TAIWAN // Taiwan is known for its pineapples, so it's no surprise that the pineapple cake is the go-to take-home treat for visitors. But Taiwan is also a place of varied influences, and this sweet treat eloquently represents this confluence of flavours. It's part flaky shortcake and part fruit pie, and although it's sweetened with natural sugar, the cake's savoury notes may be detected as well. Lee Cake in Taipei's historic Dadaocheng neighbourhood won't let you down.

EAT IT ! *Lee Cake in Taipei at No 309, Section 1, Dihua St.*

© NatashaBreen / 500px

© Lonely Planet / Pete Seaward

429

Cut a large slice of pavlova while your hosts dispute its origins

AUSTRALIA & NEW ZEALAND // Antipodeans squabble over the origins of this whipped cream, fruit and meringue dessert, but when it comes down to the eating, nobody really cares. Traditionally a celebratory dessert, you're most likely to see pavlova on family tables at Christmas. The festive colours of the fruit (commonly strawberries, kiwi and passion fruit) combined with the whipped cream topping over delicate meringue is a decorative and delicious addition to a yuletide feast. Its contentious origins concern the famous Russian ballerina Anna Pavlova after a tour down under – did the Kiwis or the Aussies first invent the dish in her honour? The Kiwi claim gained a couple of years on the Australians when Pavlova's biographer noted a Wellington chef presenting the dish to the dancer in 1926. The first credible mention in Australian records is 1929, though Aussies claim a 1926 date also. Perhaps we'll leave it at 'too close to call' and get down to enjoying its sweet, fruity, crunchy and chewy deliciousness.

EAT IT ! ***To top off a Christmas dinner during the height of the southern hemisphere summer.***

© Hemis / Alamy Stock Photo

130

Le poulet de Bresse: grab a gourmet drive-through chicken

FRANCE // Poulets de Bresse, with their red heads, white feathers and slate-blue legs, dot the meadows in the province of Bresse like miniature tricolores. They're farmed to exacting standards – allocated a minimum of 10 sq metres of land per bird and fed a low-protein diet to encourage free-range foraging for insects – and their gamey meat is anathema to the industrially farmed white matter most of us know as chicken. This is appellation-protected, best-in-world stuff sold in posh foodhalls, served in Michelin-starred restaurants... and, in one specific *aire de service* off the A39 between Dijon and Bourg-en-Bresse, turned on rotisseries till the skin is golden-brown, and sold at a fraction of the cost you'll pay elsewhere. A half Bresse chicken and a fresh baguette is the best roadstop sandwich you'll ever eat.

French *aires* often celebrate local products but the Aire du Poulet de Bresse is in another league. No longer a compromise on a journey to somewhere you really want to be, a destination in its own right.

EAT IT ! ***You can't miss it. Look for the 20m-high metal chicken sculpture. A39, 71480 Dommartin-lès-Cuiseaux.***

© robertharding / Alamy Stock Photo

© Shutterstock / wong yu liang

131

Feel the power of a pàomó bowl in Xi'an

CHINA // Enjoying a steamy bowl of *yángròu pàomó* – flatbread mutton soup – requires a bit of elbow grease. You'll be handed a frisbee-sized disk of flatbread, and asked to shred it into a bowl. Once you've done your part, a waiter will add fragrant mutton broth and slices of meat. Seasoned with pickled garlic, the Silk Road-influenced dish is both a warming winter meal and a good excuse to relax – like knitting, flatbread-shredding is a perfect time for a chat.

EAT IT ! *In Xi'an, Lao Sūn Jiā has been dishing up pàomó since 1898. 5th fl, 364 Dong Dajie.*

132

Check out Penang's best char kway teow

MALAYSIA // Char kway teow – 'CKT' to aficionados – is not a pretty meal. A swampy chaos of charred noodles, shrimp, blood cockles, bean sprouts, slices of *lap cheong* sausage, eggs and green onions, all doused in soy sauce, combines to create a dish whose looks belie its tastiness. Once a dish for labourers, it's ubiquitous at food stalls across Malaysia and Singapore. But for many, Penang's version reigns, its shrimp the most succulent, its noodles perfectly soft-crispy.

EAT IT ! *The woks at New Lane Hawker Centre in Penang's George Town heat up from around 6pm.*

133

Compose yourself for Mozartkugel in Salzburg

AUSTRIA // It's a sign of our times that you can order a cheesecake on Amazon. But one treat that resists instant gratification is the *Mozartkugel*. A ball of pistachio marzipan surrounded by nougat and chocolate, it was invented by Salzburg confectioner Paul Fürst in 1890 and named after the city's most famous son. Today, the fifth generation of Fürsts still hand-produce the candies. Their quaint cafe is filled with bags of the silver orbs, so you can buy your fill of takeaways.

EAT IT ! *Cafe Konditorei Fürst at Brodgasse 13 in Salzburg is the only place to get the original Mozartkugel.*

134

Tlayuda: the amazing snack from Oaxaca

MEXICO // Anyone who's tasted a *tlayuda* knows it's the ultimate street snack. Even its name, which translates as 'little craving', is an indication of how you'll feel after a first bite. The basic ingredients are a large corn tortilla, slathered in *asiento* (lard), packed with refried beans and *quesillo* (Oaxacan string cheese) and chargrilled. Wandering the stalls in the heart of Mexico's food scene, Oaxaca, you'll find local variations that can include slices of beef or pork.

EAT IT ! ***Start your little craving at Comedor María Alejandra's, located in Oaxaca's historic Mercado 20 de Noviembre.***

135

The Indian thali is flavour in harmony

INDIA // Throughout India, *thali* refers to both a set meal and the platter on which it is served. While there are huge regional variations, the aim of a good *thali* is to provide six complementary dishes that represent the tastes of salty, sweet, bitter, sour, sharp and spicy. Served with rice on a metal platter or, if you're in the south, a banana leaf, *thali* is eaten without cutlery. Create your perfect flavour combination by mixing and rolling your own rice ball.

EAT IT ! ***Every dish at the RRR Hotel arrives on a banana leaf, including its heavenly thali. Gandhi Square, Mysore.***

136

Mbeju and tereré: Paraguay's perfect breakfast pairing

PARAGUAY // Eat this cheesy, tortilla-like flat pancake for breakfast on a cafe terrace before you start your day of sightseeing and shopping in Paraguay's capital, Asunción. The *mbeju* has a seemingly contradictory texture that is both chewy and crisp, and it pairs perfectly with the traditional drink, *tereré* (a kind of yerber mate tea made with cold water and ice rather than warm water). Try your *tereré* spiked with freshly squeezed lime, orange or lemon juice and fresh mint.

EAT IT ! ***At El Café de Acá in Asunción's stylish Villa Morra district.***

437

Make eggs benedict your prescription for a morning after in Manhattan

USA // Most people have a favourite hangover 'cure' – including Wall Street broker Lemuel Benedict. He's said to have stumbled into New York's Waldorf Hotel in 1894 and mumbled something about toast, bacon, poached eggs and hollandaise sauce. Eggs benedict was born. The Waldorf Astoria, as the hotel is now known, is undergoing a major renovation until 2021, but don't let that worry your painfully pounding head: it's still possible to order Lemuel's namesake dish at many fine establishments throughout the Big Apple. Try Tartine, in the West Village, for a classic rendition of the dish, or brave a more modern twist at Queens Comfort in Astoria, where there's a plethora of benedicts to choose from.

EAT IT ! *Crack the mould and give Queen's Comfort a go at 40-09 30th Ave, Astoria, New York.*

437

James Syhabout

James Syhabout is the Bay Area-based chef-owner of the Michelin-starred Commis and Hawker Fare, and the author of Hawker Fare: Stories and Recipe's From a Refugee Chef's Isan Thai and Lao Roots.

01

STEAK AT A CIDERHOUSE, BASQUE COUNTRY
Basque steak is always grilled over apple-wood or grapevines, from large animals, and the fat's always glistening yellow.

02

KUAY JAP, BANGKOK It's rice noodles in this offal of crispy pork and pork blood, often with quail eggs. Find it on the streets everywhere.

03

DOUBLE SKIN SALAD, GREAT CHINA, BERKELEY, CALIFORNIA This is a creation of this restaurant that I've never seen before: translucent beans, starch noodles, sliced egg, cucumbers, and mushrooms, all tossed in a mustardy vinaigrette.

04

TACOS, TIJUANA, MEXICO
They chop the meat on a board right off the grill, use the tortilla to pick up the meat, and that's it. It's mind-boggling — Mexico is so close and yet we can't replicate those tacos.

05

PASTRAMI SANDWICH, KATZ'S DELI, NYC
I've never gone to New York without going to Katz's and it's always my first stop. They've been doing it so long I'm sure a lot of it has to do with sourcing, cure time, etc — it's just a well-oiled machine.

438

Be tutored in the wonders of mighty manuka honey

NEW ZEALAND // The Bay of Islands honey shop in Kerikeri offers the chance to learn how the local manuka honey – queen bee of honeys – is produced. This superfood, made by bees that pollinate the native manuka bush exclusive to the Land of the Long White Cloud, is said to be a natural healer that contains antibacterial properties. Dark, flavourful and not overpoweringly sweet, this is a perfect honey for grown-ups.

EAT IT ! ***At the Bay of Islands honey shop, 414 Kerikeri Rd, Kerikeri.***

439

Visit Paris for the best baguettes in the world, maybe

FRANCE // Dawn in Paris and the city's alchemists are awake and making fresh magic from their base ingredients: flour, yeast, water and salt. Nothing beats buying a warm baguette in the morning's still hours, before the City of Light stirs. An annual competition awards the best bakers the prize of supplying the Elysée palace with daily baguettes for a year. Judges look for a thin crust, a soft, stretchy interior and a length of 55-65cm. It's a tough job but someone's got to do it.

EAT IT ! ***Brun boulangerie at 193 rue de Tolbiac in the 13th was a recent winner.***

440

Eat kalitsounia pastries at Easter on Crete

GREECE // Easter is an unbeatable time to be on Crete. Not just because the island's wild flowers are in bloom (and also decorating the hundreds of simple churches) but also because bakeries are full of *kalitsounia*, sweet cheese pastry parcels served with a drizzle of wild thyme honey. At Easter a favourite *kalitsounia* is filled with *malaka*, a soft sheeps' cheese, which creates long strings of molten deliciousness when cooked.

EAT IT ! ***All bakeries sell kalitsounia during religious festivals and celebrations.***

© Getty Images / LazingBee

© Lonely Planet / Matt Munro

© Shutterstock / Lucy Brown - loca4motion

Feel the ground shake with a chicken pepián in Antigua de Guatemala

GUATEMALA // Antigua is an impossibly picturesque city – impossibly because, given its necklace of surrounding volcanoes, it's amazing it's there at all. After centuries of seismic activity lots of it isn't, but the ruins only heighten the appeal of a city filled with restored, pastel-hued baroque buildings, chief among them the Iglesias de la Merced. At the weekends everyone gathers here to catch up on news while snacking on the *pepián* sold by the vendors. Comprised of roasted meats, various chillies, pumpkin seeds (the *pepitoria* that give the dish its name) and a host of other roasted ingredients, this unctuous, slightly bitter but richly layered dish is served with rice and fresh corn tortillas. If it's going to be your last meal, it's not a bad way to go.

☛ EAT IT ! *From a street vendor, or for a more lavish version, at El Porton, next door to the Origimi resturant.*

Take a seat by the Florida beach and unlock the flavours of key lime pie

USA // Brutal hurricane seasons have had a devastating impact on crops of key limes throughout the Florida Keys, but this hasn't dimmed people's love for the region's signature dish. Cafes from Key Largo to Key West all claim to make the best version of the pie, but the key to a great one is still the use of key limes, now mostly imported from Mexico. These are yellow when ripe and have an intense tartness compared with their green supermarket counterparts. The pairing of the sharp sourness of the lime custard with volumes of soft meringue encased in a biscuit crumb is a taste sensation... pair it with a beachside pina colada for the taste of the Keys at your table.

☛ EAT IT ! *A BYO pina colada will come in handy as you queue at Key West Key Lime Pie Company, 511 Greene St, Key West, Florida.*

© Lonely Planet / Justin Foulkes

443

© Getty Images / Schollmeyer, Sebastian

Surf a wave of pleasure with a bowl of nasi goreng in Bali

INDONESIA // Bingin, on the Bukit Peninsula at Bali's southern tip, has one of the island's most spectacular surfing breaks. Despite this, and the fact that it is less than 30 minutes' drive from heaving Kuta, it's serene. The beach is accessed by a cliff-side walk dotted with tiny cafes and restaurants serving basic Indonesian and Balinese fare.

If this isn't painting a clear enough picture, imagine waking in the morning to a gentle breeze and the sound of the waves crashing below. You get up as the aromas of fried garlic, tamarind and *kecap manis* (Indonesian sweet soy sauce) reach your bedroom, and when you reach the open-air dining area at your family-run guesthouse, the chef is deftly tossing rice with shrimp paste, chicken and fresh prawns. He asks if you want some of the *nasi goreng*, and before you've had the chance to say 'yes' he lands the now stir-fried rice on a plate, tops it with a fried egg and a side of lettuce and tomatoes, and says '*menikmati*', or 'enjoy your meal'. And trust us, you will.

EAT IT ! ***For a perfect day post-nasi goreng, grab your board and hit the waves, if you're not tempted by a second helping!***

444

© Getty Images / Peter Ptschelinzew

444

© Getty Images / David Buffington

Watch the masters of pad thai work their magic from a Bangkok street stall

THAILAND // Of the multitude of Thai culinary exports that have found favour worldwide, *pad thai* is probably the most famous. The genius of the dish lies in the light balance of flavours and textures. In overseas interpretations you're likely to find that spices are added with a heavier hand, but on the streets of Bangkok the food-cart chefs have spent years and years perfecting their one dish with a deft touch. The best *pad thai* you'll ever eat will be here, and it will have rice noodles coated in a lip-smacking mix of tamarind paste, sugar, lime juice, chilli, garlic, fish sauce and white pepper. To the noodles are added shrimp, Chinese chives, minced green onion and an egg, before it's all flash-fried in a wok over a high heat. Bean shoots and chopped peanuts are added as a flourish to finish. The complex and delicate flavour profile is testament to Thailand's rich culinary history and the skill of Bangkok's street-food cooks, a skill that rivals any classically trained chef in a Michelin-starred restaurant.

EAT IT ! ***Choose just one? Impossible! Get pad thai from street stalls everywhere in Bangkok.***

Follow your nose to a Malaysian morning snack, the durian fruit

MALAYSIA // You'll see the signs posted in guesthouses and hotels throughout Southeast Asia pointedly asking that this fetid fruit not be brought inside. And if you've ever been downwind of a durian you'll know the reason why. It's an acquired aroma, to be polite. If you eat it on the roadside, however, the smell isn't as overpowering and you'll get a whiff of why it's so popular, despite the stench. Keep an eye out for stalls sporting what look like enormous jackfruits with large spikes, or just close your eyes and sniff your way to your morning snack. Want an idea of what to expect? Imagine a creamy, garlic-infused, caramel-flavoured melon. We bet that's piqued your interest.

EAT IT ! *At roadside stalls throughout Malaysia.*

Feel some old-school California love for the odd couple: surf 'n turf

USA // When ordering this classic combo of steak and shellfish, do not pronounce the and. The breezy truncated 'n' embodies the dish's SoCal Gidget-era 1950s origin, as well as its whimsical pairing. It seems to have been born out of novelty, evoking an odd mash-up of mid-century LA icons the Rat Pack and the Beach Boys. The cut of the cow and the choice of shellfish seem mere afterthoughts. What really matters is that you're tucking into your plate of surf 'n turf while sitting in a naugahyde booth beneath headshots of Hollywood stars, sipping an equally gaudy cocktail.

EAT IT ! *Tony's on the Pier in Redondo Beach, LA, is that rare seafood spot that takes steak seriously.*

© Getty Images / Peter Stuckings

117

Eyes closed tight and down the hatch – you're dining on fried tarantula

CAMBODIA // Lots of street-food dishes can be sampled outside their native countries now, but here's one that's hard to find outside Cambodia, and even then, only widely in Skuon, famous for the crunchy snack. Sounds gross? Looks worse, but in terms of interesting food experiences, fried tarantula is right up there. The story goes that the dish was born of necessity during the dark days of the Khmer Rouge when food was limited. Now these arachnids are a delicacy, eaten by locals and tourists alike. Hawkers will bring plates of spiders up to you in the street and suggest you go for the juicy abdomen first because the legs can be bitter; if you can handle thinking about a 'juicy abdomen' you might survive chomping on the legs anyway.

EAT IT ! ***Crunchy, gooey, a surprising chicken-like quality to the head… it might not be for the faint-hearted, but – Yolo!***

118

Celebrate spring with mantu dumplings in Aghanistan

AFGHANISTAN // Steamed dumplings, Chinese, right? Not necessarily. Yes, it's thought that *mantu* were introduced to Afghanistan via Mongolia, but however these spicy, meat-filled steamed parcels got here, they're a centrepiece of celebrations across the country. Most of that country remains out of bounds to visitors, but adventurous types should head for the Bamiyan Valley or Herat around the spring equinox, when the New Year festival Nauroz marks the end of the winter. Amid the sumptuous spreads you'll find platters of *mantu*, all eaten outdoors on what feels like a national annual picnic. Look out for trays of the dumplings topped with a tomato-based *kurma* sauce.

EAT IT ! ***At markets and on the streets, where vendors sell them from little stands.***

© Getty Images / HADI ZAHER

449

Make space in your festive feasting for a mince pie

UK // 'Good King Wencelas looked out on the feast of St Stephen, when the snow lay round about, deep and crisp and even.' There's only one appropriate setting for a mince pie and that's Christmas time in Britain, preferably while carols are being sung, guiding stars twinkle in the chill sky and the holly trees are laden with red berries. That's the fantasy. The reality is that mince pies are most likely to be scoffed in front of the television. But that's no reason to skimp on these sweet treats. Spiced mincemeat is no longer used for the filling, replaced by dried fruit (including raisins, currants and apple), candied peel, brown sugar, spices and fruit juice. The pastry cases are made with butter or suet then dusted with icing sugar.

☛ EAT IT ! *The best mince pies are home-made and eaten with friends and families in the days leading up to Christmas.*

450

Try chicken tikka masala where it was invented

UK // It's on every Indian restaurant menu, so you'd be forgiven for thinking chicken tikka masala is from India. But the creamy dish of yoghurt-marinated chicken was likely invented in Scotland by South Asian chefs (though this point is disputed). Wherever it's from, chicken tikka is the ultimate comfort food on a chilly Glasgow night, served with a mild tomato sauce, rice and a naan.

☛ EAT IT ! *Shish Mahal at 60-68 Park Rd, is one of Glasgow's oldest Indian restaurants.*

451

Eat elk deep in the Norwegian woods

NORWAY // After a long day in the snow you want a dinner with staying power, and Norwegians have just the thing: local elk meat, served with potatoes, lingonberries and warming shots of aquavit. Elk, which run free in the icy boreal forests of Scandinavia, have lean, flavourful meat. A traditional meal in the hunting cabins of the north, it's now seen on menus in urban Oslo.

☛ EAT IT ! *In the upland town of Geilo, elk is cooked up at Hallingstuene: Geilovegen 56.*

452

Shop for moreish mochi sweets all over Japan

JAPAN // Made from shortgrain rice pounded into a chewy paste before being augmented with flavours ranging from nutty (peanuts are a favourite) to fruity (strawberry and cherry are popular) to cacao (everyone loves chocolate), *mochi* is a much-loved sweet in Japan for children and adults. It's delicious and dense in calories, but consume with care: cases of *mochi* choking are common.

☛ EAT IT ! *Good mochi is always fresh. Shops specialising in the confection abound.*

Whose side are you on? North Carolina's east vs west barbecue battle

USA // Spend enough time in North Carolina and you'll eventually be forced to make a choice: eastern or western. That's eastern- or western-style barbecue, referring to the ferocious rivalry between two different ways of preparing the state's favourite meat: pork. In the sandhills and coastal flatlands of eastern North Carolina, barbecue (a noun, always) means a whole hog, smoked in an oil-drum cooker until the meat is falling off the bones. Then it's shredded and doused with a thin, vinegar-based sauce, which probably originates from techniques early settlers used to preserve pork after it had gone off. In the hilly West, barbecue is pork shoulder, slow-cooked and slathered in a sweeter sauce containing ketchup or another form of tomatoes. Whatever the region, the best barbecue joints smoke their meat using wood rather than gas (horrors!). These are unpretentious places, with battered Formica tables and cooks in hairnets joshing with eachother behind the counter. Order a plate, which means a heap of pork and a couple of sides, usually coleslaw and hush puppies (fried balls of cornmeal). Or get a sandwich, which comes with slaw on a squishy white roll. Wash it all down with the South's beverage of choice, iced tea sweet enough to rattle the teeth out of your head. If you're lucky, there might be peanut butter pie afterwards. If you're even luckier, you might spot the pitmaster – the high-priest of pork – shuffling around behind the kitchen, chopping wood or just having a cigarette by the hog smokers. Let him bend your ear and you'll learn more about barbecue than you ever wanted to know. Just don't ask him what he thinks of his cross-state rivals.

EAT IT ! ***OK, you made us choose – grab some of the finest eastern-style barbecue at the Skylight Inn at 4618 S Lee St, Ayden.***

© Richard Ellis / Alamy Stock Photo

Chimaek, the union of chicken and beer, is a Korean Seoul food

SOUTH KOREA // Join after-work crowds of Seoul's salarymen who pack into beerhouses, bars and restaurants to take the edge off the working day with *chimaek* and beer. Its name comes from the marriage of the English word 'chicken' and the Korean word for beer, 'maekju'. Introduced in the 1960s, the combination took off in the 1990s, and it doesn't look like the honeymoon phase is going to end any time soon. The secret to its success? First, it's the double fry. Covered in flour and potato starch for the initial quick fry in vegetable oil, the chicken is then cooled briefly before being dunked again to cook through. This renders the fat in the chicken skin, making the coating crispy. The second secret is to keep it spicy – while there are several sauces to choose from, the most popular is the fiery and sweet *yangnyeom* chicken; the sticky sauce coats the skin and is offset perfectly by the pickled radish on the side. Thirdly, it's about the beer – usually a crisp lager served in giant 3-litre jugs. The atmosphere is fun and free.

EAT IT ! ***Fried-chicken chain restaurants cover Seoul, for a more local vibe, try Chicken in the Kitchen at 4-42, Wausan 29, Mapo.***

155

Slurp on some dan dan noodles in Sichuan

CHINA // Once sold by vendors who carried their wares in baskets hanging from a bamboo pole (*dan*), *dan dan* noodles are a favourite snack in Sichuan's cities. Silky noodles are doused with a glossy sauce of chilli oil, soy sauce and vinegar pepped up with preserved vegetables and Sichuan peppercorns. Hit with ground pork and a handful of green onions, and you've got a dish to warm you on a chilly Chengdu evening or refresh you on a sweltering Chongqing afternoon.

EAT IT ! *Touristy Jinli Pedestrian St in Chengdu is a solid bet for yummy bowls of dan dan noodles.*

156

Salo: the fat of the land in Ukraine

UKRAINE // Ukrainians have forgone any complex flavours or complicated cooking techniques in the dish widely acknowledged as being their national favourite. *Salo*, otherwise known as cold pork fat, is cured, brined or smoked and these thick slices of lard are celebrated with festivals, honoured in statues and featured in record books. The traditional way to eat it is to have the *salo* frozen and then sliced thinly and seasoned with peppercorns and salt.

EAT IT ! *Take a shot of vodka with a melt-in-the-mouth piece of salo at the traditional Tsarske Selo, 22 Lavrske St, Kiev.*

157

In Mongolia, don't steppe out without a hot khuushuur

MONGOLIA // Yes, Mongolian food is simple and practical, but when you are out in the elements on an odyssey across the steppe, chances are you will crave no-nonsense belly-filling grub – and *khuushuur* is just that. Specifically, dough folded in a triangular or semi-circular shape over minced mutton (occasionally beef or cabbage) and fried until the outside is crispy. Mongolians will even clutch these meaty parcels in their hands to improve circulation.

EAT IT ! *Out in the sticks locals sell the best freshest versions from outside their house or tent in ones or twos.*

Florence Fabricant

Florence Fabricant is the long-time food and wine reporter for the New York Times, and the author of 12 best-selling cookbooks.

KAISEKI LUNCH, NAKAHIGASHI, KYOTO, JAPAN The chef walked in with an opportunistic harvest of chickweed, wild onions, mugwort, and nettles, and it all showed up in every exquisite dish he made.

CHAWANMUSHI CUSTARD, BRUSHSTROKE, NEW YORK David Bouley elevates this everyday Japanese dish. His silken rendition surrounded by Dungeness crab steeps in a black-truffle and garlic-infused broth.

LIÈVRE À LA ROYALE, FRANCE My love affair with wild hare and foie gras, bathed in a sauce enriched with blood and chocolate, began in Chinon. And I have since indulged in this classic all over France.

WILD STRIPED BASS, BOULUD SUD, NEW YORK I had this as a whole 10lb fish, stuffed with fresh black figs, wrapped in fig leaves at a private dinner at Bar Boulud. But, these days, Boulud Sud serves a snapshot of it.

SPAGHETTI WITH BLEAK ROE, ARAKATAKA, OSLO, NORWAY It's a twisted knot of butter-slicked pasta piled with crunchy, sweetly briny, reddish roe, which enhances every bite.

© Lonely Planet / Sivan Askayo

158

Breakfast on black pudding and potato in Ireland

IRELAND // If you're lucky, a traditional Irish breakfast at a B&B will feature a couple of slices of a rich, dark sausage, perhaps with a fried egg and a scoop of colcannon (potato and cabbage). Black pudding has humble origins in Ireland: farming wives would make it with the blood from a slaughtered pig, unwilling to waste any of the animal. But blood sausages go back even further, mentioned in Homer's *The Odyssey*. Today, this rich, seasoned sausage – studded with pork fat and smooth oatmeal – is worshipped by gourmets. For the best, a local Irish butcher is the first place to call but some households, such as the Egan family of Inch House B&B in Tipperary, make their own.

EAT IT ! ***Buy your own award-winning pudding from McCarthy's butcher of Kanturk; if it's good enough for Queen Elizabeth II...***

159

Why the home of the Reuben sandwich is a Big Apple institution

USA // Katz's Deli in New York has been around since 1888, since when it has perfected one of the world's best sandwiches, best eaten right here in its birthplace, where the decor is old-school, every inch of floor space is packed with hungry hopefuls, and the wall is covered with framed photos of famous guests. The real star here, though, is the piled-high plate of slow-cooked corned beef, ably supported by slices of fresh rye bread, Swiss cheese, sauerkraut and a tangy dollop of Russian dressing. You'll join a queue for the privilege, but the wait is entertainment in itself as the cast of NYC life parades before you.

TRY IT ! ***Scarf down your Reuben with confidence, knowing that you're getting a piece of history, at the famous Katz's Delicatessen, 205 E Houston St, New York.***

460

Take a walk on the wild side in Cape Town's Test Kitchen

SOUTH AFRICA // The South Africa of The Test Kitchen isn't the widescreen land that most travellers seek. But some of the best travel experiences are those that defy expectations. And besides, this much-lauded experiential/experimental restaurant represents a part of the country looking to redefine itself. The dining experience takes you through two spaces – the Dark Room (black walls, dramatic lighting) and the Light Room (industrial-chic) – which divorce you from reality and pull focus on to dishes like lamb sweetbreads, liquorice liver jus, lime gel, preserved lemon and pine-nut gremolata. Or desserts that mix mango and tamarind curd, pineapple-cured star anise and Thai green curry-flavoured meringue.

EAT IT ! *Bookings open on specific dates in advance of each quarter. Get that date in your calendar, get the restaurant on speed dial and good luck! The Old Biscuit Mill, 375 Albert Rd, Woodstock.*

461

Get your hands dirty with Singapore's original black pepper crab

SINGAPORE // Longbeach Restaurant in Singapore (at four locations citywide) is credited with inventing black pepper crab – double-fried in a wok with black and white pepper, oyster sauce, garlic, ginger, coriander and chilli – in 1959 and is still producing a tasty version (at eye-watering prices). A more affordable, authentic black pepper crab experience is at the long-standing Eng Seng restaurant. The queue starts forming at around 5pm so get in early or expect a stomach-rumbling wait. When it arrives at your table your crab will look as if it's been dragged from an oil slick, but it's infinitely tastier than it looks. So dive in with both hands – go on, get in there.

EAT IT ! *Long Beach UDMC, 1202 East Coast Parkway, East Coast Seafood Centre; Eng Seng, 247 Joo Chiat Place; both Singapore.*

162

Roll up for a cous cous carnival any night in Marrakech

MOROCCO // Every city has a week or two in the calendar where it awakens into festival mode, but in Marrakech it happens every night, as its main public square, Djemaa El Fna, transforms into a carnival of food, music, theatre and sheer human energy. For most of the day it's a sparse expanse of asphalt, dotted with stalls selling fresh orange juice, medicinal herbs and henna tattoos, mobile water sellers toting leather water bags and brass cups, old men telling stories to groups of locals, and snake charmers proffering photo opportunities to tourists. Around the edge of the square, people shelter from the sun in cafes, sipping sugary mint tea and eating sweet pastries.

The first signs of change appear late in the afternoon, when teams of men start assembling metal-framed food stalls. As darkness falls, more entertainers arrive – acrobatic troupes, Berber folk bands, more storytellers – and floodlights illuminate plumes of white smoke that rise into the night sky from portable grills and makeshift kitchens. The food on offer runs the gamut of traditional Moroccan cooking. There's lamb and prune tagines, couscous piled with slow-cooked vegetables, mountains of skewered meats ready for the grill, spicy snail broth, bowls of *harira*, and if you snag a seat at one of the larger stalls, you can sample most of it in one place. Smaller stalls tend to specialise in particular delicacies – if you're looking for roasted sheep's heads, don't worry, there's a guy. Sometime around midnight the crowds disperse, the noise subsides, the food stalls are packed away, and Djemaa El Fna is an empty expanse once more. For a few hours, at least.

EAT IT ! ***Choose a stall where you can inspect fresh ingredients before they're cooked, not the one with the loudest tout.***

© Lauri Laan no@no.ee

464

Watch Kuala Lumpur's street-side artisans serve up hokkien mee at speed

MALAYSIA // Don't let the speed of the wok masters fool you into thinking that something so quickly prepared is basic in flavour. We're in Malaysia after all, where nothing is mild or nondescript. Gifted to the Malaysian culinary scene by Chinese immigrants, *hokkien mee* is a rich, gooey concoction of thick noodles with sliced pork, prawns, cabbage and sticky dark soy sauce. Cubes of fried pork fat are also added. *Hokkien mee* is one of Kuala Lumpur's hawker-stall bestsellers, and trawling the streets for the places that stir-fry their noodles over a traditional charcoal fire to give the dish its smokiness is the key to *hokkien mee* happiness. The less adventurous can always visit Kim Lian Kee, which has been serving up the noodles since the 1920s.

EAT IT ! ***From one of KL's hawkers, or at Kim Lian Kee, 92 Jalan Hang Lekir, City Centre, Kuala Lumpur.***

NOA: Tallinn's world-class tasting menu by the bay

ESTONIA // Sweeping, modern and defiantly dramatic, NOA lies over three levels overlooking the gelid waters of the Bay of Tallinn towards the ancient Estonian capital. Thanks to some clever design and use of mirrors, every table boasts a sea view. Opened in 2014, NOA became the jewel in Estonia's culinary crown. While the main restaurant is gourmet enough for most foodies, connoisseurs can book into the NOA Chef's Hall, which promises a more private evening along with a degustation menu. As you salivate between one tasting plate and the next, the chefs are watching from the open kitchen. With an evolving menu that has included squid with 'vintage' egg yolk, mussel and jus, you can expect world-class taste with an Estonian flavour.

EAT IT ! ***Housed in a building famous for its design and views of the city and water, NOA is a must in Estonia. Ranna tee 3, Tallinn.***

© Lonely Planet /Michael Heffernan

© Shutterstock / abamjiwa al-hadi

465

Go-wild food with muskox in Greenland

GREENLAND // A relative of the sheep, muskox look more like bison, with giant heads and curved horns. After roaming the tundra for a few million years, hunting from the 19th century onwards almost wiped them out. Most of the population of 80,000 is now protected, but permissable hunting means you'll find muskox on the menu. With a taste comparable to beef, muskox is as flavoursome as you would expect a wild, clean-living, chemical-free animal to be.

EAT IT ! *Enjoy a steak with fjord views from the 5th floor of A Hereford Beefstouw at Hotel Hans Egede, Aqqusinersuaq 1, Nuuk.*

466

Savour your pumpkin pie in peace at Yura

USA // Enjoying a pumpkin pie as part of a Thanksgiving feast is a wonderfully authentic experience, but in the absence of genuine American family or friends whose table you can gatecrash for the holiday, the sweet pumpkin pie at New York's Yura bakery, with its autumnal notes of cloves and ginger, gives you all the warm and fuzzy Thanksgiving feelings, without the family rows or American football. Truly something to give thanks for.

EAT IT ! *At Yura on Madison Bakery, 1292 Madison Ave, New York, which packs great baked goods into a bright warm space.*

467

Palmiers: heart-shaped pastry perfection

FRANCE // Often known as 'elephant ears', these airy French cookies have a distinctive heart or butterfly shape. They were likely invented by a frugal pastry chef looking to use up scraps of puff pastry, a buttery dough that is folded over and over to form impossibly thin layers. Fresh from the oven, palmiers have a glossy sugared exterior and a shattering crunch. With a café au lait, they're the ideal *goûter* (afternoon snack). Just don't get flakes on your scarf...

EAT IT ! *You won't find palmiers at the boulangerie, but all pâtisseries will do them. Try Hure at 18 Rue Rambuteau in Paris.*

468

468

Bak kut teh will warm your bones in Malaysia

MALAYSIA // As tasty as meals such as *mee goreng*, beef *rendang* and *laksa* may be, there's more to Malaysia. One example is the pork bone broth known as *bak kut teh*. Of Chinese origin, it's a meal composed of pork ribs cooked slowly for at least two hours in a broth seasoned with soy sauce, star anise, cinnamon, cloves, fennel seeds, garlic and *dong gui* (a root herb similar to ginseng). You'll often also find strips of fried dough, known as *char kueh*, as well as pieces of offal, different mushrooms, choy sum and tofu puffs, which add flavour and texture. Chinese Malays see this dish as one that warms the soul, and it's commonly eaten as a late-night meal when the heat of the day has dissipated. Klang, a west coast town, claims ownership of *bak kut teh* and it's impossible to argue with the quality of the dish here. The exact balance of ingredients vary and you'll come across versions of the broth that are thick and dark and others that are light and soupy, some are heavily spiced and others more subtle. Ask for local tips.

EAT IT ! ***Start at the restaurant that started the Klang craze for the dish: Teck Teh, Jalan Stesen 1, Kawasan 1, 41000 Klang, Selangor.***

469

Cod's tongue and scrunchions? It's the food of the far north

CANADA // Newfoundland, an island off the east coast of Canada, hosts one of the world's most isolated communities, which has resulted in some 'interesting' food choices. Actually, many of these choices started as necessities born of an inhospitable climate and a scarcity of food supplies, though these days they've become PR-polished 'delicacies'. One such speciality is the obscurely named caplin, which in common terms means cod's tongue. Yummy, right? Relax, it's not quite as chewy as it sounds and they're not really tongues, more like strips of flesh from the inside of the cod's throat. Throw in some scrunchions (pork rind fried till completely rendered and crispy) and you've got yourself a tasty plate of food.

☛ EAT IT ! *At the Spanish-influenced Bacalao Nouvelle Newfoundland Cuisine, 65 Lemarchant Rd, St John's, Newfoundland.*

© Shutterstock / Elena Elisseeva

© Getty Images / maksime

470

Add trdelník to your to-do list in Prague

CZECH REPUBLIC // Sightseeing Prague's baroque delights will inevitably lead you to the discovery of an altogether different one; spirals of sugar-coated pastry hanging in shop windows or toasting on a street-side grill. A word of warning – these, *trdelník*, are about to become your new obsession. After all, who could possibly resist crispy, caramelised sugar and the waft of warm cinnamon on a winter's day? And that's before you find out you can get *trdelník* with melted chocolate inside. Visiting the city in the summer? Don't despair. Some enterprising pâtisserie has worked out that *trdelník* works like a dream as a cone, so they fill it with ice-cream. Start the diet when you get home.

☛ EAT IT ! *At pastry shops or from street carts all over Prague.*

471

Pair your pint with a steak and kidney pie where the pubs are the planet's finest

UK // Without wanting to be too antagonistic, we think that London has the best pubs in the world. There's a host of drinking holes that claim to have been around since the 15th century – places that are dripping with history, bars that have propped up some of the world's most famous writers, politicians, philosophers, even royalty; and establishments that have continuously brewed their beer for hundreds of years… and if there's one thing that can improve on the perfection of a pint of finely crafted ale, it's the humble pie. At the Windmill in London's Mayfair you'll find the award-winning (three-time national champion) steak and kidney pie. The Windmill's pies are made from suet pastry with a mashed potato top and filled with meltingly soft beef steak, ox kidney, onion, mushrooms and hints of mustard, Worcester sauce and thyme. If you think that sounds like a winner, then join the club. We mean it; the Windmill has its own pie club, which hosts regular tasting events and pie appreciation nights.

☛ EAT IT ! ***It doesn't get much better than at the Windmill, 6-8 Mill St, Mayfair, London.***

© Daniel Di Paolo

© Daniel Di Paolo

Share a family-sized banana-leaf baho in Nicaragua

NICARAGUA // There's no better food to get you acquainted with Nicaraguan cuisine than the wholesome *baho*. Made up of marinated beef brisket, plantains and cassava, steamed inside a banana leaf, this is a meal to be shared with friends and family. The meat for the *baho* is marinated in orange and lime juices, tomatoes, onions, garlic and salt, and placed on top of plantains, which are laid on banana leaves and steamed in a pot. The meat is covered with cassava and the whole thing is doused in the marinating liquid before being sealed to form a banana leaf package. At the table, each person receives their serving on a fresh banana leaf. It's a sociable way to enjoy a meal.

EAT IT ! *In lieu of a family feast, try La Nueva Casa del Baho, SE 24th St, Managua.*

Feast on roast beef baguette from Borough Market

UK // Trying to decide what to eat in a market that offers everything from Balkan bites to Levantine-inspired dishes and an Alpine deli to Argentinian treats is no easy ask, but if you're after something that is as British as roast beef, elevenses and cockney rhyming slang, you need to head to the middle of Borough Market – don't worry, your nose will lead you there. For more than a quarter of a century husband and wife team Michael and Julie Hobbs have been churning out epic lunchtime hot meat baguettes filled with roast pork, stuffing and apple sauce, or turkey and cranberry. It's like all your favourite Sunday and Christmas roasts have come at once. Join the queue and stuff your boat race.

EAT IT ! *A visit to Borough Market makes you part of its thousand years of living history. 8 Southwark St, London.*

© Shutterstock / Sofiaworld

© Dexter Choong, Courtesy of Flour and Stone

474

Season boulette dumplings to taste in Mauritius

MAURITIUS // Mauritian cuisine is influenced by African, French, Indian and Chinese flavours. Among the first meals to try are the little dumplings known as *boulettes*. You can eat them on their own or in a broth, and we think broth is best. One of the pleasures of this meal is that you get to choose any or all of the different-flavoured *boulettes* to go in your broth and then you add sauces to taste.

EAT IT ! ***At Ti Kouloir, Grand Bai, Riviere Du Rempart, Mauritius, where you'll find sauces including soy, fish, garlic and chilli.***

475

Feel the lamington love in Sydney

AUSTRALIA // There's life yet in the lamington, Australia's iconic coconut-coated cake. At the counter of Nadine Ingram's Flour and Stone bakery resist the sweet distractions and stay focused: you're after her panna cotta-soaked interpretation of this childhood classic. Grab a chair outside and bite into the soft sponge cube. And at Bennelong restaurant in Sydney's Opera House the cake has been deconstructed for a deluxe dessert.

EAT IT ! ***At Sydney's Flour and Stone bakery on 53 Riley St, Woolloomooloo.***

476

Celebrate autumn with a mooncake in Macau

MACAU // Come October, Hong Kong, Macau and southern China goes mad for mooncakes, the ornately imprinted pastries that mark the Mid-Autumn Festival. Cantonese mooncakes feature chewy pastry filled with lotus paste, red bean or salted duck egg yolk; recent years have brought new varieties – you'll see mooncakes filled with ice-cream, peanuts, cheese, caramel and chocolate.

EAT IT ! ***A status item, mooncakes are big sellers in the bakeries of luxury hotels like Hong Kong's Mandarin Oriental.***

177

Buy a Bogotá oblea, the super-sized Colombian biscuit

COLOMBIA // It's 4pm on the streets of Bogotá and you're feeling a bit peckish, not to mention worn out from exploring the high-altitude city's colonial-era attractions. Luckily, one of the world's dreamiest street snacks is right in front of you, at one of the innumerable metal carts that dot Colombia's cities. It's the *oblea*, two giant round wafers smeared thickly with *arequipe* (Colombian caramel) and sandwiched together. The best *obleas* are golden brown and bigger than your head. Common add-ons include jam, coconut and, weirdly but winningly, shredded cheese. The sugar rush should keep you going till bedtime.

EAT IT ! ***You'll find oblea vendors in busy pedestrian districts of most Colombian cities.***

477

© Marc Boettcher / Alamy Stock Photo

478

© Shutterstock / KiltedArab

178

Book into a buzzy Tuscan trattoria for bistecca alla fiorentina

ITALY // Amid the Renaissance architecture of Florence, a chef takes a steak and seasons it with salt, pepper and some olive oil... wait, back up. A truly classic *bistecca alla fiorentina* – Florentine-style steak – begins not in Florence, but in Tuscany's Chiana valley, where the Chianina steer, an enormous, ancient breed, grazes on the rich alluvial plains to produce the meat that is used for the classic dish. From there, the steak is aged to enhance its flavour before hitting the grill to acquire a luscious char. The rare meat mingles with the traditional accompaniment of lemony cannellini beans and the hustle of a noisy Florentine trattoria with a carafe of Chianti.

EAT IT ! ***Florence's Trattoria Mario (Via Rosina 2) has been turning out perfect bisteccas at lunchtime for half a century.***

479

Fuel a southern England stomp with a sticky pud

UK // The Hungry Monk, on the eastern tip of the South Downs National Park, claimed to be the first restaurant to have combined bananas and toffee in a biscuit base in 1972, and it wasn't long before other establishments took the gooey caramel-covered concoction known as banoffee pie and ran with it. The Monk's gone, but why not work up an appetite with a South Downs Way walk, stopping in Arlington for a calorie-restoring piece of the famed local pie?

EAT IT ! *Enjoy the creamy, sticky offering at the Yew Tree Inn, Arlington, Polegate, East Sussex.*

480

Thieboudienne: spicy Senegalese simplicity

SENEGAL // So often the best things in life are simple. At least in theory. Senegal's national dish is just rice and fish blended in a spicy tomato sauce. But there are as many ideas on how to perfect it as there are grains of rice in the giant communal bowl from which it's served. Typically the fish, which is smoked, has a mild flavour – it's the tangy sauce that packs a spicy punch. Regional takes on *thieboudienne* include delicious beef and broth (instead of sauce) variations.

EAT IT ! *Discover the stalls that sell to the locals in front of the busy Marché Kermel in Dakar.*

481

Discover the Thai sausage secret of sai krok isan

THAILAND // Thai food rookies should be adventurous eaters to order *sai krok Isan*, but if you're in Bangkok's Wang Lang market (and if you're in town, you should be), you'd be mad not to try this awesome sausage. Take the leap and be rewarded with one of Thailand's most satisfying snacks: fatty minced pork and rice stuffed in sausage casings, fermented until tart, cooked over a smokey grill. To serve, that sour flavour and smoke are countered by crunchy, spicy sides.

EAT IT ! *Sai krok isan are sold exclusively from mobile vendors; you'll never find the dish in a restaurant.*

482

Mark Hanukkah with an oil-fried doughy treat

ISRAEL // Hanukkah tells a story of victory over tyrants, symbolised by the miracle of a candelabra that burned for eight days on one cruse of oil. Today, Jews celebrate with oil-fried foods, including these fluffy round doughnuts. Modern-day *sufganiyot* are stuffed with everything from Nutella to ginger curd. Feast on them under the palm trees of Tel Aviv's lovely Neve Tsedek neighbourhood while playing *dreidel* (a spinning-top game).

EAT IT ! *Find Dallal Bakery's sufganiyot at 7 Kol Israel Haverim St, Tel Aviv.*

183

Experience the unique ambience of dinner in a Lyon bouchon

FRANCE // Eating in one of Lyon's *bouchons* is to participate in a social and culinary tradition from the 17th century. As the city's silk industry boomed, foreign traders sought welcoming eateries. The *bouchons*, so named for the straw provided to clean the traders' horses, offered the right combination of homely and hearty. With modestly furnished dining rooms, modern-day *bouchons* continue the tradition by creating intimate ambience without airs and graces. Expect the meaty Lyonnaise menu to list mains such as chicken liver cake or veal with morel mushrooms. Quaff a local Beaujolais wine.

EAT IT ! ***Steps from the Saône, Lyon's Café Comptoir Abel has been an atmospheric revelation behind its painted facade since 1928.***

184

Go to Singapore for the cheapest Michelin-approved meal in the world

SINGAPORE // By all accounts, chef Chan Hon Meng was bewildered by the attention that his soya sauce chicken and rice received in 2016. But it's not every day that Michelin inspectors bestow a star on a stall in a hawker centre in Singapore. And that made his classic chicken rice dish - at two Singaporean dollars per serving - the cheapest Michelin-starred meal in the world. These days the queues can last hours at Chan's stall but if you can't wait there are 260 other hawker stalls to choose from – serving black pepper crab, char kway teow, satay, bak kut teh and more.

EAT IT ! ***Liao Fan Hong Kong Soya Sauce Chicken Rice and Noodle at Chinatown Complex Food Centre, 335 Smith St, Singapore.***

© Lonely Planet / Matt Munro

© Lonely Planet / Matt Munro

185

Unearth Vietnam's hidden street food treasure, bò lá lot

VIETNAM // Some Vietnamese dishes remain unknown on the global gastronomy radar. One is *bò lá lot* – seasoned minced beef, wrapped in betel leaves and grilled over a charcoal fire. In a sheet of soft rice paper, place a lettuce leaf, pickled carrot and daikon, green herbs like coriander and basil, the betel-leaf-coated beef and fresh chilli, before rolling the lot up and dipping it in a sweet fish sauce.

EAT IT ! ***From the street stalls along Ton Duc Thang Rd, Ho Chi Minh City.***

186

Take a chance on chile relleno in Puebla

MEXICO // It's a form of food roulette: a plate of deep-fried stuffed poblano peppers. Most are mellow but will you bite into a wild one? These green chillies are stuffed with panela cheese then fried in a light batter. This ultimate drinking snack originates in Puebla; an American version uses hotter jalapenos but softens the heat with a cream cheese stuffing.

EAT IT ! ***Restaurante Sacristia on Calle 6 sur 304, Puebla. Or Puebla's Chile Festival.***

187

Go for the full works in Caracas with arepas

VENEZUELA // *Arepas* were eaten across Venezuela and Colombia for centuries before 1492. It's a type of breakfast roll made with maize dough that can be stuffed like a pita with just about anything. The dough is crunchy on top and has an airy texture inside that's sweetened by the corn. Popular fillings include black beans, cheeses, fish and pork.

EAT IT ! ***Start your day with one of Arepa Factory's fresh and original fillings: Cristal Palace Transversal 2, Caracas.***

488

A pile of placky is a Slavic potato obsession

SLOVAKIA // Eastern Europe's love for the potato is epitomised by this hunger-busting potato pancake. Most Slavic countries have a version, but people in the Czech Republic and Slovakia are obsessed. A stay at a family house nearly always results in *placky*, or the similar *lokše*. Raw potatoes are grated, then mixed with egg, flour, ground pepper and marjoram to form the dough. The results are so belly-pleasing that, despite being a snack, folks here will wolf a pile as a main meal.

EAT IT ! ***Get an invite to anyone's house, ideally in the mountains, and look all large-eyed at whoever might be cooking.***

489

Mop up sauce sweet or savoury with Yemeni lahoh

YEMEN // The best comparison for *lahoh* would be a pancake. Traditionally made with flour, yeast and water, this circular, spongy flatbread is a popular snack any time of day. For breakfast, Yemenis layer *lahoh* with honey and ghee for a sweet morning hit. Light and airy, they're also perfect for mopping up curries and soups. It even makes an appearance in the dessert *shafout*, where it's drowned in yoghurt, fresh mint and pomegranate.

EAT IT ! ***When the conflict abates, stalls in Sana'a's souk in the Old City will sell sizzling lahohs.***

490

Alcapurria: a Puerto Rican roadside classic

PUERTO RICO // With its dough made from bananas wrapped around a spicy meat filling, *alcapurria* is a unique take on the fritter. You'll find these tasty (if greasy) snacks on roadsides across Puerto Rico, but if you want one loved by the locals follow the patchwork road east from San Juan to Piñones. Amid the pristine mangroves, surf and sunshine, Afro-Puerto Ricans keep their cultural traditions alive with dance, *plena* music and amazing *alcapurria*.

EAT IT ! ***Kiosko El Boricua is the freshest and best beachside stall – with the queue to prove it.***

© Lonely Planet / Mark Read

© Lonely Planet / Mark Read

491

Power a hedonistic Havana night with a medianoche

CUBA // The tearaway little sister of the renowned Cuban sandwich, the *medianoche* is most likely encountered late at night when you're running with a wild party crowd in Havana. The name literally means 'middle of the night', and the *medianoche* packs its roast pork, ham, Swiss cheese and pickles into a sweet eggy bread as opposed to the crispier and crunchier Cuban. This, of course, makes for much easier eating after one too many mojitos.

EAT IT ! ***At cafes and takeaways near Havana clubs, like La Chucheria, 1era entre C y D Vedado, La Habana; or on El Malecon.***

492

Try the Southern soul-food classic, shrimp and grits

USA // Finger-licking, belt-straining, soul-stirring fare is an intrinsic part of the culture in the South, and Charleston restaurants have stepped up to the plate by celebrating the homey, low-country meal shrimp and grits, which are a kind of creamy corn porridge. Here, the interpretations of the dish stretch from the no-frills version you'll find at places like Hannibal's Kitchen to fine-dining examples such as the ones served up at chef Robert Stehling's upmarket Hominy Grill. Try both.

EAT IT ! ***At Hannibal's Kitchen, 16 Blake St; and Hominy Grill, 207 Rutledge Ave; both Charleston, South Carolina.***

Allow the Viennese to please with their apple strudel

AUSTRIA // The humble *strudel* has been a Viennese icon for centuries (the city library famously holds a handwritten *strudel* recipe dating from 1696). The word itself is German for whirlpool and refers to the technique of rolling up the dough to envelop the apple filling. The use of apple probably came about during hard times when this was the only fruit in plentiful supply. After the apple is combined with sugar and spices, it is rolled in layers of velvety, paper-thin pastry.

EAT IT ! ***Opposite the Opera House, Gerstner's opulent cafe serves the prettiest strudel in town. Kärntner Str 51, Vienna.***

493

© Stockfood / Twellmann, Birgit

494

Make it a proper event with espetinho in Brazil

BRAZIL // Be it for an open-air concert, major sporting events or a festival, the sight of *espetinho* vendors getting their grilling stations in gear is a sure sign that a party is happening. Translating from Portuguese as 'little skewer', the *espetinho* is a kebab-like treat. Unlike with many iconic national foods around the globe, *espetinhos* are not boasted about: Brazilians joke about the meat that really goes into these snacks. Spot the best vendor by the queues around the stall.

EAT IT ! ***Anywhere a big gig is on, espetinho sellers are on stand-by.***

195

Greet the day in Istanbul over a simit-bread dip

TURKEY // Turkey's sesame-studded hoops of *simit* bread have been baked in Istanbul for over 500 years. The perfect simplicity of a breakfast with *simit* and the tangy yoghurt dip known as *haydari* could be the clue to its enduring popularity. Or perhaps it's the way the crusty exterior contrasts with the chewy inside. Either way, when served with butter, some feta cheese and a Turkish coffee, it's hard to beat first thing in the morning as Istanbul swings into mesmerising activity.

EAT IT ! ***From a simit seller cart on Istanbul's streets, or stop a simit seller with a stack on his head.***

196

If it's good enough for ghouls… Irish barmbrack

IRELAND // Similar to Welsh *bara brith*, this Irish 'speckled loaf' is made with strong black tea, yeasted flour and dried fruit. Likewise, it is usually served in buttered slices, with a cup of tea. But it's the tradition behind *barmbrack* that sets it apart. A remnant of All Hallow's Eve (when ghosts could pass over from the spirit world), *barmbrack* was left outside homes to appease mischievous phantoms, while symbolic items were baked inside for the lucky people who found them.

EAT IT ! ***Enjoy your barmbrack with great coffee at the Hansel and Gretel Bakery & Patisserie, Clare St, Dublin.***

197

Study soufflé with its Gallic masters

FRANCE // Notoriously fragile, soufflé has a reputation for being hard to pull off. So, if you do want to prepare this light, fluffy, savoury or sweet delicacy then take some tips from the French, its inventors and masters. In Angers, the restaurant La Soufflerie is one grand masterclass in soufflé cookery, from savoury stars like the St Jacques, featuring scallops, sole and crayfish, to irresistible desserts like shortcrust biscuit with caramel sauce. Go on, try it. Then try it again at home.

EAT IT ! ***At speciality soufflé restaurant La Soufflerie, 8 Place du Pilori, Angers.***

198

Meloui: street-fried spirals of piping-hot dough

MOROCCO // Most popular at breakfast, the thick, bready Moroccan pancake *meloui* is seared in a hot pan or on a griddle then served with syrup. However, variations come stuffed with minced meat, cheese, lamb fat and a preserved meat known as *khlii*. *Meloui* is served in traditional riads and restaurants but one of the best ways to eat it is straight off the hotplate from a street vendor, when all the layers are hot and crispy on the outside, and soft and steamy on the inside.

EAT IT ! ***Buy meloui from street vendors all over the country.***

Drop into the Lower East Side bakery that hasn't changed its knish recipe for over a century. And with good reason

USA // Jewish immigrants from Eastern Europe are credited with bringing the *knish* to NYC around the turn of the 20th century; on Lower East Side (LES) streets they'd hawk these baked stuffed-dough dumplings from street carts and baskets. One such peddler was Yonah Schimmel, a Romanian Jew who used his meagre savings to convert his cart to bricks and mortar and open a bakery in 1890. The business is still going strong, making it the oldest *knish* bakery in the US. It's also still in the family, managed by Yonah's great-nephew. The *knishes* at Yonah's stick close to tradition, the original potato and *kasha* (buckwheat groats) recipe is still as it was over 100 years ago, but today there are alternative stuffings such as spinach, broccoli, mushroom and sweet potato. The flaky pastry around a warm, soft centre is like comfort in the palm of your hand, transporting you back to when the LES was home to a burgeoning immigrant Jewish community that would go on to have an indelible effect on NYC's culture and character.

EAT IT ! ***At Yonah Schimmel's Knish Bakery, found since 1910 at 137 E Houston St, New York.***

© xPACIFICA / Alamy Stock Photo

© xPACIFICA / Alamy Stock Photo

© Shutterstock / Shi Yali

© Lonely Planet / Matt Munro

500

Make straight for the stinkiest street food in the Taipei night market and your reputation will be assured

TAIWAN // The name stinky tofu really tells it like it is – this famous Taiwanese street-food snack smells really nasty. Walking the narrow bustling alleys of Taipai's famous night markets, the stench of stinky tofu is likely to find you before you clap eyes on it. A waft of something similar to a mouldy gym sock combined with bad body odour is the first sign that you've found what you're looking for. Now it's just a matter of steeling yourself for the challenge ahead and the bragging rights to follow. We suggest going for the deep-fried version and perhaps skipping the one with the congealed duck blood. Choose chilli and pickled cabbage as an accompaniment. Then it's time to use all your mental powers to override your impulse to gag, and swallow the stinky tofu down. The chances are that you'll find the flavour salty and the texture soft and delicate, with a tangy punch supplied by the chilli and cabbage. Once you've finished, you can go tell all your friends.

EAT IT ! ***Shilin Night Market, No 101, Jihe Rd, Shilin District, Taipei.***

Index

A

Afghanistan
- ❏ Mantu 290
- ❏ Qabili palau 168

Albania
- ❏ Fëgëse 128

Algeria
- ❏ Makroudh 144

Angola
- ❏ Chicken muamba 142

Argentina
- ❏ Asado 96
- ❏ Choripán 131
- ❏ Empanadas 273
- ❏ Humita 129

Armenia
- ❏ Harissa 159

Australia
- ❏ Adelaide Central Market 231
- ❏ Anzac biscuits 184
- ❏ Avocado on toast 236
- ❏ Barra 245
- ❏ Bush tucker 102
- ❏ Lamington 305
- ❏ Meat pie 254
- ❏ Moreton bay bugs 265
- ❏ Mud crab fishing 206
- ❏ Oysters 29
- ❏ Pavlova 280
- ❏ Scallop pie 157
- ❏ Wallaby tail soup 268

Austria
- ❏ Apple strudel 311
- ❏ Mozartkugel 282
- ❏ Sachertorte 110
- ❏ Wiener schnitzel 197

B

Bangladesh
- ❏ Shingara 206

Belgium
- ❏ Mitraillette 261
- ❏ Moules frites 36
- ❏ Waffles 94

Bolivia
- ❏ Quinoa stew 198
- ❏ Salteñas 242

Bosnia and Herzegovina
- ❏ Cevapi 144

Botswana
- ❏ Seswaa 248

Brazil
- ❏ Acaí na tigela 202
- ❏ Bolinho de bacalhau 249
- ❏ Brigadeiro 160
- ❏ Espetinho 311
- ❏ Feijoada 116
- ❏ Pudim 241

Bulgaria
- ❏ Banitsa 137

C

Cambodia
- ❏ Bai sak chrouk 58
- ❏ Fish amok 147
- ❏ Fried tarantula 290
- ❏ Pumpkin custard 92

Canada
- ❏ Caplin and scrunchions 302
- ❏ Maple syrup 169
- ❏ Nanaimo bars 221
- ❏ Poutine 257

Cape Verde
- ❏ Cachupa 181

Chile
- ❏ Cazuela de mariscos 234

China
- ❏ Baozi 62
- ❏ Biang biang noodles 266
- ❏ Chongqing hotpot 253
- ❏ Cong you bing 134
- ❏ Congee 159
- ❏ Dan dan noodles 294
- ❏ Dim sum 24
- ❏ Dragon beard candy 153
- ❏ Egg waffles 137
- ❏ Hong Kong crispy duck 218
- ❏ Hong Kong roast meats 262
- ❏ Jiaozi 99
- ❏ Lamian 200
- ❏ Mapo tofu 138
- ❏ Mooncakes 305
- ❏ Peking duck 37
- ❏ Rou jia mo 236
- ❏ Wonton noodles 241
- ❏ Xiaolongbao 112
- ❏ Yángròu pàomó 282
- ❏ Yangshuo beer fish 216

Colombia
- ❏ Baneja paisa 176
- ❏ Obleas 306

Comoros Islands
- ❏ Langouste à la vanille 106

Costa Rica
- ❏ Casado 238

Croatia
- ❏ Black risotto 226

Cuba
- ❏ Chicharrones 195
- ❏ Medianoche 311
- ❏ Ropa vieja 191

Czech Republic
- ❏ Trdeknik 302

D

Denmark
- ❏ New Nordic Cuisine 140
- ❏ Smorrebrød 18
- ❏ Toverhallerne 95
- ❏ Wienerbrød 109

E

Ecuador
- ❏ Llapingachos 122
- ❏ Salón de Chocolate 216

Egypt
- ❏ Feteer 115
- ❏ Ful medames 209
- ❏ Kushari 123
- ❏ Ta'amiya 195
- ❏ Umm ali 152

El Salvador
- ❏ Pupusa 70

Estonia
- ❏ Baojaam 271
- ❏ NOA 299

Ethiopia
- ❏ Doro wat and injera 179

F

Faroe Islands
- ❏ Koks Restaurant 269

Fiji
- ❏ Fresh coconut 61
- ❏ Kokoda 247
- ❏ Palusami 145

Finland
- ❏ Korvapuusti 79
- ❏ Kraftskivas 208
- ❏ Leipajuusto 180
- ❏ Ravintola Juuri 249
- ❏ Reindeer stew 104
- ❏ Vorschmack 255

France
- ❏ Baguette 285
- ❏ Boeuf bourguignon 77
- ❏ Bouchons 308
- ❏ Bouillabaisse 126
- ❏ Cassoulet 139
- ❏ Cheese 30
- ❏ Clafoutis 105
- ❏ Crème brulée 229
- ❏ Crepes 99
- ❏ Croque monsieur 150
- ❏ Eclade de moules 256
- ❏ Escargot à la Bourguigonne 158
- ❏ Galette Bretonne 165
- ❏ Galette des rois 90
- ❏ Gateau aux noix 250
- ❏ Macarons 113
- ❏ Marche Bastille 271
- ❏ Palmiers 300
- ❏ Poulets de Bresse 281
- ❏ Quiche lorraine 238
- ❏ Ratatouille 232
- ❏ Rillettes 221
- ❏ Salad niçoise 182
- ❏ Soufflé 312
- ❏ Soupe au pistou 181
- ❏ Steak tartare 52
- ❏ Tarte au citron 172
- ❏ Tarte tatin 47
- ❏ Tartiflette 183

French Guiana
- ❏ Blaff 250

G

Georgia
- ❏ Khachapuri 175
- ❏ Khinkali 149

Germany
- ❏ Bratwurst 116
- ❏ Cherry torte 161
- ❏ Currywurst 149

❑ Glühwein and stollen 118
❑ Schweinshaxe 277
❑ Weisswurst and pretzels 230

Global
❑ Airline food 180

Greece
❑ Domatokeftedes 68
❑ Greek salad 165
❑ Kalitsounia 285
❑ Kourou pie 172
❑ Moussaka 186
❑ Souvlaki 40
❑ Taramasalata 162

Greenland
❑ Muskox 300
❑ Restaurant Ulo 271

Guatemala
❑ Chicken pepián 286

Guinea-Bissau
❑ Cashew fruit 268

Guyana
❑ Metemgee 172
❑ Pepperpot stew 142

H

Hungary
❑ Chimney cake 255
❑ Dobos torte 229
❑ Flódni 279
❑ Goulash 212
❑ Lángos 125
❑ Töltött káposzta 184

I

Iceland
❑ Hot dogs 216
❑ Icelandic lobster 144

India
❑ Bhel puri 115
❑ Chai 202
❑ Dal 91
❑ Gulab jamun 242
❑ Keema matar 131
❑ Laal maas 207
❑ Masala dosa 64
❑ Murgh makhani 220
❑ Paranthe Wall Gali 160
❑ Raan biryani 190
❑ Rasgulla 232
❑ Samosas 72
❑ Sandesh 175
❑ Tandoori chicken 152
❑ Thali 283
❑ Vada pav 120

Indonesia
❑ Bakso 185
❑ Black rice pudding 278
❑ Gado gado 115
❑ Nasi campur 248
❑ Nasi goreng 287

Iran
❑ Baghali ghatogh 167
❑ Tehran bakeries 58

Ireland
❑ Barmbrack 312
❑ Black pudding 296
❑ Irish stew 65

Israel
❑ Hummus 46
❑ Miznon 100
❑ Shakshouka 80
❑ Sufganiyot 307

Italy
❑ Aperitivo 151
❑ Arancini 201
❑ Bistecca alla fiorentina 306
❑ Cannoli 167
❑ Cicchetti 272
❑ Gelato 44
❑ Grilled octopus 83
❑ Insalata Caprese 56
❑ Orecchiette 188
❑ Osteria Enoteca Ai Artisti 252
❑ Pizza margherita 22
❑ Porcedu 47
❑ Ragu 54
❑ Risotto alla Milanese 207
❑ Spaghetti alle vongole 74
❑ Spaghetti carbonara 118
❑ Suppli 229
❑ Tiramisù 224
❑ Torta di ceci 194
❑ White truffles 101

J

Jamaica
❑ Ackee and saltfish 221
❑ Curried goat 192
❑ Jerk chicken 32

Japan
❑ Convenience store chicken 170
❑ Ekiben 260
❑ Goya champuru 265
❑ Kaiseki 66
❑ Katsudon 176
❑ Kobe beef 274
❑ Miso ramen 134
❑ Mochi 291
❑ Okonomiyaki 258
❑ Onigiri 213
❑ Papabubble candy 244
❑ Ramen 130
❑ Sanuki udon 210
❑ Sea urchin 73
❑ Shojin ryori 248
❑ Sushi 14
❑ Taco rice 279
❑ Takayoaki 205
❑ Tempura 198
❑ Wagashi 216
❑ Yakitori 228

Jordan
❑ Mansaf 148

K

Kenya
❑ Giraffe Manor 204
❑ Nyama choma 161

Kuwait
❑ Machboos ala Dajaj 233

Kyrgyzstan
❑ Manti 185

L

Laos
❑ Khao piak san 84
❑ Larb 124

Lebanon
❑ Fatteh 166
❑ Halloumi 105
❑ Knafeh 120
❑ Manoushe 193
❑ Shish tawook 189

M

Macedonia
❑ Pastrmajlija 192

Madagascar
❑ Romazava 165

Malaysia
❑ Assam laksa 122
❑ Bak kut teh 301
❑ Beef rendang 196
❑ Char kway teow 282
❑ Curry laksa 12
❑ Durian fruit 289
❑ Hokkien mee 99
❑ Ikan bakar 75
❑ Kaya toast 240
❑ Roti cani 266
❑ Wantan mee 213

Maldives
❑ Mas huni 227

Malta
❑ Lampuki pie 162

Mauritius
❑ Boulettes 305

Mexico
❑ Chalupa 240
❑ Chapulines 156
❑ Chile relleno 309
❑ Cochinita pibli 124
❑ Elotes 83
❑ Fish taco 236
❑ Huevos divorciados 153
❑ Lechón 187
❑ Mole 229
❑ Sopa de lima 162
❑ Tacos al pastor 198
❑ Tamales 266
❑ Tlacoyo 273
❑ Tlayuda 283

Mongolia
❑ Khuushuur 294

Morocco
❑ Cous cous 298
❑ Harira 181
❑ Lamb tagine 32
❑ Meloul 312
❑ Pigeon pastilla 186
❑ Sardines mariées 246

Mozambique
❑ Piri piri chicken 68

Myanmar
❑ Lahpet thoke 256
❑ Mohinga 95
❑ Tiger prawns 71

N

Nepal
- ❏ Dal bhat 136
- ❏ Momo 223
- ❏ Thukpa 151

Netherlands
- ❏ Musk strawberries 220

New Zealand
- ❏ Crayfish 20
- ❏ Hangi 217
- ❏ Hokita Wildfoods Festival 238
- ❏ Manuka honey 285
- ❏ Pavlova 280
- ❏ Whitebait fritters 71

Nicaragua
- ❏ Baho 304

Nigeria
- ❏ Akara 276
- ❏ Jollof rice 223

Norway
- ❏ Elk 291
- ❏ Kraftskivas 208

P

Pakistan
- ❏ Apricots 252
- ❏ Seekh kebab 219

Paraguay
- ❏ Mbeju and tereré 283

Peru
- ❏ Caña de azúcar 224
- ❏ Ceviche 26
- ❏ Cuy 259
- ❏ Picarones 154

Philippines
- ❏ Adobo 178
- ❏ Halo-halo 159
- ❏ Sisig 146

Poland
- ❏ Chlodnik 273
- ❏ Pierogi 143
- ❏ Zurek 152

Portugal
- ❏ Cataplana de marisco 168
- ❏ Franceshina 230
- ❏ Pastéis de nata 26
- ❏ Percebes 121

Puerto Rico
- ❏ Alcapurrias 310

R

Russia
- ❏ Borscht 185
- ❏ Caviar 125
- ❏ Syrniki blinis 153

S

Senegal
- ❏ Black-eyed pea fritters 89
- ❏ Slow-cooked chicken 156
- ❏ Thieboudienne 307

Serbia
- ❏ Pljeskavica 240

Seychelles
- ❏ Fresh fish 46

Singapore
- ❏ Black pepper crab 297
- ❏ Chicken and rice 308
- ❏ Chilli crab 34
- ❏ Hainanese chicken 78
- ❏ Nasi lemak 193

Slovakia
- ❏ Bryndzové halusky 175
- ❏ Placky 310

South Africa
- ❏ Biltong 251
- ❏ Boerewors 122
- ❏ Braais 235
- ❏ Bunny chow 244
- ❏ Pap en vleis 223
- ❏ Test Kitchen, The 297

South Korea
- ❏ Barbecued pork 59
- ❏ Bibimbap 21
- ❏ Chimaek 293
- ❏ Gimbap 278
- ❏ Hotteok 120
- ❏ Kimchi 270
- ❏ Noryangijin fish market 222

Spain
- ❏ Churros 41
- ❏ Gazpacho 187
- ❏ Jamón ibérico 160
- ❏ La Boqueria market 42
- ❏ Pa amb tomaquet 144
- ❏ Paella 106
- ❏ Paletilla de cordero 171
- ❏ Pintxos 10
- ❏ Restaurant Les Cols 261
- ❏ Salmorejo 103
- ❏ Suquet de peix 191
- ❏ Tapas 76
- ❏ Tarta de Santiago 198

Sri Lanka
- ❏ Egg hoppers 241
- ❏ Ministry of Crab 231
- ❏ Polos curry 150

Suriname
- ❏ Pom 210

Sweden
- ❏ Köttbullar 49
- ❏ Kraftskivas 208
- ❏ Nystekt Strömming 115
- ❏ Pepparkakor 162
- ❏ Semla 224

Switzerland
- ❏ Café Schober 190
- ❏ Confiserie Sprüngli 233
- ❏ Fondue 115
- ❏ Raclette 134

Syria
- ❏ Fattoush 69

T

Tahiti
- ❏ Poisson cru 207

Taiwan
- ❏ Beef noodle soup 104
- ❏ Bubble tea 166
- ❏ Coffin bread 180
- ❏ Pineapple cake 279
- ❏ Stinky tofu 314
- ❏ Tainan Night Market 52
- ❏ Tea eggs 156

Tanzania
- ❏ Ngorongo Crater Lodge 218

Thailand
- ❏ Gaeng keow wan 86
- ❏ Khao soi 203
- ❏ Mango sticky rice 123
- ❏ Massaman curry 60
- ❏ Pad ka pao 194
- ❏ Pad thai 288
- ❏ Sai krok isan 307
- ❏ Som tum 16
- ❏ Tom yum goong 152

Trinidad & Tobago
- ❏ Corn soup 247
- ❏ Crab and dumplings 206
- ❏ Doubles 89

Turkey
- ❏ Balik ekmek 110
- ❏ Midye dolma 62
- ❏ Simit 312
- ❏ Testi kebap 194
- ❏ Turkish delight 144

U

Uganda
- ❏ Rolex 144

UK
- ❏ Arbroath smokies 146
- ❏ Balti 252
- ❏ Banoffee pie 307
- ❏ Bara brith 250
- ❏ Borough Market 304
- ❏ Chicken tikka masala 291
- ❏ Crab sandwiches 93
- ❏ Cream tea 109
- ❏ Fat Duck, The 238
- ❏ Fish and chips 50
- ❏ Full English breakfast 173
- ❏ Haggis 145
- ❏ Khichari 134
- ❏ Langoustine 174
- ❏ Maltby St Market 177
- ❏ Mince pies 291
- ❏ Ploughman's lunch 225
- ❏ Pork pie 157
- ❏ Rex Whistler Restaurant 227
- ❏ Scotch eggs 128
- ❏ Smoked salmon 59
- ❏ St John 242
- ❏ Steak and kidney pie 303
- ❏ Summer pudding 114
- ❏ Sunday roast 74
- ❏ Yotam Ottolenghi 209

Ukraine
- ❏ Salo 295

Uruguay
- ❏ Chivito 174
- ❏ Dulce de leche 183
- ❏ Postre chaja 167

USA
- ❏ Apple pie 98
- ❏ Barbecued pork 292
- ❏ Beef brisket 16
- ❏ Beefburger 48
- ❏ Beignets 63

❏ Breakfast diners 211
❏ Buffalo wings 57
❏ Cheesecake 143
❏ Chez Panisse 75
❏ Chili con carne 232
❏ Clam cakes 129
❏ Clam chowder 173
❏ Cobb salad 175
❏ Coney Island hot dogs 265
❏ Crab cake 247
❏ Crawfish boil 195
❏ Cronuts 233
❏ Cuban sandwich 241
❏ Eggs benedict 284
❏ Eggs sardou 154
❏ Fried green tomatoes 170
❏ Grilled green chillies 105
❏ Haden mango 244
❏ Hot fudge sundae 83
❏ Key lime pie 286
❏ King crab with mac & cheese 205
❏ Knish 313
❏ Lobster roll 208
❏ Lox bagels 267
❏ Mission-style burritos 219
❏ Muffuletta 117
❏ New England Ice cream 261
❏ Oysters Rockefeller 251
❏ Philly cheesecake 245
❏ Pizza slices 275
❏ Plate lunch 240
❏ Po' boy 101
❏ Poke 133
❏ Pumpkin pie 300
❏ Reuben sandwich 296
❏ Salt water taffy 256
❏ Shrimp and grits 311
❏ Sourdough 88
❏ Southern fried chicken 132
❏ Spago 268
❏ Steamed crab 191
❏ Surf 'n turf 289
❏ Vegetarian tacos 259
❏ Voodoo Doughnuts 69

Uzbekistan
❏ Plov 249

V

Venezuela
❏ Arepas 309

Vietnam
❏ Bánh bao vac 201
❏ Bánh mì 119
❏ Bánh xèo 78
❏ Bò kho 210
❏ Bò lá lot 309
❏ Bún cha 227
❏ Cha ca 177
❏ Chilli-salted fruit 93
❏ Goi cuon 274
❏ Pho 38

Y

Yemen
❏ Lahoh 310

Z

Zimbabwe
❏ Kapenta 187
❏ Mopane worms 166

Top Fives

Eric Ripert 28
Martin Morales 40
José Andrés 63
Amanda Hesser 79
Curtis Stone 92
Ping Coombes 98
Tony Singh 103
Mark Hix 117
Dan Hunter 120
Monica Galetti 142
Ford Fry 171
Gail Simmons 176
Tessa Kiros 200
Ben Shewry 212
Wylie Dufresne 230
Elena Arzak 237
Rowley Leigh 257
Andrew Zimmern 276
James Syhabout 284
Florence Fabricant 295

First Edition
Published in August 2018
by Lonely Planet Global Limited
ABN 36 005 607 983
www.lonelyplanet.com
ISBN 978 17870 1421 3

Printed in Malaysia
10 9 8 7 6 5 4 3 2 1

Managing Director, Publishing Piers Pickard
Associate Publisher Robin Barton
Art Direction Daniel Di Paolo
Editors Nick Mee, Yolanda Zappaterra
Image Research Regina Wolek
Print Production Nigel Longuet
Thanks to Chris Downey, Ashley Garver, Laura Hamilton, Laura Lindsay

Commissioned by Ben Handicott
Written by: Andrew Bain, Celeste Brash, Joshua Samuel Brown, Austin Bush, Will Cockrell, Jen Feroze, Emily Matchar, Kalya Ryan, Mark Scruby, Craig Scutt, Luke Waterson, Yolanda Zappatera

Top Five interviews by: Will Cockrell

Lonely Planet offices

AUSTRALIA
The Malt Store, Level 3, 551 Swanston Street, Carlton Victoria 3053 Phone 03 8379 8000

IRELAND
Digital Depot, Roe Lane (off Thomas St), Digital Hub, Dublin 8, D08 TCV4

USA
124 Linden St, Oakland, CA 94607 Phone 510 250 6400

UNITED KINGDOM
240 Blackfriars Road, London SE1 8NW Phone 020 3771 5100

STAY IN TOUCH
lonelyplanet.com/contact

Paper in this book is certified against the Forest Stewardship Council™ standards. FSC™ promotes environmentally responsible, socially beneficial and economically viable management of the world's forests.